ROY HUDD'S
Book of
MUSIC-HALL,
VARIETY
and
SHOWBIZ ANECDOTES

ROY HUDD'S
— Book of —
MUSIC-HALL,
VARIETY
and
SHOWBIZ ANECDOTES

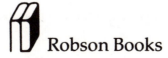

Robson Books

To my Brother Water Rats and my friends in the business whose tales have made me laugh, cry and think.

This Robson paperback edition first published in 1994
First published in Great Britain in 1993 by Robson Books Ltd,
Bolsover House, 5-6 Clipstone Street, London W1P 7EB

British Library Cataloguing in Publication Data
A catalogue record for this book is available from the British
Library

ISBN 0 86051 876 0 (hbk)
ISBN 0 86051 929 5 (pbk)

Typeset in Meridien by Columns Design and Production
Services Ltd, Reading
Printed in Finland by W.S.O.Y.

FOREWORD

I am a collector. Well, a hoarder really. I collect almost anything to do with the business I love. Showbusiness. I have a house full of sheet music, programmes, photographs, posters, scripts, 'props' and Max Miller's guitar. Those are the things you can see. I collect invisible things as well. Stories, overheard remarks, memories and all sorts of seemingly useless information. On an early school report my head teacher wrote: 'He has a rag-bag mind. It is stuffed with facts and fantasies that are of no possible interest to anyone but himself.' I hope this book will prove that supercilious pedagogue wrong.

The book is exactly what its title says it is: a collection of stories from the 'light entertainment' side of showbusiness. I hate that prissy, homogenised handle so I've used the rather dated but far more colourful terms 'music hall', 'variety' and 'showbiz'.

The music hall, which grew from amateur free-for-alls in the back rooms of pubs to become the major leisure industry of its time, spans, roughly, the period from the mid-1800s to the end of the First World War. The easiest way to distinguish music hall is to assume the entertainment was run by a chairman who would introduce the 'turns' and encourage the audience of drinkers to buy more booze.

Variety happened when drinking was relegated to bars outside the auditorium, the chairman was dispensed with and the acts followed each other as per a printed programme. A lighted number would appear on the proscenium to correspond with a number in the programme – so you'd know who was on. Variety, after surviving the onslaught of films and radio, finally bit the dust when, in the late 1950s, television turned a whole nation into non-participating couch potatoes. We don't despair, though. Comedy clubs are growing apace and, by returning to the spirit of the music hall, things are looking up once more.

I'm sorry I can't expand the remit into 'straight' theatre as I can't include some of my favourite 'legit' stories. I was lucky enough to have a wise agent who, when the writing was on the wall for variety, led me, rather unwillingly, into theatre proper. I'm glad he did. His foresight has enabled me to see both sides of the business – 'turns' and 'actors'. I still find it odd that comedians and variety people still talk of 'working' while actors always say they are 'playing'. Having a foot in each camp has brought me immense pleasure not least from being in the company, off-stage, of both 'workers' and 'players'. It is a shame I can't include stories of some of the incidents that have happened to me in the 'legit'. I would have liked to have told you of playing Sir Andrew Aguecheek in *Twelfth Night* alongside two exciting, witty and knowledgeable Shakespearians, Edmund Bailey and Sidney Bromley. They had been together years before in Sir Philip Ben Greet's company. I found their explanations of what nearly every line in the play meant fascinating and very helpful. On the opening night, however, as we three – Andrew, Sir Toby and Fabian – bobbed up and down interpolating snappy one-liners in the famous hedge scene, Sidney looked over the hedge and said, with great conviction, 'Sontar will cry on it though it be as rank as a fox!' followed by, for our ears only, 'Whatever the **** that means!'

I would have enjoyed quoting a story Leonard Rossiter told me about the leading man and leading lady in a rep season seated, as a Lord and Lady, on a sofa. The 'Lord' turned to the 'Lady' and said, 'Darling what has gone wrong with our marriage?' at which point a moth flew out of the flies of his hired tail suit.

I would have loved to have told you about playing Bottom in *A Midsummer Night's Dream* at that most magic of venues, the Open Air Theatre in Regent's Park. (The place where so often the audience's attention wanders from the actors speaking the bard's beautiful words to two wood pigeons having it off.) It was in the Park that, after what I thought had been a particularly successful matinée, I was having a drink with some friends on the lawn when a lady came up to me and said, 'I did enjoy the show.' I nodded graciously. 'Yes,' she continued, 'it was lovely, but tell me – didn't you use to do comedy?'

I would like to have included the night during Ray Cooney's *Run For Your Wife* when one of the actors, who had read for the new James Bond, assured us that Cubby Broccoli (the producer of the 007 films) was out front. He told us that as Mr Broccoli's preference for the new master spy seemed to be for a Scot he would play his part, that night, Scottish. His accent throughout the evening came and went leaving myself and the late Ralph Bates helpless with barely stifled giggles. Windsor Davies was in the play and he is the worst 'corpser' in the business. My evening was spent clinging to Ralph and admiring Windsor's beyond-the-call-of-duty self control. He deviated from the script just once. Towards the end of the play he was asked a question to which he replied, 'Don't ask me – ask' (pointing to the would-be Bond) 'Jock!' That was the finish. We all totally lost control. Cubby Broccoli wasn't out front but Ray Cooney was! He was backstage before the curtain had touched the stage and gave us all a terrible dressing-down. He was quite right, but I still blame 'Jock'.

Sadly, I can't include any of those stories; so I won't. Instead let me tell you the source of the majority of the tales I have included. Dressing-rooms and pubs, of course, but – most importantly – the Lodge Room of the Grand Order of Water Rats.

The Rats are a collection of showbiz blokes. They are performers, musicians and general dogsbodies whose pleasure in each other's company and soft charitable hearts bind them together. Some of my happiest hours have been spent with them. Our meetings, once the formalities are over, are glorious swap shops. Ad libs, interruptions and, best of all, stories are the order of the day: old ones, new ones, loved ones, neglected ones, as the pianist Semprini used to say.

There are lots of them in this book. I've included a little glosssary of terms used in some of the tales because there are several rather 'pro-ey' ones. Though they are rather 'in', they are funny, I'm sure, to everyone. Someone once asked Groucho Marx what was the difference between what made the customers laugh and what made the professionals laugh. He said, 'The customer would laugh if he saw a man dressed as an old lady in a wheelchair careering out of control down a hill. A pro would only laugh if it was a real old lady and she hit a wall at the bottom!'

'Enough!' you cry, and quite right too. I sincerely hope this, by necessity, skimming of the surface of the great pool of pro-ey parables will give you as much joy to read as it has given me in the putting together.

Russ Abbot One of the true originals the business has produced in recent times began as the drummer with The Black Abbots comedy group. He has developed and extended his range till he has become a genuine top of the bill. Russ remembers an adventurous pantomime in Oxford.

A few days after the opening of *Cinderella* the producer suggested putting in a ghost routine: 'Look out! He's behind you!' Russ asked for a volunteer, and the Town Crier/Flunkey/Company Manager stepped forward.

They rehearsed and all seemed well until the night of the 'ghost's' debut. In his hastily conceived costume, a white sheet and pointed hat with two eye holes, he looked like a member of the Ku Klux Klan. The tag of the sketch, of course, is when the ghost sees the comic, throws up his hands in fright and runs off. Alas, when Russ's ghost raised his arms he also raised the costume's eyeholes above his head.

Suddenly he could see nothing, but he did run off. Not offstage but past the footlights into the orchestra pit. After a spectacular somersault over the brass section he came to rest, like a bag of laundry, behind the drummer.

A lesser 'ghost' would have resigned immediately, but not this one. Within a few performances he was back, with suitably adjusted eyeholes. Russ wants to dedicate this tale to that brave ghost/Town Crier/Flunkey/Company Manager and embryo stuntman, Terence Nolan. Believe me, they don't make many like him these days.

Russ also recalls, when he was part of The Black Abbots, travelling from club to club in a caravan. The caravan made good sense. Money was tight, there was none to pay for digs, so they simply put themselves in the nearest car park. In Middlesbrough they parked on what they thought was a plot of waste ground, only to wake up the next morning to find themselves in the middle of the town's weekly market. Hundreds of people were milling around them and Russ says, 'It was the best crowd we had all week.'

Leslie Adams A collector and purveyor (via his after-dinner speeches) of many a cracking showbusiness story, Les told me this story about an un-named (rotten old Les!) singer he shared a summer season with in Bournemouth. The young, good-looking vocalist used to stop off at an hotel for a bevvy after the show on the way back to his digs. One particular evening, in the bar, a pretty lady smiled at him. He smiled back and they chatted. They liked each other. So much so that he didn't go back to his digs that night but booked himself, and friend, into the hotel. The next morning he smilingly asked for his bill. His smile vanished as he read £286.

'What's this?' he asked. 'I only stayed one night.'

'I know,' said the sphinx-like receptionist, 'but your "wife" has been here a fortnight.'

Frank Adey Frank was a producer. Not a producer in the current sense – the man who finds the money – but a producer from the days when the title meant someone who put the whole show together from choosing the artistes, constructing the programme and lighting the scenery to directing the performers. The old-style producer literally did produce the show from thin air. Frank began as a dancer and graduated to production through West End shows like *Hellzapoppin'* and *The Bird Seller*.

The Bird Seller was a huge, spectacular flop in which Richard Tauber, no one knows why, conducted the orchestra. At one of the auditions where Tauber was choosing the singers, Frank saw him select a very pretty girl with no voice at all. 'But she can't sing,' Frank protested.

'Ah,' explained the notoriously promiscuous *chef d'orchestre*, 'she's for the first interval!'

Frank himself eventually produced the famous Clacton-on-Sea summer show, *The Ocean Revue*, for more than forty years. I had the great joy of working there for him and loved his down-to-earth approach and total dedication to his show. He once said to me, 'All the old toffee that's talked about lighting! Come in and watch me for an hour tomorrow and I'll teach you all there is to know – open white for the comical bits and colours for the singers.' He was lying. *He* could light a show in an hour but he's the only one I've ever seen do it, and beautifully.

Conducting a morning rehearsal, he noticed one of the girl dancers was missing. 'Where's Margaret?' he asked.

'I'm sorry Mr Adey,' said the Head Girl, 'but as we were coming out of the digs this morning, she fell down the steps and broke her ankle.'

'You see,' Frank exploded, 'everything happens to me!'

Agents According to showbiz folklore, the very first agent was called 'Nosenheimer' and was just an enormous nose. The stereotype is still a Jewish wheeler-dealer who treats his clients like sides of beef and should be played by Sydney Tafler but the truth is very different. They don't have to be Jewish. Today's agents are smoother, more subtle, better dressed and look more like stockbrokers than market-place hagglers but, thank heavens, they still retain that sense of humour that enables them to get away with it.

A very famous small agent *was* a Jewish gentleman, Harry Wright. His office was in a basement in Charing Cross Road and legend has it that his desk was once showered with a sack load of nutty slack when a coalman opened the wrong manhole.

A favourite apocryphal story about him goes like this. His phone rang and a beautiful, familiar to all, voice said, 'Richard Burton here. I'm doing a tour in the UK, and I'd like you to handle my business. Can you?' Harry removed his cigar (from half-way down his throat) and spluttered, 'Of course! of course!'

'And, oh,' added the great Thespian, 'my wife, Elizabeth, will be working with me. Could you look after her, too?'

'Certainly! Certainly!' said Harry, mentally totting up his commission.

'Just one thing,' said Burton, 'you aren't Jewish, are you?'

Like a flash Harry replied, 'Not necessarily!'

A classic agent/booker of shows story is where an agent phoned the man who booked the attractions for Walthamstow Palace. The agent, desperate to fill in vacant weeks for the tour of a musical comedy he was representing, asked 'How do you think *Goodnight Vienna* would go in Walthamstow?' Replied the booker, 'About as well as *Goodnight Walthamstow* would go in Vienna!'

My favourite agent, apart from my own, shall remain nameless (to protect him!).

This particular gentleman was very fond of paying artistes in 'Nelsons' (rhyming slang: Nelsons – Nelson Eddys – readies), or ready cash rather than by cheques which would have to go through the books. Alas for everyone involved, he got caught by the tax people who demanded a five-figure sum – immediately! He hadn't got it, but he had got an enormous network of relatives who rallied round and came up with the lot – in cash. The debtor duly appeared in front of the taxman and emptied a huge bag full of notes on to his desk. The money was painstakingly counted and he was asked, 'Would you like a receipt?'

'No thanks,' replied our hero. 'You never have a receipt for "Nelsons"!'

Another agent of my acquaintance didn't abide by this golden rule and was indeed writing a note of 'Nelsons' paid when the VAT men burst into his office. He ate the note!

My favourite apocryphal agent's story concerns one of that much-maligned breed asking his son: 'What do you want to be when you grow up?' The son dutifully replied, 'I want to be an agent and work for –' (and he named the biggest agency in London).

'Ah,' said his dad. 'You must make up your mind. It's one thing or the other!'

Ray Alan The ventriloquist with the most perfect technique and the wittiest partner was thrilled, in the days before he invented the unique Lord Charles, to tour in variety with Laurel and Hardy. He tells of changing on the top floor of a theatre (the smaller your name was on the bill the higher up the building your dressing-room was). One evening at the end of the week he heard a heavy pair of feet ascending the stairs. It was 'Babe' Hardy. 'Forgive me intruding,' said the best straight man of them all, 'but Stan and I like to remember everyone we've worked with. Would you sign our autograph book, please?' For the unknown that Ray was at the time, it was a moment to treasure.

During a week in Newcastle Ray, encouraged by the double act's genuine friendliness, asked Mr Hardy if press reports that he and Laurel had gone through a long period of not speaking to each other off the set were true. Babe Hardy chuckled and said, 'Well, I'll tell you, Ray. It wasn't until Stan and I read that report that we realised we shouldn't be talking to one another.'

Chesney Allen I got to know Ches, Bud Flanagan's partner, very well towards the end of his career. He was charming, urbane and great company.

He told me one of my favourite stories during rehearsals for *Underneath The Arches*. I liked it so much I put it in the show.

In the days of the music hall, a rather fly-blown soprano had just finished her first song to howls of rage, and advice, from the rougher denizens of the gallery. Amid this chaos a loud voice was heard from the stalls advising the galleryites: 'Knock it off, please, give the poor cow a chance!'

'Thank you,' responded the soprano. 'It's good to know there's *one* gentleman in the audience.'

Bob Andrews A wonderful raconteur whose tales are always spiced with the most devastatingly accurate local accents, Bob was appearing with Vic Oliver in Dublin and 'The Old Vic' had to go back to London for a Sunday concert.

On the Saturday night he told the hotel receptionist, 'I have a very important engagement in London tomorrow and I must get the early morning plane. Would you please give me a five-thirty call?'

'No trouble at all,' said the lady, 'but a five-thirty call will cost you five shillings. Do you mind that?'

'Not at all,' replied Vic.

'Right, sir,' said the receptionist. 'Five-thirty you will be called.'

Vic was awoken the next morning by a cheery Irish voice that said: 'Good morning, sir. This is your five-thirty call, and there's nothing to pay.'

'Why not?' enquired Vic.

'Because,' smiled the voice, 'it's *nine*-thirty!'

Bob and Davy Kaye shared digs in Wigan. The landlady, a sweet dumpy sixty-five-year-old, said to them on the Tuesday morning: 'Ee, lads – you'll never guess who I've got coming to stay with me next week.'

'Who?' they asked.

'None other than Stanelli!'

'Stanelli!' said the two lads, with barely a glance at each other. 'Oh dear, oh dear.'

The lady looked alarmed. 'Why, what's up?'

'He's a sex maniac!' said the evil pair.

'Oh no!' she said. 'He wouldn't bother with a body like mine.' 9

Bob and Davy warmed to the subject. 'Oh, yes, he would.' 'You've got what he wants – you're a woman.' 'You've got to be very, very careful.' 'Don't give him any encouragement.' 'Keep your hand on your ha'penny. Believe me he doesn't care,' and so on. They kept this up for the rest of the week.

A few weeks later Bob bumped into the great Stanelli. 'What did you tell that landlady in Wigan about me?' he asked.

Bob, the picture of innocence, said 'Why?'

'Why!' roared Stan. 'I'd travelled all the way up from Plymouth and arrived at her place starving hungry and in need of a kip. She insisted on showing me every detail of the bedroom. Eventually I said it was fine – now how about some *manjari**? She threw herself on the bed and said, "Oh, well – if you must you must!"'

Anthea Askey The vivacious and talented daughter of the great Arthur recalls surprising people by calling her Dad by what became his favourite nickname, 'Wave'. Arthur was constantly on tour, and Anthea's earliest memories are of being held up in her mum's arms and being told: 'There he goes! Wave!' Similarly, when he arrived home, she would be instructed: 'Here he comes – wave!' For years she thought that was his name.

Arthur Askey The most successful graduate of seaside concert party, he became a star through radio – and in particular through *Bandwagon* with Richard Murdoch. He was just as successful on television and, like all the greats, put several phrases into general use. 'Before your very eyes' and 'I thenk yew!' are two that he gave us. I did panto with Arthur at Wimbledon and, though I only lived down the road, I made a point of having lunch with him every day before the matinée. He was a good raconteur and a brilliant ad libber.

The Wednesday matinée audience always contained lots of pros, because they could get in 'on the Wilkie'. (Rhyming slang – Wilkie Bard – card – an Equity member shows the union card, and gets in free.)

Everyone knows the pantomime line: someone falls over and

* *manjari* (= Italian 'mangiare', to eat) is the old pros' term for food.

is asked, 'What are you doing down there?' The reply is inevitably, 'Getting up!'

One Wednesday afternoon, as we prepared to deliver this belter, with a large number of our out of work mates in the audience, I fed Arthur the classic line: 'What are you doing down there?' Before the audience could join in, Arthur, in apparent disgust, said, 'I'm not giving my good material away with all these pros in!'

My favourite of all the stories he told me was one about his very early days in concert party. He played the summer at the Lido, Cliftonville. The concert party did their show on a circular bandstand surrounded by rows of deck-chairs. Unlike lots of the alfresco seaside shows, who could adjourn to a town hall or similar if it was raining, this one had nowhere to go. Rain meant no takings. The season began patchily in May and June, but July brought disaster. Torrential rain all through the month meant they hardly played at all. August arrived and the weather was glorious. The deck-chairs were all taken and the bad month was forgotten by almost everybody. One gorgeous afternoon Arthur and his chums were on the bandstand soaking up the sun and feeling delighted with themselves. The boss, who was in the show too, sat next to Arthur and the heat, plus a liquid lunch, made him nod off. Arthur nudged him whenever it was his turn. He'd get up, do his bit and then sink into oblivion again. He was gently snoring as the soprano sang her first song. Excellent reaction and into the next number which she announced, 'I would now like to sing for you "April Was A Lady".'

The governor opened one eye and said, 'But July was a bastard!'

At Arthur's memorial service (a joyous, fun-filled thanksgiving if ever there was one) Dickie Henderson told of being with Arthur in that very church, St Martin-in-the-Fields, attending another memorial service. Just as the business was about to start, down the aisle came an old wino, ex-army overcoat tied with string, no socks, and cider bottle in the carrier bag. He walked down the centre aisle then, for no reason at all, turned right and pushed his way past all the seated congregation along a pew. When he got to the end there was a sigh of relief from the trodden-on parties. He then moved one row back and did the same back to the centre aisle. Arthur's comment was, 'That's what you get when you book your ticket through Keith Prowse.'

Arthur wrote his own story (in longhand) and it was published   11 under the title *Before Your Very Eyes*. It is one of the very best showbusiness autobiographies, full of anecdotes, and Arthur himself comes through on every page. Do try and read it. I like his story of going, after Dunkirk, to entertain at an army hospital in Preston. He took his entire show along, including the orchestra. It went like a bomb and at tea after the performance the commandant took Arthur on one side and thanked him profusely. Arthur, in the glow of a job well done, said, 'We don't want thanking after all those lads did for us at Dunkirk.'

'Dunkirk?' said the boss, 'none of this lot have been farther than Blackpool. This is a VD hospital!'

Tom O'Connor was very fond of Arthur, who had been very kind to Tom when he first came into the business. He sat in the audience for a farce Arthur was on tour with. It was a small unresponsive house but Tom, like every good pro would, dutifully went backstage afterwards to see the great little man.

'I'm sorry to see the business is a bit duff, Arthur,' said Tom. 'Were the reviews bad?'

'No,' said Arthur, 'the critics were very kind. It's the word of mouth that's killing us!'

Charlie Austin A greatly-loved sketch comedian, Charlie was famous for his invention of 'Parker-P.C.'. So loved was Charlie that he was King Rat of the Grand Order of Water Rats six times. This story has been told about many different people, but Ted Ray assured me this was the original.

With Charles Coburn (the singer of 'Two Lovely Black Eyes' and 'The Man Who Broke The Bank At Monte Carlo') Charlie attended the funeral of Harry Tate. As they stood beside the grave, Charlie said to Charles, 'You're getting on a bit now aren't you, Charles?'

'Yes, I am,' replied Charles. 'I'm over ninety.'

'Blimey,' said Austin. 'It's hardly worth you going home!'

Morris Aza is my agent. We've been together ever since I came into the biz – 'and it don't seem a day too much'. He is a wise, classy, shrewd and, best of all, witty man and I enjoy his company enormously. One of his early jobs was sweeping up the cutting-room floor at Lime Grove Studios, a job he shared with Bud Flanagan's tragic son, Buddy. Morris was a second assistant director at Elstree Studios when Max Miller was making films and tells this story of how 'careful' Max was.

Morris saw Max, in between takes, lounging against a wall outside his office. Max nodded, produced a silver cigarette case and took a fag out. 'I would offer you one,' he said, 'but you wouldn't like 'em. They're menthol.'

'Oh,' said Morris (well aware that Max never gave anything away if he could help it), 'I like those.' Max was lumbered. He reluctantly handed one over and even lit it for him. Morris inhaled deeply and beat a hasty retreat round the nearest corner. It nearly killed him. He did think about giving it back but, after scoring so heavily over the Cheekie Chappie, he couldn't. I think he's still got it.

Morris was Gracie Fields' nephew. His uncle Archie Pitt was Gracie's first husband and his dad, Bert Aza, was Gracie's agent. One morning she was sitting in the back of Morris's car while Boris, her last husband and a hi-fi freak, was shopping in Tottenham Court Road. She watched the young office workers passing by and commented, 'All the young girls think about these days is where to buy their next frock and who to take it off for.'

Joe Baker was half of a double act, with Jack Douglas. Joe is a great off-stage inventor and carrier-out of practical jokes. I had, but have lost a wonderful recording he made of his havoc-causing telephone calls. Joe now lives in America so his leading of innocents up his own extremely twisted garden path is denied to his chums here, more's the pity. He was doing a *witty* 'Jeremy Beadle' before the whole thing became a pain in the whatsit.

I once did a panto with Joe and he introduced the show's leading lady to our governor, the late Tom Arnold, as 'the touring version of the wife'.

At the end of a long summer season Joe asked Freddie 'Parrot Face' Davies if he'd meet him the following morning and drive him to an out-of-town golf club. 'I've left my bag of clubs there,' explained Joe. 'Of course,' said Fred. He enjoyed Joe's company. The next day they set off through the country lanes. Joe was directing and, after an hour of 'Left – no, right – no, wait – back again', Fred stopped the car. They were at the end of a narrow, high-hedged cul-de-sac. 'Where *is* this golf club?' he asked. Joe leaned forward, put his hand on Fred's knee, squeezed it and huskily said, 'What golf club?'

Joe was in a once-nightly West End farce which finished fairly early. On his way home he drove past a surburban theatre where an old pal of his was billed in panto. (He shall remain nameless – to protect the guilty.) He decided he'd pop backstage and say hello.

'Great to see you,' said the panto star, 'hang about. I've only got to do the Giant's Kitchen and the "Who's best?"' (A phrase coined, I believe, by Eric Morecambe to describe a pantomime finale where all the characters enter for their applause one at a time. Whoever gets the most applause answers the question 'Who's best?')

Joe sat till his friend returned with the invitation, 'Do you fancy one over the road?' Joe did and they retired to a little club opposite the theatre. Twenty minutes later the star's dresser appeared and whispered disparagingly, 'They're here.'

'Thank you, Shankers,' replied Joe's pal, finished his drink and dragged Joe back to his dressing-room. There, waiting for them, were two distinctly friendly young ladies.

Joe was speechless. Out went the lights and the four of them enjoyed half an hour of good, clean fun. Eventually the lights came on, the kiddies' favourite peeled off a couple of tenners and dismissed the girls with a cheery, 'Here's your taxi fares, darlings.' The ladies left, the star put on his hat and coat and propelled Joe, who hadn't said a word throughout the entire happening, towards the stage door. 'I think you'll agree,' announced the perpetrator, 'a very entertaining evening!'

Another story told about the above jolly Lothario concerned his (*not* Joe's) early days in variety. After a long spell on the road he had to confide to his father that he had contracted an unpleasant social disease. 'Right!' said Dad. 'It's the special hospital for you.' With his blushing son in tow he marched into the Soho Square establishment, banged his fist on the reception desk and announced to the startled nurse, 'Good morning, miss. We've called in answer to your advert in Leicester Square gents.'

This same infamous loo was, for many years, a meeting place for those who were a bit light on their feet – all right, then – 'ginger'. When the old place was finally closed, the day after the heartless deed was done, a wreath was found hanging on the padlocked gates. The message attached read: 'In Loving Memory'.

Barry Balmayne Barry, who is the *Stage and Television Today* reviewer and editor of the British Music Hall Society's magazine, *The Call Boy*, worked very successfully, in the clubs with his brother Dave as the Mumford Brothers.

In the late sixties the boys were working a Leicester club – Saturday night, Sunday lunchtime, Sunday night. After the Sunday lunchtime show they were asked if they would do a free show that afternoon. The organiser couldn't tell them where it would be but assured them that they would be driven there and back, a meal would be laid on and they would play to the best audience they'd ever met. It was an invitation they couldn't resist. They would only be required to do one twenty-minute spot and could only take two pieces of music and their stage suits. This intrigued them even more and they duly were collected to be delivered at Gartree Maximum Security Prison near Market Harborough. It took them more time to get in and out through security than they spent on stage in the prison gymnasium. The organiser was right – the inmates were a marvellous audience. Barry wonders if it had anything to do with the two pieces of music they took along: 'Gee, But It's Good To Be Here' and 'Born Free'!

I remember, when in concert party in Babbacombe, Devon, going to Dartmoor Prison to do a Sunday afternoon show (only the number ones for yours truly). The organiser, a local probation officer, had approached all the big stars appearing in the area and they had all turned him down but we, as total unknowns, would go anywhere to perform. One top of the bill did say yes. Ken Dodd. He finished the show and, of course paralysed 'em. From his opening song, 'There Is A Key That Will Open All Doors To Me', to his final remark: 'You've been so good I'm going to take you all on a cross-country run', he could do no wrong. The trouble came when the entire company, as was usual then, sang the national anthem. This was greeted with foot-stamping, jeers and loud raspberries. The curtains closed hurriedly and we exited in total disarray. A 'screw' told me, 'They hate that. Most of them are here at her pleasure!'

Ida Barr One of the great lady chorus singers of the music hall, whom I saw at the Metropolitan Music Hall, Edgware Road, on the night of its closure. Her big hit song was 'Oh! You Beautiful Doll'. She, like all the lady chorus singers, was a big girl. They had to be built like Pavarotti to top the sound of two thousand-odd people singing their songs with them. She once heard two blokes talking, outside her dressing-room window, about the show they'd just seen. 'How about that Ida Barr?' asked one.

'Ida Barr?' said the other. 'She could 'ide a bleedin' brewery!'

The Barron Knights The evergreen comedy vocal group are as fresh and original today as they were when they first got together in the 1960s.

They had just come off stage at a club in Swansea to a standing ovation from 400 people. The compère brought them back while the whole audience (nearly) rose and sang 'We'll Keep A Welcome In The Hillside' especially for them. As they sat in their dressing-room basking in the warmth of the adulation, a knock came on the door. 'Excuse me,' said a broad Welsh-accented voice, 'I hope you don't mind me saying this, but I brought a coachload of forty people tonight and two of them didn't like you!'

At another club in Wales, a man came up to them after the show and insisted on telling them how much they had cheered him up. 'Oh yes,' he went on. 'You made me very happy, very, very happy.'

'Thank you,' said the lads.

'I can't tell you how happy you made me, 'cos my brother died at half-past six you know!'

Fairly recently they were on their way home after a late night-club appearance in Harrogate. The weather was foul and a gust of wind blew their car off the road and aquaplaning into a ditch where they came to rest – upside down. Luckily, their safety belts had done their job and minor cuts were the only injuries. They still looked a sight, though, covered in wet mud and blood. A passing lorry driver called an ambulance which duly arrived to find a group of shaken, cold and wet Barron Knights.

Did the ambulance driver enquire, 'Are you hurt?' or 'Do you need blood?'

No. His opening remark was, 'Oh no, not you lot. I saw you at the California Ballroom, Dunstable, in 1960!'

The tag came, as it so often does, from the man who had booked their Harrogate appearance, Michael Black. He'd read about the accident in the following morning's papers and rang the lads' office. 'Are the boys all right?' he anxiously enquired.

'They're fine,' said Dave.

'Thank God,' said Michael. 'Thank God it didn't happen on the way *to* the gig!'

Michael Barrymore I knew Michael would make it big from the days when we were together in the *Black and White Minstrel Show*, and he is now one of our brightest television personalities. His off-beat approach appealed to me then, and millions of television viewers have since agreed with me. I, and they, love his anarchistic approach to the medium and his amazing rapport with the featured punters. Not many top-of-the-bill performers would tell a story like this but, well, Michael is Michael. He says:

This story takes place on the road. I have always loved listening to LBC, one of London's best independent radio stations. Some of my happiest listening has been late at night, travelling back from cabaret and television recordings. This night was no exception. I was with a mate of mine listening to Clive Bull, a DJ who presents a phone-in show in the early hours of the morning. On this particular occasion the phone-in was a talent competition – on radio! Listeners were invited to call the station and show their talent. They would be judged by a panel of 'experts'.

I decided to enter, just to see how talented, if at all, I was. So we pulled off the M25 and on to a trading estate. It was now well past midnight. The switchboard operator at LBC told me they would be delighted for me to appear (I kept my identity secret by using an assumed name) but she thought there might be problems with me using a mobile phone. I was devastated, but using my own particular brand of charm (?) I managed to talk her round and she told me I was next. I quickly got my pal to scribble down an act for me to do. I would do impressions, we decided, and having only about ninety seconds to perform, I braced myself. Suddenly I was on.

I opened with Danny La Rue, worked my way through Loyd Grossman, Tommy Cooper and David Frost finishing with – myself. You have no idea how difficult it is to impersonate yourself! So this make-believe contestant finished his performance and we began the drive home, listening intently to LBC for the comments on my act. It was a long wait as I had to sit there while the other contestants performed – there were ten in all. Eventually the big moment came. The first expert liked my Danny La Rue. The second got a bit mixed up between my Loyd Grossman and my David Frost but the third was the best of the lot. Basically I was quite confident, she said, although my impressions were rusty. The whole performance had not impressed her and worst of all was my Michael Barrymore. That was dreadful and sounded nothing like him! To top it all I came seventh out of ten.

I have never told this story before and have never told LBC it was me. So now they know!

Harold Behrens An amazing nonagenarian who, since his national exposure with radio's *Ignorance Is Bliss* continues to entertain in cabaret, after-dinner speaking and notably in films with character parts like the bandleader in *Hear My Song*.

Harold is in great demand as the entertainer at Jewish weddings and after a successful spot at the Marble Arch Synagogue was approached by a lady who enquired whether he would be available for her daughter's wedding. The date was suitable for him, so the lady gave him a telephone number to ring.

Harold rang and a very Jewish-sounding voice answered. 'Who's speaking, please?'

'Harold Behrens.'

'You're not the geezer who's on the television, radio and films are you?'

'Yes.'

'So what do you want?'

Harold explained that the bride's mother wanted him to do the cabaret at the forthcoming wedding. 'Well,' said the organiser, 'it's very difficult – how much do you want?'

Harold told him and was informed that the lady would be spoken to and he would be rung back. Three days later he was rung and was told, 'I've had a long chat with the lady and we've been unable to decide whether to have you or a fish course!'

'Alas,' says Harold, 'the fish won.'

Billy Bennett A 'one off' on the music hall and variety stage, Billy popularised parodies of famous dramatic recitations like 'The Green Eye Of The Little Yellow God'; his version was 'The Green Tie On My Little Yellow Dog'. He, with Albert Whelan, was also Alexander and Mose a black-faced double act. They mounted their own variety shows starring Billy Bennett, Albert Whelan *and* Alexander and Mose!

During a variety season at the Palace, Shaftesbury Avenue, the bandleader Jack Payne – a not very popular chap – asked, 'Can anybody lend me twopence? I want to phone one of my friends.' Billy handed him a coin saying, 'Here's sixpence, phone the lot.'

It was Billy Bennett who coined a phrase still used in the business today to describe a duff audience. He was on a variety bill preceding the popular West Indian entertainer at the piano, Hutch. As he came off stage at the end of his act, Hutch enquired, 'What's the audience like?'

'Cor,' snorted Billy, 'not worth blacking up for.'

Here's a story remembered by Benny Lee, and told to him by a well known Water Rat from the music-hall days, George Buck (who incidentally was a mad keen golfer, and got a hole in one at the age of ninety).

Billy had bought a new car and took delivery of it on the very day that the late King George the Fifth was dying. Every newspaper placard had reports on the King: 'The King is sinking fast' and so on. Billy proudly parked the new vehicle outside Thurston's Billiard Hall in Leicester Square and went inside for a game and a swift one. About an hour later he decided to go home and came out of the hall to discover a drunken tramp urinating against his pride and joy.

'You dirty, filthy old swine!' exploded Billy. 'What the hell do you think you're doing?'

The tramp, with scarcely a pause, looked around and asked, 'Any news of the King?'

David Berglas Practically sitting in his lap, I have seen *the* great 'man of mystery' do things other magicians only dream about. He is a dear friend and will he let me into any of his secrets? Of course he won't. He daren't. He's the President of the Magic Circle.

For seventeen years he was almost a permanent fixture as *radio's* mystery man. You would think magic on radio would be about as effective as bunjy jumping, but David did achieve the impossible with 'experiments' perfectly tailored for the medium. He explains:

Most of my broadcasts included split studio presentations where I would be in one location and talk to an audience in another. On this particular occasion the compère was the multi-talented Alfred Marks.

Alfred was in front of a studio audience at the Playhouse Theatre near London's Embankment, and I was at Broadcasting House, the other side of London. I asked Alfred to pick five volunteers from the audience and to stand them in line on the stage. The first person was to select one of many newspapers lying on a table, the second to pick any page, the third to tear that page out, the fourth to tear it into small pieces and the fifth, who was a lady, to choose any one of those pieces.

I intended to ask her to select a few words from either side of that small piece of paper. It never reached that stage as I heard laughter from Alfred's audience. When I asked what was happening he told me she was eating the piece of paper! Apparently she had misheard me and instead of 'choosing' the paper she was 'chewing' it! I quickly told her,

'For goodness sake, spit out the words,' as it was essential for her to select a few words from the piece of paper. After the wet and bedraggled paper was removed from her mouth, I asked her again to select any three or four words.

Those words were indeed the ones David had predicted and were printed in the previous week's *Radio Times*.

Says David, 'From that moment on I've always ensured that I "choose" my words very carefully.'

The Beverley Sisters The Bevs, the three legendary singing sisters, retired at the height of their popularity and are now back again, more popular than ever.

The girls tell of the time Bill Cotton, Junior, called to see them after their show at the Prince of Wales Theatre. The stage door keeper told him they'd left a message: 'Sorry they can't see anyone tonight – they have a headache.'

The Bevs were sharing a bill with Benny Hill, who had one of the first portable television sets in his dressing-room.

Their father was very impressed with it. 'It is quite handy,' said Benny, 'but these tiny screens are a bit of a nuisance. When the Bevs are on I can only see two of them, and when Dolly Parton's on I can only see one of 'em.'

Issy Bonn A very popular Jewish comedian who I never thought was very funny. He got away with it through his singing. He had a great cantor-type voice, and tore the place apart with the 'My Yiddisher Momma' type of ballad.

One Christmas he was booked as top of the bill in the pantomime *Cinderella*. However, he did not appear until the end of the first half, when the Fairy Godmother had revealed herself to our heroine and promised she would grant her three wishes.

'First, I'd like a beautiful ball gown.'

'Your wish is granted.'

'And secondly I'd like a lovely coach to take me to the ball.'

'Your wish is granted. And what would you like for your third wish?'

'I'd like to hear Issy Bonn sing "It's My Mother's Birthday Today . . .".'

'Your wish is granted!'

Blackout. Exit Cinders and Fairy. Orchestra Issy's signature 21 tune. Enter in smart double-breasted suit and trilby, Issy to do twenty minutes. Interval. Back to the plot.

Peter Bray A drummer I worked with in my early days, Peter is not an old man but, believe it or not, he played for Harry Champion. He was in his early teens when he did his first week as a pit drummer. The great chorus singer was on the bill in a sort of 'Thanks For The Memory' company.

'I'll never forget him,' said Pete. 'At the end of the week I knocked on his dressing-room door and asked for his autograph, and do you know what he said?'

'What?'

'"Bugger off!" I'll never forget him.'

Alan Breeze For many years the featured vocalist with the Billy Cotton band, Alan could handle every conceivable type of song from schmaltzy ballad to raucous comedy – often in drag. No wonder Bill kept him on. Alan rarely spoke in public. Sadly he had the most terrible stutter. It really was painful to hear him trying to answer with even a simple 'yes' or 'no'. The amazing thing was when he sang there was no sign of the stutter at all. I shared a dressing-room with him and a young Welsh singer for a BBC/TV *Billy Cotton Bandshow*. The Welsh chap tore the place apart and the ever-generous Alan said to him, 'Young m.m.m.m.an. U.u.u.u.u. 're goo goo goo goo – going places!' Alan was right – it was Tom Jones.

This story – of Alan overcoming his frightening affliction – was told me by Michael Hurll who directed Billy Cotton's TV shows (and in his long career almost everybody else's, too).

Alan had been nabbed for a driving offence and was forced to go to court and explain his actions. The band, and Michael, sensing an eccentric occasion, all went along to witness the event. 'Mr Breeze,' said the magistrate, 'tell me in your own words exactly what happened.'

Alan rose. 'W.w.w.w ell – u.u.u.u.u. 're on.on.on.on er.'

'Take your time, Mr Breeze.'

'I.I.I.I.I'm t.t.t.t.t. trying t.t.t.t.to! I.i.i.i.t's n.n.n.n. NO GOOD. W.w.w.w.would i.i.i.it b.b.b.be p.p.p.possible? – er.er.er.er – OK? – i.i.i.i.if I s.s.s.s *sang* m.m.m.my e.e.e viDENCE?'

A hasty confab took place and the magistrate, thinking he could be there all morning, said, 'Very well, Mr Breeze. Sing your evidence.'

With an audible sigh of relief, Alan, setting the tempo with his foot, gave forth in perfect rhythm and at great speed:

'I was proceeding down the Goldhawk Road at the regulation thirty miles an hour when, suddenly, out of a side turning on my left shot a man in a Mini Minor . . .' till eventually '. . . and that is the reason, sir, I stand before you today!'

A round of applause rang round the court. The magistrate, after letting Alan take a decent call, banged his gavel and solemnly announced, 'Case dismissed.'

Bernard Bresslaw The excellent and extremely versatile actor whose early death saddened all who knew and loved this gentle giant. His *Carry On* characterisations and creation of the legendary Private Popeye in *The Army Game* were only tiny parts of the complex whole that was Bernie. It is a tragedy that what was to come never happened.

Bernie was officially a 'giant'. He was also Jewish and once stayed with a landlady who was a devout Catholic. 'Have you ever been to Lourdes?' he once asked her. 'Oh yes,' she replied, 'and it was wonderful! Wonderful! There was only one thing that spoilt the visit. I was taken ill there, and had to be brought home on a stretcher.' This reversal of most people's idea of a visit to Lourdes *would* have appealed to Bernie.

Duggie Brown Yet another 'overnight' discovery, Duggie's success is based on years of hard graft in every branch of show-biz. In the early 1960s Duggie was one of a group called the Four Imps and appearing in *Babes In The Wood* at the Pavilion, Glasgow. Duggie was playing one of the Sheriff's men. The Sheriff himself was a big gambler and unfortunately for the Sheriff, there was a bookie's just up the road from the theatre.

One matinée the show had reached the point where Duggie had to utter the deathless line: 'Here comes the Sheriff now.' He did, but no Sheriff appeared. He said it again, no Sheriff – only a stage hand who whispered, in broad Glaswegian, 'He's no comin'. He's in the bookie's getting on a horse.' Duggie quickly instructed one of the 'villagers': 'Go and help the Sheriff.' Off went the villager while Duggie filled in. The Sheriff eventually ran on, straight from the bookie's, in full costume to exclaim, 'Sorry I'm late. I've had trouble with my horse.'

As Duggie says, 'Only in Glasgow would no one turn a hair at 23 a Sheriff in a crowded betting shop in full make-up, tights and tricorn hat.'

Albert Burdon The well-known Northern variety comedian and father of Bryan Burdon, Albert had a magic cabinet routine that was a classic of the variety stage. Bryan has many tales of his illustrious dad. Here's one of the printable ones!

During the many pantomime seasons the Geordie Albert did at the Theatre Royal, Newcastle, it was his habit, during a break, to go over to the pub opposite the stage door. He would appear there minus his dame's wig but in full make-up and costume. Some members of the company thought this meant they could do the same. The Company Manager felt he couldn't allow this and pinned up a notice to the effect that no one was to go to the boozer in costume and make-up. On reading this Albert got the needle and at the end of the performance packed his case and announced to the distraught manager that if he couldn't have his relaxing interlude in the pub he was off back to London.

The next day a new notice appeared which said, 'Members of the company are not allowed in the pub during the performance in costume and make-up with the exception of Mr Albert Burdon who is excused for medical reasons.'

Here's another one. As well as the magic cabinet routine Albert had a second spot, a military line-up sketch which would always finish with a close harmony song. Albert was always on the look-out for good numbers and, after a week in variety with the American singing group the Deep River Boys, decided their piece 'The Whiffenpoof Song' (Baa-Baa-Baa!) would be ideal to end his second spot with. Albert's master stroke was to have a real sheep come on at the end. The scene was set for the spectacular at the Empire Theatre, Middlesbrough. Albert had borrowed a tame sheep from a farmer pal and the stage hands had built a stall at the back of the stage to house the embryo star.

On the Monday night the orchestra struck up the overture and the sheep didn't like it. It bleated, kicked and generally made its presence felt while Bryan, under instructions from Dad, tried to shut it up. He failed.

The first act, a sophisticated ballroom duo, were accompanied by bangs, crashes, muffled bleating and cursing from Bryan – as was the second turn, a patter comic. The act that preceded the Burdons, though, suffered most. It was a unicycle act and no sooner had the gent wobbled on than the sheep decided it was time to relieve itself. Disaster; the relief trickled from the back of the stage towards the orchestra pit. The unicyclist exited in total disarray. Albert Burdon and Company were on and somehow got through to the big finish. The tabs opened behind them and the sheep was catapulted onto the stage. It was no pro. Its eyes rolled and, seeing its every exit was blocked, it promptly leapt into the orchestra pit and landed on top of the conductor. The house tabs were rapidly lowered.

A year later the Good Shepherd and his company were again at the Empire. 'I hope you're not using that bloody sheep in your act,' said the stage manager.

'No fear,' said Albert. 'Now we finish on "Mule Train" and we have a donkey!'

Bryan Burdon Bryan is a brilliant visual comic, a master of pantomime and the pratt fall and he's no slouch when it comes to the acerbic riposte.

He auditioned for an Andrew Lloyd Webber musical and, when asked by the maestro what he would sing, he informed him 'The Impossible Dream'. Sir Andy had obviously heard that one a few times before and audibly sighed. The eagle-eared Bryan heard that reaction and said, 'Well you can't write them all.' I'd have given him the job there and then.

Peter Butterworth Peter (the husband of Janet Brown) was a stalwart of post-war British comedy, an excellent dame in panto and a successful film actor.

My pal Tony Hare, the writer, was part of a group sitting chatting round a table in the BBC canteen. So was Peter. The rest of the participants were rather pretentious young people who were avidly discussing foreign films. One turned to Peter and asked, 'Do you know Fellini's *Eight and a half*?'

'No,' said Peter, 'but I've heard the rumours!'

Douglas Byng The popular revue, pantomime, musical comedy and night-club entertainer, was a very 'high camp' performer on and off and I had a marvellous evening at the Dome in Brighton when, as a very old man, he was interviewed and asked questions by the audience. In reply to one query, 'Did you ever see Lady Beerbohm Tree?', he replied, 'Yes, I saw her once at a charity matinée. She walked on in a purple crinoline with purple ostrich feathers, a purple fan and elbow-length gloves, and wearing a diamond necklace, tiara and bracelet. She picked up a kitchen chair, put it downstage, sat on it and said to the audience, 'Now I want you all to imagine I'm a plumber's mate!'

Patrick Newley, the *Stage and Television Today* columnist, presented Dougie and Billy Milton in a show where Billy did the first half, entertaining at the piano, and Dougie the second, chatting, singing his famous songs and answering questions. It was at the end of their careers, and as Patrick says, in his own subtle way, 'They hated each other.' As the tour proceeded, their upstaging of each other got worse. One night Dougie asked for £50-worth of flowers which he intended to present to the lady pianist at the end of the show. Billy spotted the flowers backstage in a bucket, promptly grabbed them and, while Dougie was taking his applause, presented them to the lady pianist – from himself.

Dougie was banned by the BBC in the 1940s for being too blue. He used to tell about two matronly ladies visiting a friend. Once inside their friend's house they heard, through an open kitchen door, the end of a children's programme about bird life. Alas they only caught the back announcement as the presenter said, 'So remember, children – tits like coconuts.'

'Oh!' cried one. 'Turn that wireless off. They're listening to that dreadful Douglas Byng.'

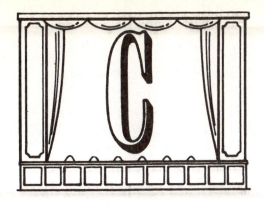

Norman Caley 'The Mad Earl' was one of my early heroes, an eccentric comedian who was way ahead of his time. When I worked in the next theatre to his in Margate for a summer season I discovered he was as delightful off stage as he was on. When he went particularly well he would throw out his arms and cry, 'Waves of love!' This always cracked me up and I asked him where the phrase came from.

'From here,' he replied, tapping his heart, 'at the moment I say it it's true. I can feel the waves of love from them and they can from me.' Norman, was also the first I ever heard use this expression to describe one's feelings after 'dying the death' – 'So I peed on my props and thought sod the profession!'

John Styles, the famous Punch and Judy man, remembers chatting to Norman when, in mid-conversation, he leapt to his feet and left the room. A few seconds later he returned and carried on as if nothing had happened. 'What was all that about?' asked John.

'Just observing an old showbusiness tradition – never fart in a dressing-room without windows!'

Eddie Calvert The trumpet player who became a variety top of the bill with his hit recordings of 'Cherry Pink' and 'Oh! My Papa'.

Eddie was sitting in his dressing-room, relaxing before his finishing spot, when he heard a commotion at the side of the stage. He rushed out to discover that a lady trampolinist had, in the middle of her act, broken her bra strap. She panicked (a bra-less trampolinist is not for everyone's eyes) and, in trying to get off quickly, bounced to the edge of the trampoline and caught her foot on the edge. She described a perfect arc into the wings, where she grabbed the first thing she came into contact with. It 27 was the handle of the sprinkler system! Suffice to say the theatre was flooded from gallery to stalls and didn't open for two days.

Wyn Calvin 'The Welsh Prince of Laughter'. The popular Welsh comedian and well-known pantomime dame is noted for the butchness of his female impersonation – he often finishes his spot in panto with 'Old Man River' in a voice that makes Roger Whittaker sound a cissy.

His 'dame' is usually called Blodwyn and, despite beautiful costumes, make-up and wigs, he fools no one, especially the kids. He was doing panto in Birmingham, in the stalls, in full female gear doing his 'giveaway' spot – throwing sweets to the kids – when a tiny Black Country voice from the gallery called to him 'Sir! Sir! Up here, sir!'

Wyn, of course, is very popular in Wales, especially in Llandudno having done some six or seven long summer seasons there. One morning he bumped into two ladies from a village in the Snowdonia mountains. They recognised him and one said, in that beautiful thick accent of the area, 'Oh, Mr Calvin, I hope you don't mind us stopping you like this, but we come to see your show at the Arcadia every week and we always sit in the same two seats, a regular booking, and d'you know when you come on that stage it's all my sister and I can do to keep from laughing.'

Wyn says that playing dame often means you can pass through the crowd at a stage door without being recognised. But one night at the Theatre Royal, Nottingham, a lady recognised his voice, unmistakable, and grabbing her four-year-old daughter's programme thrust it at Wyn saying, 'Sign this for her.' Turning to a photograph of himself in 'skirts' (never 'drag' – female impersonators wear 'drag', dames get into 'skirts'; there is a big difference) Wyn duly obliged, personalising the signature 'To Avril'. The little girl took one look and burst into tears.

'Whatever's wrong darling?' enquired mum.

Replied the tear-stained darling, 'He's scribbled all over my programme.'

Harry Champion The songs which, for most people, are *the* songs of the music hall, 'Any Old Iron', 'Boiled Beef and Carrots' and 'I'm 'Enery The Eighth I Am', were made famous by Harry Champion. (Incidentally, Sir Alexander Korda heard a cabbie singing "Enery the Eighth', and it inspired him to produce the Charles Laughton film *The Private Life of Henry the Eighth*.)

Harry Champion, whose real name was Crump, hit upon a great way of supplementing his income. He started his own hansom cab business. He was very successful at it and one Sunday morning he was washing down his cabs when two 'toffs' walked by. They stopped and one said, 'Good God, Harry Champion. I saw you at the Bedford Camden Town, last year you were jolly good. I'm sorry it's come to this,' and gave him half a crown.

Charlie Chaplin Little more can be said of Charlie. He became a Water Rat in the 1930s and, at his initiation, told this story.

Toots Shor had a very famous restaurant in New York. It was so popular *everyone* had to queue to get in – even the great Chaplin. One night he was standing in line when Toots came out to assure the crowd 'it wouldn't be long now'. 'Be patient, folks,' he said and, spotting Chaplin, remarked, as he made his way back into the restaurant, 'Charlie! Be funny for the people.'

Although not so rife in Britain, there are certain restaurants that the pros like to go to. The Caprice Restaurant, on the seafront in Penarth, is a favourite. Apart from the grub, the company of the genial governor, Eddie Rabaiotti, is a big draw. Eddie is a great supporter of showbiz charities and tells of he and his wife going to a big 'do' and being asked by the toast-master for his name. 'Rabaiotti', Eddie adlibbed brilliantly. 'Ladies and gentlemen,' announced the Master of Ceremonies, 'the Rabbi and Mrs Otti!' And him a good Catholic boy!

Dougie Chapman The proprietor and chairman of his own music-hall company presents all types of shows from pantomime to farce.

Dougie had a pantomime at the Southport Theatre, *Dick Whittington*. Marie Ashton, later of the famous Roly-Polys, was his choreographer and was playing the Cat. On dress rehearsal night Marie wanted to see one of her production numbers from the front, but the Southport Theatre had no pass door from backstage into the auditorium. To get there she had to go out of the stage door, along the side of the building and get inside by a 29 little door at the end of the theatre. Marie came off stage in her cat-skin and dived out to see what she wanted. The alley by the side of the theatre was dark and standing in front of the door into the auditorium was a bloke having a wee.

'Excuse me – can I come through, please?' said Marie, tapping the fellow on the shoulder.

The sight of a giant, talking cat sent him fleeing into the night, fastening his flies as he went!

Chas and Dave The Cockney duo's songs have given me much joy over the years, from 'Rabbit' to 'I Wish That I Could Write A Love Song'. They write tunes you can remember and terrific lyrics. I like 'em.

Chas and Dave often team up with a great pal, Joe Brown, for one-night stands. They are a great threesome; no egos, just excellent musicians who love what they do. Anyone who sees those three names on a bill together is guaranteed a good night out. All three always insist that their names must be the same, and that all three are top of the bill, so they were somewhat miffed to arrive at one venue and discover that, outside the theatre, it said: 'APPEARING HERE TONIGHT – CHAS 'N' DAVE'. Their respective agents assured them the theatre had been given the correct information, so they tackled the theatre manager. 'You'd better see the man who puts the letters into the frame,' he advised.

Said letter putter-upper duly appeared.

'Did you put the letters up?'

'Yes.'

'Were you told it was Chas and Dave and Joe Brown?'

'Yes.'

'Well, why no Joe Brown?'

'I can only work with what I'm given.'

'What do you mean?'

'Well I was only given three N's and I'd used 'em up before I got to Brown. I couldn't put Joe Brow, could I? It wouldn't have looked right, so I left it out.'

'It's got to be the best excuse I've ever heard: 'I ran out of N's.'

Charles Chilton The radio producer who really turned me on to the songs of the music hall. He researched and wrote a long
radio series which he called *Roy Hudd's Vintage Music Hall*, and it

was working with Charles and his brilliant musical director, Alfred Ralston, that opened my eyes to the wonderful world of the music-hall song. This story, though not strictly music hall or variety, I include because it makes me laugh.

Among his many successes, including *Oh! What A Lovely War!* and *Journey Into Space*, Charles had a big hit on radio with *Riders Of The Range*. The cowboy's dog, Rustler, was the character that everyone remembers. Rustler was a real dog who, in those days, had to be in the studio to do his barking on cue – live. He was, Charles recalls, a real pro and never missed an entrance. One day, however, he didn't turn up. His trainer sent a message saying Rustler wasn't well, so Charles had to find a replacement.

Another dog duly turned up but wouldn't do a thing. His owner tried everything – bribery, shouting, bullying – all to no avail. Things were getting fraught when the stand-in's boss said, 'I know what it is. He's embarrassed with all these people in the studio. If I get under the piano with him he'll be all right.'

The pair duly disappeared under the piano, which was covered with a cloth. Came the moment for Rustler to bark, and the air was rent with a long mournful howl. 'Wrong,' said Charles and lifted up the cloth to disclose the owner squeezing the dog's 'orchestras'. Rhyming slang – orchestra stalls . . .

Bernie Clifton Bernie is one of our most creative and off-beat comedy talents *and* an inveterate practical joker.

In 1980 Bernie was compèring a week's variety at the Theatre Royal, Nottingham. Top of the bill was Jimmy Tarbuck. On the Friday evening Jim went into his Tom Jones routine where he swings the microphone around his head. Disaster! The mike head came off the lead and shot like a bullet towards the fifth row of the stalls. Miracle! A bloke in the fourth row stuck his hand in the air and caught the missile, thus saving the woman behind from certain pole-axing. Jim came off white and shaking. 'I nearly killed someone tonight,' he said to Bernie. 'I'll never do that routine again as long as I live.'

'Hmmm,' thought the evil Clifton.

The following night Jim was in a bad mood. He kept getting called to the stage door telephone, and every time he picked up the receiver the caller hung up. He wasn't any more pleased when he got to the part of his act where he normally did the Tom Jones bit. The band went straight into 'It's Not Unusual' despite him telling the conductor the number was out. He tried to stop   31 them but they ignored him so he thought, 'Well, if they won't pack it in, I might as well do the bit.' Off he went. 'Tom Jones!' and he started to swing the mike round his head. Suddenly all the lights in the auditorium went on and Jim saw the entire audience and the orchestra don hard hats of the building site variety. Jim collapsed. Who had set him up?

That morning Bernie Clifton and the stage manager had toured all the building sites in Nottingham and borrowed every hard hat they could find. Every time Jim was called to the phone Clifton gave out the hats and rehearsed the audience!

This painstaking preparation is typical of Bernie. 'Hard work, but so worth it.'

Harry Clifton One of the very earliest music-hall stars came to the halls direct from the old song and supper rooms – really posh pub sing-songs. He was a highly successful writer as well as a singer of songs. Many of his songs were 'motto' type numbers, full of good sound advice for the working man, and it was rumoured that he was paid by the bosses to sing his songs in the halls to brainwash the working classes. All the words of his songs he wrote himself, but the tunes he knocked off. He lifted them from everywhere and the earliest version of an old chestnut was first told about him. He was with a pal in a pub listening to a man playing the concertina. It was a tune neither of them had ever heard before and Harry remarked, 'What a beautiful melody. I wish I'd written it.'

The friend smiled and said, 'You will, Harry. You will.'

John Clive The actor who has had enormous success as a writer, particularly with his fascinating Second World War story, 'KG 200'. John's early years were steeped in variety. His first job was as a page boy at Liverpool's Shakespeare Theatre and his first professional performing job was as a member of Will Murray's *Casey's Court*. Charlie Chaplin had been a member of the troupe in 1909. John, during a fascinating career, has also written several Top 10 hit songs and this is his story of a never to be forgotten meeting.

I was in a song publisher's office in Bond Street, waiting to see the head man with my hopeful hit. Sitting opposite me in the narrow waiting-room was an elegant dapper fellow wearing a light grey suit and holding a silver-topped cane. It was Charlie Chaplin. I stared, he erected his 'private' sign . . . a copy of *The Times*, and I was utterly confused. What to do? Then I remembered what my mother had said time and time again: 'If you've got something nice to say about someone, always say it.'

I cleared my throat. 'Excuse me, sir,' I said respectfully.

Slowly he lowered the newspaper and peered at me over the top. 'Yes, young man.'

I swallowed hard and plunged on. 'I was once in a show you were in.'

He gazed at me, faintly surprised. 'Really. What show was that?'

I smiled triumphantly. *'Casey's Court,'* I said proudly.

He stared at me incredulously, waited, then said devastatingly, 'Good heavens, you must be a good deal older than you look!'

I realised my gaffe. 'No,' I stammered. 'It ran until 1949, that's when I was in it . . .'

He lowered *The Times* still further. '1949?'

'Yes . . .'

'Was Will Murray still playing Mrs Casey?'

'Yes . . .'

'He must have been very old.'

'Yes sir, he was.'

He paused fractionally. 'Terrible show,' he said.

'Yes,' I said. I'd have said yes to anything.

'What did you do?'

'I sang and worked with the comic in the sketches.'

'What sketches?'

I thought frantically. 'There was one in the lunatic asylum . . .'

He interrupted. 'Were you the warder?'

'Yes,' I said again.

'And did you have to hit the comic over the head with a rubber hammer?' I nodded dumbly. 'I played that part too,' he said.

I stared at him open-mouthed, dumbfounded.

At that moment the door to the inner sanctum flew open and Chaplin was whisked away from me. I never did get in to see the publisher, but as I walked down Bond Street my feet seemed to be ten feet off the ground. I'd played the same part as Chaplin, in the same show, forty years apart.

Clubland It must be left to the brave souls who cut their teeth (and lost them!) in the tough world of working-men's clubs to tell their own stories. There are lots in this book. I'll just fill you in with a couple of the well-known ones. Who they actually happened to has been forgotten in the mists of time. I include these familiar fables just so that they're not lost to posterity.

The club comic, with top lip stuck to his teeth, desperately trying to 'get 'em' was interrupted by a totally unexpected roar of excitement from his audience. Quite frightened, he asked the chairman, 'What's happened?'

'Don't worry,' said that gent. 'It's just the hot pies have come.'

The same club chairman told his audience of the death of a well-loved member and called for two minutes' silence. After a hundred and twenty seconds of reverent hush, he banged his gavel and announced, 'And now – here's the comic!'

I like the Concert Secretary (the man who did all the hiring and firing) following up a complaint by a customer that he couldn't hear the Bingo numbers being called because the trumpet player was practising backstage. He collared the unfortunate musician and said, 'Be quiet.'

'But I've got to warm up,' said the trumpeter.

'Now come on lad, warm up? You've been here a fortnight.'

Dec Cluskey With his brother Con, Dec is a founder member of The Bachelors, and a highly successful record producer. Before their chart-topping times with the group, Dec and Con were, as kids, touring Ireland with the legendary Bailey's Road Show. Dec vividly describes those long vanished days.

We'd arrive at the venue with our truck full of props. We'd unload and an awning was stretched out from the side of the vehicle to make a dressing-room. The flat part of the truck, now empty, made the stage. A proscenium arch was attached to the front and an upright flat behind completed the illusion. Add a simple one-pole tent and you had your theatre. A flap at the back of the dressing-room awning even gave us a proper stage door.

In Dingle one winter's night we were doing the usual second-half drama *The Birth of a Nation* (with a cast of six). The 'non legit' acts, as variety turns were called in Ireland in those days, had done the first half, collected the money on the gate, filled the generator full of diesel (nicked from a local farmer), and sold the ice cream, lemonade and raffle tickets during the interval. Their second half was spent moving the scenery and props, and working the lights and tabs for the drama.

Dingle, as we all know, is that little part of the south-west of Ireland that juts out into the wild Atlantic. The best, and most dramatic, part of the play was the firing of the prop cannon. To get the most out of it we rigged an old fifty-gallon oil drum with a wire over the top and a military maroon primed inside the whole affair. You can imagine when we set off the maroon the truck, the tent, the audience and a fair bit of the surrounding area really shook.

This sensational effect was such a success on the opening night that, surprise, surprise, we had to retire to the nearest Guinness house to celebrate. We were well into 'afters' when suddenly the door crashed open. There stood a dripping, yellow-coated and sou'wester-hatted angry man. 'Who was responsible for the bang?' he enquired. As one man we all pointed to the boss, Bailey. 'Ye bloody eejit,' roared the visitor. 'Ye launched the lifeboat!'

Denise Coffey A best friend of mine, Denise has been involved in every aspect of the biz from concert party in Scotland to stunning performances in theatre, television and radio. She has become a top-class director and writer and a witty and erudite contributor to radio panel games.

In the very early days of her career Denise was the 'low' comedy woman in Johnny Victory's company at the Palladium in Edinburgh. Denise says, 'It was true theatre. That twice-nightly mixture of blue jokes, sentimental monologues, dancing, singing, sketches with slapstick (that was where I came in) and the whole company in ensemble of patriotic or 'sophisticated' or sentimental mood. Long-vanished but warm-hearted, rough and vital.' The programme was changed frequently and Denise was once told to learn 'The Tay Bridge Disaster' and recite it to the audience. She did, disguised as a grieving mother, and hearing a sound behind her turned to see a model train chunter across stage and fall off its 'Tay Bridge'.

Johnny Victory was an Edinburgh comedian who played throughout Scotland (and once at the Metropolitan Music Hall, Edgware Road). As he stepped out of his yellow Rolls-Royce to go to rehearsal on the first day of the season, a woman was at the 35 stage door handing out biscuits to the company, a tradition she'd established. When she saw Johnny, she screamed and fainted, biscuits flung to the wild winds of Edinburgh. When she revived she said, 'Oh Johnny, is it really you?'

'Yes,' he said. 'It's really me. What's up with *you*?'

'Oh dear,' she said. 'It's a shock. You see they told me you had "died" at Kilmarnock.'

A woman called Mrs Forbes brought her dinner in to the first house every Wednesday, and always sat in the front row of the stalls, eating her fish and chips or whatever, from the café next door. The custom was for the opening chorus to pause while Johnny asked her what was on the menu then announced it to the audience, who would cheer. One week she had haggis. Cheers from the audience and a sort of smirking snigger from an English tap-dancer.

Johnny beckoned the boy, who time-stepped over to him. 'Do you know what haggis is?' Johnny asked him.

'No,' the boy chortled. Johnny whispered in his ear. The boy's face took on a greenish hue.

'Mrs Forbes,' Johnny asked, 'lend us your dinner.' It was obligingly handed up from the front row via the Musical Director to Johnny on stage. He then force-fed the boy haggis, with the audience cheering and stamping. The green-faced boy made a quick exit to the wings, and there was the sound of a bucket being hurriedly brought! They then continued the opening chorus. Scotland's pride had been restored. Denise says, 'I think the number was "We'll All Go Riding On A Rainbow".'

Barney Colehan For many years Barney Colehan produced and directed BBC TV's *The Good Old Days*. Despite objections from the music-hall purists, the show was extremely popular and is still very sadly missed. Its great attraction for me were the speciality acts Barney found and his insistence on the inclusion of, at the time, unknown comics. Ken Dodd, Hylda Baker, Les Dawson and Norman Collier all made early appearances at the City Varieties, Leeds, for Barney.

Barney was a highly respected member of the Leeds community and, as such, was involved in all sorts of local activities. He was President of this, Patron of that – he never stopped. He was involved with a local amateur operatic society who, every year took their current production to the local mental hospital. Barney, never a supporter of anything in name only, went along and in the interval joined the staff and inmates for a cup of tea. He spotted an old friend who was now a resident. It was the comedian Jimmy Gay.

Jimmy had been a terrific front-cloth comic. He'd stand perfectly immobile centre stage, smoking a Capstan Full Strength, while he dispensed his acerbic one-liners. 'I played Scotland last week, and on the Tuesday night business was so bad they shot a stag in the gallery!' When he exited after singing his get-off song (just one line: 'Why should a comic have to sing?') he left behind a pile of cigarette ash about three inches in diameter. He made many appearances on *The Good Old Days* but sadly, the last time I saw him he was the lavatory attendant at a Northern nightclub. Barney was delighted to see him and enquired 'How are you?'

'Not so bad,' replied Jimmy. 'Some days I'm fine, other days I haven't a clue where I am or who I am.'

'What do you think of the show?' asked Barney.

'Ah!' said Jimmy. 'I think it's part of the treatment.'

Norman Collier Truly an original. His routine as a club chairman coping with the badly connected hand mike and his famous chicken impersonation are present-day comedy classics.

During rehearsals for a summer season in Bridlington Norman was having fish and chips at a café across the road from the theatre. Norman says:

No sooner had I got a chip on my fork when there he is – knotted hankie, dangling braces, pot belly, sandals and no socks. A hole opened revealing wet gums. 'Now then,' it said, 'it is you,' pushing the chip away from my mouth.

I said, 'Who?'

He said, 'You know, the chicken fella.'

I said, 'Yes that's him,' another hand came over, once again pushing the fork away from its intended destination.

Reaching for a serviette it shouted across to another table, 'It is him, Flo – put your bloody moniker on here.' It shoved the serviette in front of me. 'It's for her,' it continued. 'She thinks a lot about you, by hell she laughs at you. Mind you, she laughs at anything!'

Norman's first appearance at the City Varieties in Leeds was a memorable one. At the end of his act he exited stage right and found himself facing a brick wall. (The only exit at the Varieties is stage left.) As he desperately tried to find his way off the next act was on. Franklin and his Doves. The tail-suited Franklin, blowing smoke into the air to the music of 'Smoke Gets In Your Eyes' produced live doves from everywhere. He hadn't spotted Norman but the audience had, and were merrily encouraging him. Norman clocked Franklin and gave him a thumbs up – why? – Franklin worked his way over to Norman and subtly whispered 'P*** off!'

'I don't like your act anyway,' said Norman and directed, even more subtly, by Franklin, exited stage left. Franklin and his Doves had never gone so well.

Jess Conrad The Peter Pan of showbusiness is one of the most amusing and entertaining senders-up of himself in the business today.

Not everyone remembers that there was *Joseph and The Technicolor Dreamcoat* before Jason Donovan, but Jess himself starred in a West End production a few years previously. Going to work on a bus which stopped a little way past the theatre where he was appearing, he sat behind two ladies. Jess's name was up in lights and the ladies noticed it.

'Oh look!' said one. 'Jess Conrad. He's one of my favourites. I wonder if Jess Conrad is his real name?'

Her friend replied, 'Is Jess Conrad whose real name?'

Russ Conway The evergreen pianist whose Top 10 hits are still constantly heard and who, more than ever, packs theatres wherever he appears.

Russ began as an accompanist and everyone from Gracie Fields to Dorothy Squires availed themselves of his services. He wrote many hit songs under his real name, Trevor Stanford, and this story is set in the No. 2 studio at the EMI Recording Studios in Abbey Road, North London.

Geoff Love was conducting the orchestra for a Danny Williams recording. Danny and Geoff are, of course, both black. Both sides of the 78 had been written by Russ so he was on piano. In one song the key was changed from D Flat (a black-note key) to E Flat (another black-note key) but Russ inadvertently slipped from D Flat to D Natural (a white-note key) thereby cocking up the recording completely. The ever-patient Geoff loudly tapped his baton on the stand, bringing the orchestra and the recording

to a standstill. 'Oh dear,' he said, glaring at the blushing

Conway. 'I've heard of a colour bar but this is taking it too far. Gentlemen, one more time.'

Bobby Cook Perhaps the last of the great show drummers. A good show drummer should be able to 'follow the act' – watch what the performer is doing and put in all the appropriate effects: drum rolls, cymbal crashes, wood blocks, cowbells and so on. Anything to enhance the comic or dramatic moments. Bobby, like most musicians, is a collector of musicians' stories. This one is my favourite.

A big symphony orchestra had a guest conductor join them – a very fiery, Continental gent. At the first rehearsal things were decidedly dodgy. The maestro was determined to impress his authority upon the orchestra, not always a good idea. He bellowed, laughed, wept and picked the band up on every bar. As he couldn't understand or speak English too well a very nasty time was being had by all.

Eventually he got to a certain point in the score, stopped everyone and said, 'Vhere is da third floot player?' Nobody answered. He said again, 'Vhere is da third floot player? I cannot continue wizout a complete orchestra.'

The lead fiddle player looked around and, as everyone else was looking at their feet, volunteered, 'Well maestro, he's only got a couple of bits in the whole thing and as he's played it hundreds of times he er . . .'

The maestro roared, 'I do not care. I vill not continue wizout the complete ensemble. Get him at vunce!'

Someone left and dragged the offending third flute out of the pub next door. Alas, he'd overdone the Handel's lager. He staggered into the rehearsal, falling over the percussion, through the harp, knocking over music stands wherever he walked till he eventually collapsed on to his seat.

'You,' screamed the conductor, 'are da free shits to da wind! As drunk as a newt. You have got da boot! You are F.I.R.E.D. Sacked! Vat do you say to dat?'

The offender got slowly to his feet, blinked and said, 'What do I say? I say I couldn't give a monkey's, you pompous, no-talented bag of Continental wind!'

'Ah!' riposted the maestro. 'It's too late for apologies!'

I love Bob's story of the stripper who rang her agent and complained, 'This club you've booked me into. It is just impossible. I'm sorry, I just can't take it. I've never had to work under conditions like it.'

'It can't be that bad,' said the agent.

'Can't it?' she said. 'You get yourself up here and see for yourself.'

He duly turned up at the club and as soon as his client appeared about thirty blokes rushed up on to the stage. While some tore all her clothes off, the others poured beer over her and the remainder did unspeakable things with anything they could lay their hands on.

'There you are,' said the bruised and battered lady as she staggered off. 'What did I tell you?'

'You're right!' said the trembling agent. 'You can't work here.'

'Exactly,' added the lady. 'I can't work under these conditions – did you *hear* that drummer!'

Bobby, like all the good musicians, is a great fan of other good musicians and told me this story about the late, great bass player Dennis Bowden. It's one Dennis himself always told. Dennis was in the orchestra of *Jesus Christ Superstar* and, leaving through the stage door one night, was approached by a small boy. 'Shall I get his autograph, Mum?' the child asked.

'No,' said mother, 'he's nobody!'

You were always quite 'somebody' to us, Dennis.

Henry Cooper 'Our 'Enery' is a past King Rat of the Grand Order of Water Rats and our greatest living advert for the continuation of boxing. His down-to-earth philosophy, quick wit and fondness for people has made him a national institution – *and* he's never done panto!

Henry is a mad keen golfer and was flying up to Glasgow to play in a tournament. The plane, a little one plastered with adverts for a tobacco company, was nicknamed 'the flying fag packet'. The pilot was Henry's golfing partner, the late great racing driver Graham Hill. Before they set off, Graham asked Henry, 'How high would you like me to fly the plane?'

'About thirty-seven inches,' replied our 'Enery.

'Why thirty-seven inches?' asked Graham.

'Because,' his passenger informed him, 'that is my inside leg measurement and if necessary I can step out!'

Tommy Cooper The incompetent conjuror's bemused approach led him to being so much more; he was one of the few performers who started getting laughs as soon as he walked on.

His off-beat timing was a source of great envy to lesser mortals and I remember asking him once how he did it. 'I dunno,' he said. 'I'm usually just trying to remember what I say next.'

Being so loved, he was another who would jump in where angels fear to tread and at a Royal Variety performance he asked the Queen: 'Do you like football?'

'Not particularly,' she replied.

'Ah,' said Tommy, 'then can I have your Cup Final tickets?'

Many a taxi driver will tell you the story of having Tommy in their cab. The tag is always the same. 'As he got out he paid his fare and saying, "Have a drink with me" pushed something into my hand – it was a bleedin' tea bag!'

While we are on the subject of taxi drivers, I was playing Fagin in Lionel Bart's *Oliver!* at the Albery Theatre in St Martin's Lane. I had overspent my time with friends at lunch and, very unusual for me, took a cab to the theatre to be just in time for the matinée. I was sweating on getting there in time so didn't notice the price conversion table stuck on the window. We arrived at the theatre and I paid what was on the clock, plus a tip, and started to dash to the stage door.

The cabbie called after me, 'Oi, Roy! If you're as good at playing Fagin in there as you are in real life I'll be in to see you.'

My other cab story is of a driver saying to me, without looking round, 'Here, you're Roy Hudd, aren't you?' I preened and said 'I am.' He said, 'Right, I thought I recognised that voice. Roy Hudd, aye. Wait, till I get home and tell my missus I've had Roy Hudd in the cab.'

I ventured, 'Oh, she's a fan?'

'No,' he said, 'she thinks you're bloody awful.' Served me right for preening.

Kenneth Earle tells of being on a bill with Tommy at the Hippodrome, Birmingham. To pass an afternoon (they'd seen all the films in town), Kenny suggested Tommy joined him for a Turkish bath. 'It was worth it to see Tommy stripped,' says Kenny. 'He was, if possible, even funnier with no clothes on!'

Kenny had a massage while Tommy was in the steam room. 'How can I describe my masseur?' says Mr Earle. 'Let me just say he seemed to devote all his efforts to the region of my wedding tackle.' Thinking the whole thing was in his imagination, Kenny tried to ignore what was happening. He failed! At the end of the ordeal, the sibilant pummeler smacked Kenny's bottom and heartily declared, 'That's you finished.' He then leant over and whispered confidentially, 'I'm here every Wednesday.'

Kenny fled and found Tommy, to whom he related the whole

episode. His recital was interspersed with comments of: 'I don't believe it,' 'He should be sacked!' 'The man's a pervert,' and so on from Tom. After about a minute with, as Kenny says, 'The timing of the gods', Tommy said, 'Well, I suppose I'd better have my massage now – which one was it?'

Bill Martin remembers his brother George Martin touring with Tommy in the early 1950s. They got on well and shared each other's cars during the run of the show. Tommy, as was his wont, drove up a one-way street. A copper appeared and, putting his head in the car window, said, 'I'm sorry, sir, I'll have to book you.'

'Well,' said Tommy, 'you'll have to do it through the Grades.' (Lew and Leslie Grade were famous agents of the day.)

It was on this tour that Tommy and George shared digs where the landlady, as she served them their soup on the Monday night, said, 'I used to be a turn – semi-pro.'

'Really?' said George. 'What were you – a dancer?'

'No,' she replied, 'I used to do animal impressions.'

Well, that was all the evil pair needed. With barely a flick of the eyes between them they were off. 'Do one now,' said Tommy.

'Oh no,' giggled their reddening hostess. 'I can't do it in front of anyone any more,' and hurried out of the room. Once she was outside the door, there was a slight pause and then an enormous 'Moo-oo-oo!' hit their ears.

Back she came with the main course. Tommy greeted her with a broad smile. 'You don't have to tell us. That was a cow you did, wasn't it?'

The lady mumbled her affirmation.

'Terrific!' added George. 'Do another one.'

'Not in front of people,' she said, and once again left the room. The same pause and then a loud, 'Quack! Quack! Quack!' came through the closed door.

The sweet came next. 'That was marvellous,' said Tommy. 'The ducks were even more lifelike than the cow!'

From then on their every waking hour was filled with the cries of dogs, sheep, goats – you name 'em. Served 'em right.

Tommy's first big summer season was at the Princess Theatre, Torquay. On the bill were Edmund Hockridge, Joan Regan and, before they'd cracked it on telly, Morecambe and Wise. During rehearsals Eric and Ernie were told they'd be doing the warm-up spot – 'death valley' – directly after the opening, while the audience were still coming in. The two old hands looked around and decided the rather green Tommy would have to suffer and they convinced him that the opening spot was the best in the show. 'Get them there, and they'll love you when you come back for your main spot,' they insisted. Tommy swallowed it and tried out his jokes on them. The two rotters fell about at everything he said and Tommy was convinced they were doing nothing but trying to help.

Came the first night. On walked Tommy, cracked a couple of one-liners to an audience still searching for their seats *and* a very audible, 'Tut! Tut! Tut!' was heard. Now that is the worst sound in the world – someone disapproves of your stuff, and their reaction can affect everyone in the place. But it didn't sound as if it was coming from the auditorium. Tom desperately tried to 'clock' the cluckers and he did. There in the wings were the great double act, shaking their heads and tutting to each other. The following night they were in the opposite wings. But not the third night. The 'tutting' was still to be heard, but Tommy couldn't see where it was coming from. Not in the right wing, nor the left – no, they were up in the flies (above his head). They weren't there the next night. They were sitting with the orchestra, each with a saxophone, still tutting and shaking their heads. On the fifth night, even louder tutting. Tommy glanced from left to right, looked up and into the orchestra pit – no sign. The conductor drew Tom's attention to the front row of the audience, where from behind two raised newspapers, came 'Tut! Tut! Tut!'

A group of Water Rats were discussing the strengths and weaknesses of their various cabaret acts. Knowing Water Rats, it was most probably their strengths. Entering into this ego-massaging debate, Tommy explained that his great gift was his ability to turn anything that happened in the room while he was on to his advantage. 'My eyes are everywhere,' he explained. 'I miss nothing. I might not have the greatest material in the world but just let anyone say or do anything and I'm on 'em like a ton of bricks. I'm like lightning.'

Some weeks later several comics, who'd heard this rare boast of Tommy's, were together in a town where the great man was working in cabaret. Of course they all trooped in to see him. (No one who appreciated a brilliant clown would ever pass up the opportunity.) He had done all his classic bits and was about to launch into his monologue with the different hats when, right in front of him, a waiter crossed the floor armed with a trayful of a dozen pints. As he reached centre stage he tripped. Up went the tray and down went the waiter followed by the twelve glasses which distributed their contents over the front three rows. 'This is it!' thought the comics. They leaned forward to hear what Tommy's 'like lightning' riposte would be. He paused, fireman's hat in hand. He looked at the beer-spattered punters. He looked at the tray. He looked at the waiter and then looked back to the punters again. 'That's nice,' he said and went on with the act.

Coram and Jerry The comedian Billy Whittaker, son of the famous ventriloquist Coram, remembers that his stepmother, the formidable Mrs Pat Coram, would always stand at the side of the stage when his Dad was working. Woe betide anyone making the slightest noise during his act! She even insisted that all the stage hands wore rubber-soled shoes. Ever a beater of the drum for her husband, she turned to a member of the stage crew one night and whispered, 'Isn't Mr Coram wonderful? You can't see his lips move, can you?'

'No, lady,' replied he of the rubber-soled shoes. 'Only when the dummy's talking!'

Ray Cornell One of our most successful director/choreographers started, like so many, as a dancer.

He recalls being in the chorus of Lionel Bart's ill-fated Robin Hood musical, *Twang!*. The director Joan Littlewood had a habit, during rehearsals (and during the show!) of cutting lines and scenes as the fancy took her. During the rehearsals one actor realised he had time to relieve himself before his next entrance, so dashed off. On his return he picked up his script and entered the scene as previously plotted.

Joan jumped up. 'No darling. I've just cut you from this scene.'

'I see,' said the actor. 'It's a good job I only went for a pee. If I'd had a crap I'd have been out of work!'

In 1991 Ray directed *Aladdin* at the Liverpool Empire. The star was 'Mr T' from television's *The A Team*. He was playing the Genie. It was his first appearance in panto and, I think, his first brush with the stage. (Wyn Calvin, who played Dame in this production, told me that 'Mr T' was somewhat distressed to find he had to say lines. 'I thought it was panto *mime*,' he told Wyn.) Ray directed the Genie to 'enter O.P.' (usually the right-hand side of the stage, 'opposite prompt'). 'Mr T' had no idea what he was talking about and asked a young Liverpudlian stage hand what 'O.P.' meant. The young man, who didn't know either, ad-libbed 'On the Princess'. 'Mr T' looked out front to where Ray was sitting in the darkened stalls. 'If you wouldn't mind, sir, I think I'd prefer to walk on by myself.'

The Cox Twins Identical twins who married the identical Miles Twins. Fred and Frank have worked in every branch of the business from their early days as members of Steffani's Silver Songsters (a boys' choir of twenty-one miners' sons from Wales) through to TV commercials in the 1990s.

At the Theatre Royal, Portsmouth (renowned for the forward-ness of its almost all-naval audience) they were featured in Cyril Dowler's revue *Nudes Of All Nations*. As was the fashion in those days, the nudes appeared statically posed in a frame while a compère announced the title of the 'picture'. One girl would be seen holding a bunch of flowers. 'This is summer,' the compère would say. Another would appear in a cape and fur mittens to be introduced as 'This is winter.' One lady, not as well endowed as her fellow artistes, was shown holding a dove and introduced: 'This is peace.' One night a sailor in the gallery added, 'Gawd! If that's peace give me f*****g war!'

One wet afternoon Fred and Frank were parking their car in Covent Garden when Fred thought he saw Charlie Chaplin walking by. They caught the man up and indeed it was our greatest comedy export. In the pouring rain they chatted happily about theatres they had played and performers they had known. Suddenly Chaplin asked, 'Do you know where I can get some kippers?' The twins, as they always are, were only too happy to help and eventually they found a shop. 'Great,' said Charlie. 'Now all I need is an English newspaper to wrap them in.' Another search and the paper was bought. 'Walk with me back to the hotel,' said the smallest millionaire. They did and outside the Savoy they stood, wet through, while Chaplin thanked them profusely and went inside alone!

Mike Craig The radio writer and producer who nurtured the talents of The Grumbleweeds, Jimmy Cricket and many more for BBC Light Entertainment North, Mike is a brother Water Rat, brilliant raconteur, after-dinner speaker and a great lover of showbiz stories. This one I first heard from him:

A pair of Siamese twins got together a variety act, dancing in unison: 'Me and My Shadow', that sort of thing. On their first tour they worked a week at one of the big Northern clubs. The manager took a fancy to the cheeky one of the twins and he told her so. She said, 'Well, let's go out for a drink.' They did and things progressed. One evening she said to him, 'Would you like to come back to the digs?'

He said, 'Sure.' They went back, all three of them, and the cheeky one and the manager got very friendly.

Eventually she said, 'Would you like to stay the night?'

He said, 'I would but what about your sister?' She said, 'Oh that's all right. We lead totally separate lives. She'll do a jigsaw or something.' He stayed the night, the sister did the Rubik Cube, twice, and a good time was had by all. The week finished and the girls went on to the next date.

Twelve months later the girls' agent said, 'I've fixed your next tour and you start at that club up North. Where you started your last tour. You should enjoy that!' He winked at the cheeky sister. 'I hear you had a great time with the manager there.' She blushed and said, 'Yes, I did, but that was a year ago. He won't remember me.'

Jimmy Cricket In a world of carefully manufactured and marketed comedians Jim stands out like a beacon. He is a throwback to the great variety funny men, an original with a unique and lovable personality. Gushing, you think? Well, go and see him 'live'.

Both of Jim's stories involve Blackpool, a town where they really know a funny man when they see one. The Blackpool season is, because of the illuminations, one of the longest in the country. Jim was at the South Pier in October, a very chilly venue at that time of the year. The night was bitter and there was no heating in the theatre. Jim walked on to see his audience wrapped up to the eyebrows in overcoats, mufflers and caps. Half-way through his act a man on the front row stood up and said, 'Will someone please open the doors and let the heat in!'

A rather bizarre thing happened to him during a stint at the Grand Theatre in Blackpool. He was on stage when, three rows from the front, a man in the audience died. The St John's ambulance man was summoned, but didn't believe the man was dead! He kept reassuring the wife that he was 'only pretending'.

The wife insisted her husband had indeed well and truly snuffed it. Finally the ambulance man was convinced and commented, 'Oh dear, oh dear. I've only done bandages and fainting!'

Leslie Crowther He is one of our most versatile and underrated comedian/actors, greatly loved by his fellow pros and, like all the good ones, gives tremendously of his time and talent to charity.

Leslie tells of being in digs in Bradford. All the houses had outside toilets which were in a long row at the bottom of the gardens of the long row of terraced houses. There was no lighting in the loos so the landlady provided a torch. As Les approached the toilets one night after the show a casement window in the house opened and the landlady's head came out.

'Are you going to the lavatory?' she shouted.

'Yes,' he whispered back.

'Well, don't go in that one, luv. It's next door's and we're not speaking!'

Barry Cryer Comedy writer supreme, radio and television panel game participant, brilliant after-dinner speaker and superb music-hall chairman, Barry is a right clever dick!

Like Johnny Dennis, he often chairs at the Players Theatre Club where part of the job is chatting to the customers in the bar after the show. A certain case of asking for it! He was approached one night by a lady member who enquired, 'Were you the chairman tonight?' Barry humbly nodded. There was a pause and then she added, 'Yes. I suppose you're the sort that grows on people.'

Some years ago Barry watched 'an excellent series', about the life of a scriptwriter, starring George Cole. A friend, on asking Barry if he'd enjoyed it, commented, 'Wasn't it good? It must have been written by a writer.'

Barry's face is familiar to everyone and, as is the case with all nice blokes, he is accepted by the public as just that – an ordinary nice chap. He was filming a bit for a Kenny Everett TV show outside St Thomas's Hospital on the south bank of the Thames when a hospital worker came up to him and asked, 'Can I have your autograph, Bal?'

'Of course,' said our friendly hero. 'Leave it out,' said his 'fan'. 'You didn't think I was serious?'

The story has a sequel. Some weeks later he was crossing Westminster Bridge in a taxi. Seeing the hospital he was reminded of the incident and, ever in search of an audience, he told the taxi driver the story. 'Oh dear,' chortled the cabbie. 'Imagine that happening to someone well known!'

Now this is another true story – so says Cryer. A well-known comedian visited a friend in an old folks' home. As he was leaving, the matron said: 'There's been a bit of a buzz among the residents – they know you're here. It's a bit of an imposition, but as they're all in the lounge, could you pop in and say hello?' He did and, like any comedian would when he gets a few laughs, finished up doing a half-hour spot.

Afterwards an old lady resident came up and said, 'I did enjoy that. You're very good at it.'

'Thank you,' said the comedian and then, his vanity getting the better of him, said, 'Do you know who I am?'

'No,' she said, 'but don't worry – matron will tell you.'

Billy Dainty The wonderful eccentric dancer and comedian who, alas, died just as he was set for the accolades that were his due.

On the opening night of a summer season in Torquay he had just finished his act and stepped forward to take his bow. As he bowed, the tiny hairpiece he wore to cover his bald spot fell forward and to the stage at his feet. What would a lesser mortal have done? Bill calmly picked it up, dusted it and said, 'Oh well, you may as well know the lot!' and took out his three false teeth. It stopped the show.

Bill and Bert Weedon did a summer season together and one evening Bert came to Bill and, in a barely audible whisper, explained that he had lost his voice and would Bill announce his numbers for him. Bill, with the light of anarchy in his eye, said, 'Of course Bert. What do you do?'

Bert then gave him a list of the pieces he would be playing. Scrupulously writing them down, Bill listened. 'I'll start with "Guitar Shuffle Boogie" then "Wheels Cha Cha" ...' and so on till "... and I finish with a bit of a gimmick. I play the guitar faster than it's ever been played before with "Twelfth Street Rag".'

'Got it,' said Bill.

That night on he went, telling the audience Bert's problem and assuring them that he would announce the numbers. 'So to start, an old favourite: "... Bye Bye Blackbird".' Bert somehow got through this, Bill leading the applause as he re-entered, then proclaimed: 'And now a good old goodie, "Daisy Daisy".'

Poor Bert. Bill just announced anything that came into his head, except the right one but he saved his masterstroke till the end. 'And finally he's going to play the guitar faster than it's ever been played before. It's one you all know and love, of course – "Just A Song At Twilight".' And Bert played it!

Finally a Dainty story from Rod Hull – he of Emu fame. Bill and 49

Rod worked together a lot, not only in panto and variety but on TV as well – in 'E.B.C.' (Emu's Broadcasting Corporation). They did a season in South Africa and on the last night Rod, while Bill was doing his act, carefully unpacked all Billy's bags and cases and put the dressing-room back to exactly how it had been at the beginning of the season.

There is no record of how Bill reacted when he came off but he did miss his flight back to the UK that night. Rod says:

> Billy never mentioned it, ever, but, months later we were in panto together. I made my entrance from the flies, with Emu, coming down in a hot air balloon. I used to watch Billy doing his routine from the roof of the theatre. He opened with a 'give away' routine and this night, he'd never done it before, he asked the audience if anyone liked whisky. He then passed several bottles of Scotch over the footlights. 'Anyone like gin?' he enquired – bottles of gin went out. 'How about red wine?' Business as before. 'White wine?' Again more largesse. I thought, 'He's gone raving mad!' But there was more: 'How about champagne? Oh, never mind bottles, have a case.' To my horror I saw a case of Dom Perignon go down into the audience. It was mine! He'd given away the entire stock of booze I'd got in for the season! Dainty's revenge.

Freddie 'Parrot Face' Davies After years of learning his business, Freddie shot to the top via *Opportunity Knocks*.

One Christmas Freddie was in pantomime with Joyce Blair. They didn't get on – it does happen sometimes! Both of them are, individually, great company but at this time and in this place something didn't gel. They agreed about nothing, to the point where they would stand in the wings and give each other hell. One matinée they were at it again, and it was getting personal, when a chorus boy rushed off stage, hissing, 'You're on!' and dragged both of them back on with him. Without missing a beat, Freddie placed his hand on Joyce's shoulder (à la Flanagan and Allen) and they both sang 'Friends! – Isn't it rather nice to have friends?'

They both told me that story.

Dabber Davis The comedy writer now runs a highly successful cabaret and after-dinner speaking agency. Dabber is one of the most popular guys to work with and for because, unlike so many, he loves our business. He sent me this memory of times long gone.

In 1943, as a terrible and terrified young comedian, I was working a week's variety at the Palace Theatre, Halifax (only the number ones for me). At the band call on Monday morning I put my band books in the footlights in front of the musical director and waited my turn. While waiting I noticed that the Exit door to the street, just by the drummer, was wide open. 'Odd,' I thought but didn't think about it again until I rehearsed 'Side By Side' with the band. I finished my act with that number. 'Happy Days Are Here Again' was my play on and that was OK, but then they started to play my finish.

'Nice and bright,' I said, 'one, two, three, four.' I sang, *'Oh we ain't got a barrel of money,'* at the end of which the drummer shouted very loudly through the open street door, 'Whoa!'

'Maybe we're ragged and funny . . .'

'Whoa!' went the drummer again.

'But we travel the road . . .'

'Whoa!'

'Sharing our load . . .'

'Whoa!'

'Side by side.'

'WHOA!'

By this time I thought the drummer had gone mad. I told the conductor to stop playing and addressed the eccentric percussionist. 'Why are you shouting?' I enquired. 'There's nothing written on the part.'

'I'm ever so sorry, Dabber,' apologised the drummer. 'But I'm a milkman during the day. I come here for the rehearsal just after my first delivery and I have to leave the horse and cart outside the door. Every time the bloody horse hears the music he walks away!'

Les Dawson The tragic early departure of Les from show-biz has left a gaping hole. He was a broad comedian in the mould of Norman Evans, Albert Modley and W.C. Fields (what a combination!). He was much more than a successful purveyor of jokes and 'gurning'. He was a brilliant, deep-thinking and prolific writer. He sent me the following as soon as he heard I was putting this collection together.

Many years ago, when my career was on the free list, by

some odd freak of chance, I found myself booked on *The Billy Cotton Band Show* at the Manchester Opera House. Apart from Billy and his merry Cro-Magnon orchestra, the rest of the bill consisted of Gilbert and Partner (a man and a chimpanzee), myself as compère, four sinister-looking lady tap-dancers, a comedy duo whose bill matter escapes me but I do recall they were so unfunny that when they once did get a laugh it threw their timing and they left the business and, last but not least, a gaunt elderly man who walked across a wire only four feet off the stage. The climax of his extraordinary performance was a lumbering attempt to play a bassoon whilst jumping up and down on one leg.

The business at the Opera House was so bad, people with one eye were let in for half-price ... the theatre was so empty night after night, monks started using it as a short cut to vespers. One ghastly evening, the silence that greeted us from the auditorium was so intense that the mere shifting of a cough lozenge from one molar to another reverberated like a musket volley. The Gaunt Man On The Wire trudged on to the stage reeking of Old and Mild. He belched, glanced at the rows of empty seats, stood on his wire and boomed out: 'You can walk along here sometimes and never see a soul.' He then tucked the bassoon under his arm and trudged back into the wings, but under his breath I heard him mutter: 'Not worth risking your life for – sod 'em.' He was fired the same night.

Sonny Day The Thanet-based song and dance man and producer of shows whom I first met when he was a minstrel in *The Black and White Minstrel Show*.

Sonny took a friend, Joe, to see his hero Max Wall. The compère came on and began to warm up the audience with the usual: 'Anyone here who's been married ten years?' A chorus of 'Yeses'. 'Twenty years?' More 'Yeses'. 'Thirty?' Not so many 'Yeses'.

'Anyone here been married for forty years?'

'Yes,' shouted a lone voice. It was Joe.

'How long, sir?' asked the compère.

'Forty years,' said Joe.

'Marvellous!' said the compère. 'Your name?'

'Joe.'

'Marvellous. Stand up, please. A nice round of applause for Joe.' The audience obliged. 'Tell me, are you happy, Joe?'

'Happy?' riposted Joe. 'I'm delirious. She buggered off two years ago!'

Sonny worked a lot with the late great 'drag' act Billy Wells and after a show in Stevenage they travelled back together on the last train to King's Cross. Billy, surprise, surprise, got talking to a young soldier who asked him, 'Have you just finished work?'

'Yes,' said Billy.

'What do you do?' enquired the soldier.

'We're actresses,' answered Billy.

At King's Cross Billy started getting his bits and pieces together and his new young friend offered to help. 'I'll carry your cases to the taxi rank.'

'Thank you,' said Billy and, turning to Sonny, added, 'Watch him. He's got all my props and stuff there.' They followed the gallant young man to the front of the station.

Suddenly, in the middle of the concourse, one of Billy's cases burst open scattering bras, corsets and knickers everywhere. Sonny fled as the soldier shouted to whoever would listen 'They're not mine, honest. Nothing to do with me – they're his!'

Roger De Courcey The 'controller' of Nookie the bear began as a straight singer and took his first steps as a 'vent' in the rough tough world of London's East End pubs and clubs. Roger's story is one to make every pro tremble.

In the early seventies I was working a stag night at a pub in Bermondsey. On the bill were Jim Davidson, Barry Craine, Trevor Little and three dippers (strippers).

When I arrived it was a question of who was going on first because in those days everyone had another show to do on the same evening. Even if you hadn't, you lied to get on in the first half. Nobody wanted to do a second-half spot on a stag. Having got the running order sorted out, the show started. It was held in the back room of this pub and we were only allowed in one at a time. Barry compèred and put on a dipper. I was next and went on to find no more than 30 people in the audience with some girls sitting on the fellows' laps. In those days I had a bear with an attachment that used to spray water on people if they got too lippy. All went well till I got some aggro from a bloke in the front row. I duly sprayed him to good laughs from all and sundry. I went well, collected my ten quid and departed for the next

53

gig. I just had time for a quick beer with Jim in the bar. He asked me if I knew the people who were in that back room. I didn't so he enlightened me.

'You know the Krays are inside?'

'Yes.'

'You know the Richardsons are in too?'

'Yes.'

'And that the Tibbs have been put away as well?'

'Yes.'

'Well, that do in the back room is the party for the bloke who's taking over.'

'He's not a small Mediterranean-looking man, is he?' I asked.

'That's him,' said Jim.

'Oh dear!' I said – or something like that – 'He's the one I've just covered in water!' At this point they dragged the said gentleman out. He could hardly stand. I looked at the barman and spoke the immortal words, 'Where's the back door?'

'There isn't one,' he said.

'Where do you want one?' I responded.

Too late! The damp gentleman had spotted me and asked a rather large chap in a Crombie overcoat to bring me to him. He eyed me up and down and, in a charming unfocused way, slurred, 'I really enjoyed the show.' ('Thank God,' I thought.) He continued, 'And the parrot, yeah, the parrot was great.'

As *was* my wont, I corrected him. 'Actually, it's not a parrot it's a bear.'

His minder looked me straight in the eye, and said, 'If he says it's a parrot it's a f*****g parrot!'

Johnny Dennis Johnny is an actor who has carved a highly successful niche for himself as an excellent chairman in old-time music hall, especially at London's Players Theatre and at the famous City Varieties, Leeds. As chairman he often joins the punters after the show in the bar and has been on the receiving end of some wonderful comments. One lady came up to him at the Players and said, 'I hope you don't mind me saying this, but you look just like my lesbian sister!'

At the Varieties a man approached him and enquired, 'How much do you earn?' 'Why?' asked Johnny. 'Well, my son wants to be a comedian and he doesn't know what to charge.'

Audiences for music hall are never shy in voicing their opinion of what they are watching and one night Johnny heard, while pausing after getting a very good laugh, a man on the front row turn to his wife and comment, 'I know, dear, but he's doing his best!'

Another regular chairman at the Players is the giant-sized actor Michael Kilgarriff (the author of the very best handbook on putting on a music-hall show *It Gives Me Great Pleasure*). One night, after what he thought was a successful performance, he passed two customers leaving the hall. The two elderly ladies were tottering gingerly down Villiers Street. 'Well,' said one, 'at least it's not too far from the coach – that's something.'

Digs The old-fashioned theatrical 'digs' have, of course disappeared. It's all bed and breakfast or, if the telly people are paying, characterless, 'tea-making facilities in every room' hotels. Oh, those evil plastic thimbles full of white emulsion! I missed the golden days of theatrical landladies but I did meet some good, some not so good and some 'never again'. My favourite was a lady in Cardiff who invited the whole of our *Red Riding Hood* company for Christmas dinner. She was so thoughtful she even cooked a vegetarian meal for our Wolf, who was one.

I stayed in a small hotel for several weeks while shooting a film and knew we'd backed a loser when, after the main course at dinner on the first evening, the landlord stood in the doorway to his kitchen and barked à la *Fawlty Towers*, 'Right, who *doesn't* like apple pie?'

The worst digs I ever stayed in shall be nameless, to protect me! Suffice to say they were in a university city where I was doing panto. I shared a room with a pal and we knew we were in trouble from being shown the room, right under the eaves – the ceiling was so low even the mice were hunchbacks (Jimmy Gay, 1952). The room smelt damp and my pal switched on the one-bar electric fire and held it over the bed – the sheets steamed! Worse was to come. For supper we were given a plate of baked beans apiece. We rehearsed in the city for a fortnight and every night for supper were – baked beans.

The night of the dress rehearsal was Christmas Eve. (All pantos used to open on Boxing Day in those days.) The dress rehearsal went on and on and it was just after midnight when we walked back to our chambers. Give the landlady her due, she was waiting to serve our supper. We sat at the table, fed up, 55 we'd both been given a hard time by the director. I said to my pal, 'If it's baked beans again tonight I'll throttle her.'

Then came the flop flop of 'ma' making her way down the passage with, of course, two plates of the dreaded. She plonked them down and shuffled off to where landladies seemed to spend their lives. I toyed with the glutinous heap. 'What a festive season this is turning out to be! An eight-hour dress rehearsal where everything I did was wrong, no hot water in the dressing-rooms, this khazi to stay in and bleedin' baked beans again!'

But wait. There was something in the pile of beans. A sausage. I got the red mist and shouted down the passage, 'Oi, Ma! I think you've made a mistake. I've found a sausage with my baked beans!'

'I know,' came from the kitchen. 'Merry Christmas!'

This story is a legendary one and has been attributed to everyone. My source was Arthur Lane, the actor, impresario and lovable rogue who, almost till his death, presented *The Golden Years of Music Hall.*

Arthur was in rep and at the theatre for a midweek matinée. Just as the half-hour call was announced he remembered he'd left an important prop back at his digs. He dashed back and let himself in through the back door. He was surprised (something Arthur rarely was) to see his landlady at it with the milkman on the kitchen table. He (as only he would) merely said, 'Good afternoon,' and carried on with his errand.

That evening, when he returned, the landlady brought him his supper and said, 'I do apologise for this afternoon, Mr Lane,' and added becomingly, 'You must think I'm a terrible flirt!'

Another digs story concerns a comic who returned to the place he'd stayed at two years previously. The landlady was waiting for him. 'So, you've come back!'

He said, 'Yes, ma – I had a very nice week here last time.'

'I know you did,' she roared. 'The last time you were here you put my daughter in the family way.'

'Did I?'

'Yes you did!'

He, for once at a loss for a snappy ad lib, could only say, 'Oh I'm sorry.'

'Sorry!' she said. 'Never mind sorry. What are you going to do for her and the nipper?'

He quickly replied, 'Well, how about a couple of complimentary tickets for first house tonight?'

My pal, the *Huddlines* writer Tony Hare, who has been such a help in sorting out all the memories in this book, remembered this classic story. Tony says:

Three pros were staying in digs where the landlady, a kindly soul, liked to leave 'her boys' a little surprise treat on the supper table for when they got back from the theatre. One night they returned to find three jellies awaiting their delectation. Somehow, after having downed a large amount of post-performance alcoholic beverage, they couldn't face the red, yellow and green gelatinous comestibles that lay there quivering in a festival of colour on the white tablecloth. One of the trio suggested they threw them into the dustbin and tell the landlady the next morning that they'd eaten them. The others didn't think that was such a good idea as there was the strong possibility she would discover them the next time she emptied the rubbish. Suddenly, a brainwave! Flush them down the khazi. So the troupers crept up the stairs with the three offending articles. Down the pan went the first jelly, the chain pulled and it disappeared from sight. A few moments to wait for the cistern to fill up again and down went the second jelly. Horror! As the cistern refilled, the first jelly returned! In a panic the third jelly was deposited and the loo flushed. Both jellies disappeared but the *second* one reappeared!

Now it so happened that all three performers were rather keen on the occasional flutter or ten and, not wishing to let a golden opportunity slip by, one of them suggested they make a book on which colour jelly would return on the next flush. During the next hour or two some serious gambling took place with the chain being virtually wrenched from its ballcock as the various jellies vanished and came back slightly smaller each time till they had all dissolved. The following morning 'Ma' asked them if they had enjoyed their supper. White-lying through their teeth they nodded enthusiastically. 'Are you sure the jellies agreed with you?' she continued. 'Only someone had an upset stomach – the toilet didn't stop flushing all night.'

Jack Dixon This human fireball, by his own enthusiasm and hard work, has put Newcastle-upon-Tyne's Tyne Theatre on the map. The historian, actor and general Geordie-about-town Joe Ging told me this story.

At one time a well-known subsidised theatre company had a short sojourn at the Tyne. They were not Jack's favourite tenants and when they proposed presenting an all-black production of *The Importance of Being Earnest* he was asked for his comments.

'A good idea,' enthused Jack. 'Then our lot can do an all-white version of *Zulu*.'

Ken Dodd

Everyone who has only seen him on television should rush to whichever theatre he is appearing in to see a master audience manipulator, perhaps the greatest 'front cloth' comic since Max Miller, in action.

I like a letter Ken had sent to him by a little girl when he was appearing in pantomime at the Hippodrome, Birmingham. He was playing the title role in *Humpty Dumpty*. The letter said –

Dear Humpty Dumpty,
   I think you should marry Mary, Mary Quite Contrary and not Tommy Tucker (the principal boy) as he is a girl and doesn't Mary know?

Val Doonican

The Irish singer and entertainer who has become a national institution. His comfortable, laid-back, witty approach to the business – and his musicianship, of course – have made him the most enduring of all family entertainers. His magnetic personality is reflected in his writing and the following tales I include verbatim.

Through the 1950s I toured the British Isles as a member of an Irish vocal quartet. Year after year, week in, week out, we covered just about every music hall and cabaret room on the circuit.

   Our business affairs at the time were in the hands of a very nice little man named Syd Royce. In my eyes, at least, he was a caricature of a Jewish agent, short, plump, very bald, and spoke with a rich Jewish accent. He organised our working lives from behind a desk in his minute office, situated over a music shop in Charing Cross Road.

   Syd rang me one day, asking if I could do him a favour. He'd taken under his wing a young comedian/impressionist, still in his teens, and was anxious to try him out in a few cabaret rooms in London. The young hopeful had got his act together, and needed some music arranged to accompany it. I was offered the sum of eight pounds for the job, and it was agreed that I should pop along to the office a few days later to see what could be done. More than a few laughs were in store as I mounted the rickety stairs to Syd's tiny place of business. The young Peter Kaye was already there, bubbling with youthful enthusiasm, and sounding more like a fellow about to open in Las Vegas. He wore a very smart suit, neat white shoes and his *pièce de résistance*, the very latest thing in trilby hats, à la 'Ol' Blue Eyes' himself. It was not the kind of headwear seen around London in those days, and Peter made quite a point of how difficult it had been to lay his hands on 'the real McCoy'.

I took a seat, my guitar to hand for checking keys, etc., plus a few sheets of manuscript and a well sharpened pencil. It was high summer at the time, and in spite of the fact that all the office windows were wide open, it was stifling hot, and dear old Syd mopped his bald pate incessantly.

He couldn't wait for me to see what his young find had in store. 'Go on, son,' he encouraged, 'show him the opening . . .' Then, turning to me, 'This is sensational.'

'What's the first song?' I enquired, wanting to write something on the top of the page.

'Mack The Knife,' they both said in unison. Syd turned to the lad. 'Go out on the landing, son, then you can make a proper entrance.'

Peter buttoned up his jacket, adjusted his precious hat to its most jaunty angle, then, giving the brim a final flick with the fingernail of his middle finger, disappeared on to the tiny landing. After a short pause filled with expectancy, he began shouting instructions through the closed door, as to what the musical introduction ought to be.

'Barah bah rahbah pow,' he sang, sounding like a one-man impression of the entire Nelson Riddle Orchestra. Suddenly the door burst open, as he exploded into the centre of the room, his fingers clicking out the tempo.

'Oh the shark has . . . Parah pow.' This was accompanied by a few fancy, well-rehearsed movements. *'Pretty teeth, deah . . . Barah row.'*

I just sat there, pencil poised, wondering where the hell all those imaginary brass figures were to come from when a badly played organ and drums were the substitutes for Nelson Riddle. Peter stopped. 'Now, at this point,' he said, 'I take off the hat and send it flying into the wings, and the

music goes *Zeeeeeee . . . POW.'* There followed a demonstra-
tion which sent both Syd and myself into roars of laughter,
and poor Peter into a fit of depression. *'Barah row,'* he
repeated, removing the hat and, with a sophisticated
flourish, sent it flying like a frisby across the tiny office.
Sadly, in his state of ecstasy, he'd forgotten that all the
windows were wide open. Away went the brand new hat,
sailing out over Charing Cross Road, landing like a flying
saucer on the roof of a passing trolley bus, never to be seen
again. Bless him, he'd made the cardinal mistake of doing
his best gag first.

Peter, however, went on to find great success in television
and theatre and today lives and works in Sydney in
Australia. In fact, we appeared together on a talk show over
there a few years ago, when the story of the hat was the
highlight of the evening.

This story is a cautionary tale. It warns would be hecklers not to
tangle with a real pro. Now read on Val says.

We occasionally did a week's engagement at the Astor Club,
one of London's best-known nightspots, situated in Berkeley
Square. It was what we pros categorised as a 'hard room',
most of the clientèle being far more interested in food, drink
and chatting up the hostesses, and not necessarily in that
order. The place came to life quite late at night and it was
not unusual for the cabaret to end at about one in the
morning.

However, the room was very popular and welcomed many
world-famous personalities among its guests. Part of its
tradition was that immediately after the floor show and prior
to the final dancing session, there came an interlude when
everybody who was anybody among the patrons would be
introduced in a blaze of spotlights and applause. If there
was the slightest hint that some extra encouragement might
inveigle the said party to come to the stage and say hallo, or
say a few words, or even sing a few bars of a song, then no
effort was spared.

On one memorable night while we were appearing there,
the old routine went as usual. We did our act, took our
applause and retired to our dressing-room. The master of
ceremonies mentioned some lesser names among the guests,
then went on to the 'biggies'.

'Ladies and gentlemen, making a welcome visit to the
London Palladium, a very talented group of musicians and
singers from the United States . . . will you please welcome

CHARLIE AUSTIN: 'It's hardly worth you going home.'

LADY BEERBOHM TREE — 'the plumber's mate.'

CORAM and JERRY — 'only when the dummy's talking.'

STANELLI – 'he's a sex maniac.'

RUSS CONWAY: 'I've heard of a colour bar but this . . .'

TOMMY COOPER: 'Can I have your Cup Final tickets?'

LES DAWSON: '...the mere shifting of a cough lozenge from one molar to another reverberated like a musket volley.'

BILLY DAINTY: 'You may as well know the lot.'

JIMMY CRICKET: 'Open the doors and let the heat in.'

BILLY BENNETT: 'Not worth blacking up for.'

WYN CALVIN: 'Sir! Sir!'

KEN DODD: 'Tommy Tucker is a girl.'

VAL DOONICAN: 'That bloody fool of a drummer.'

CHRIS EMMETT: 'A shameful nervous breakdown in the middle of Cinderella's forest.'

SID FIELD: 'Working?'

ARTHUR ENGLISH: 'Where is the grand piano?'

FLORRIE FORDE: 'I've Got A Feeling I'm Falling.'

GRACIE FIELDS: 'Can any of you buggers do that?'

BUD FLANAGAN and CHESNEY ALLEN: 'I thought we all might go back to your place.'

GEORGE FORMBY: 'You'll look like that one day – if you keep playing with yourself.'

MIKE and BERNIE WINTERS: 'Christ – there's two of 'em!'

GERTIE GITANA: 'I think I'll play my saxophone.'

TOMMY GODFREY in the new CRAZY GANG: 'They must be from a circus.'

HINGE and BRACKET: 'It's very sad when women get to this age and do not know when to retire.'

LARRY GRAYSON: 'Whenever I watch *The Last Night of the Proms*, I always get a little twinge.'

JIMMY JAMES: 'Twenty-five years and we've never spilt a drop.'

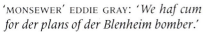

'MONSEWER' EDDIE GRAY: *'We haf cum for der plans of der Blenheim bomber.'*

NAT JACKLEY: 'Well, that will have to do!'

(*Above left*) R. G. KNOWLES: 'This is a monologue.'

(*Above*) G. H. MACDERMOTT – 'an aggressive warlike character.'

DAN LENO: 'Is that clock right?'

SIR HARRY LAUDER: 'Tell your friends
I'm here.'

MARIE LLOYD: 'I want you to take all
those knives, forks, spoons and
circular saws...'

RADIO REVELLERS: 'I spotted you.'

THE KRANKIES: 'I disguise myself as a woman.'

the fabulous Trenniers.' There was wild applause as the lads rose from their seats for a few brief seconds to accept their welcome to the club. 'And seated at the very same table, we're proud and pleased to introduce one of the world's great comedy talents, Mr Alan King!' Alan King's reception was really something. He'd appeared in London for a short season with the great Judy Garland not so long before and made a most amazing impact with the public, the press and British entertainers.

The applause simply went on and on while he took bow after bow, waving an open hand in appreciation, the customary huge cigar perched between his first and second fingers. He sat down for what he hoped was the last time, turning his attention once more to his guests. The applause continued, reinforced with shouts of 'More' and 'We want Alan'. Mr King tried to ignore it, hoping it would go away, but it didn't. Mein host took what he judged to be the most logical step.

'Would you like to just come up here, Alan, and say a quick hallo to the folks?' Alan King declined, waving once again, this time adding a shake of the head as if to say, 'Thanks, but no thanks.' The clapping and cheering at last began to fade, when from one of the tables a somewhat disapproving voice shouted, 'Oh come on, mate, stop playing hard to get. Tell us a few jokes . . . it won't cost you anything.'

There was a smattering of self-conscious laughter mixed with a sort of shocked silence, and all eyes were on Mr King. He positively glared at his critic, then slowly but deliberately rose from his table and approached the cabaret floor. Once again the room rang with applause while the atmosphere changed to that of an audience watching a gladiator entering the arena. He bowed to the crowd, shook hands with the host and calmly took the microphone. Now, I can't claim the ability to quote word for word what went on in the next ten minutes or so, even though I look back on it as a memorable moment in my career. The script would read something like this.

(It will help, of course, if you are familiar with Alan King's work and style, that kind of Marlon Brando-ish way of talking, his whole script seeming to consist of complaints about everything. I should also mention that his assailant in the audience was a short, bald-headed, middle-aged but prosperous-looking man, who sat at a table for two, accompanied by a very young, very busty hostess. He also looked very Jewish, and since Alan King's humour can be very much in that idiom at times we were set for a good encounter.)

ALAN: Good evening, ladies and gentlemen and thank you very much. I'd like to say that it's good to be here, but I can't, because it's not. It is good to be in London, I like London. I'm over here to do some television shows ... I've been in the studio all day, rehearsing ... I got through at about eight o'clock ... went back to my hotel and took a shower ... I then picked up my friends the Trenniers at the Palladium and we thought we'd go out and have a quiet meal ... Then some joker told us to come here ... (Pause) ... I've just had the worst meal I've ever eaten ... some clown of a waiter poured the most expensive whisky in England all over my pants ... and now, just to round things off ... you've got me working again.

INTERRUPTION: Aw come on, you'll make us cry in a minute. Tell us a few bloody jokes.

ALAN (pausing, puffing on his cigar, then gazing thoughtfully at the burning end, the way cigar smokers do): Do you think we could have a little light on this guy over here for a moment?

(He slowly approaches his victim. The spotlight operator duly obliges. The two men are now face to face for the first time. Alan looks him over, then looks at his young companion. With a wicked smile he gazes around the room, as if inviting everybody to take a look. The crowd are loving it.)

ALAN: Good evening, sir. Would you mind telling me your name?'

(Man, looking very annoyed, refuses to be drawn.)

ALAN: Come on now, what's your name? You're not going to tell me, are you? OK, tell you what, I'll have a guess. (He steps back, places his fingers over his pursed lips in a thoughtful pose, then smiles.) Let's call you Louis for now, all right? Now, tell us Louis, what do you do for a living?

(Man stares in silence.)

ALAN: You're not going to tell me that either, so I'll have to guess again? (Stands back as before, sizing up his new found partner.) I'd say, Louis, ahm, you make ladies' skirts in a little back street in London, am I right?

(Man looks more determined than ever to take no part in the encounter, but the expression on his face indicates that he could happily strangle Mr King. At this point, Alan leans on the edge of the table and faces the audience.)

ALAN (*waving his cigar like a conductor's baton*): I'd like to give you a hypothetical situation, ladies and gentlemen. I want you to imagine that Louis has had a really hard day in his little factory in that back street in London. At nine o'clock in the evening he locks up his front door and climbs in to his car to travel home, when up comes Alan King. 'Just a minute, Louis,' I say, 'before you go home, I'd like you to give me fifty ladies' skirts.' Now, I wouldn't be a bit surprised if Louis told me where to go. He'd have every right to say, 'Why the hell didn't you come during the day when I was open for business?' (*Pauses and turns to the man.*) Isn't that right Louis? (*By now, nobody expects a reply, so their eyes go back to Mr King who then delivers his crushing blow.*) But you haven't heard the worst yet Louis, not only do I want the fifty skirts after working hours, BUT I WANT THEM FOR NOTHING!

The room erupted to what was the best part of the evening's entertainment as Alan prepared to retire to his table. Then he turned once again to the man with yet another stinging remark. 'I do hope I haven't embarrassed you too much, Louis,' he said apologetically, 'especially in front of your daughter.'

He then returned to the cabaret floor, thanked the patrons and, to everybody's surprise, introduced the Trenniers once again. The boys rose as one and joined him at the microphone. He turned to the pianist; asked for a chord of E flat and together they closed the proceedings with a marvellous rendition of the old standard 'Up A Lazy River'.

Some years later I watched him do his full cabaret act at Caesars Palace in Las Vegas. He was quite superb, but for me the name Alan King will always mean that little interlude at the Astor Club, all those years ago.

Finally here's a story of Val's earliest days.

I was brand new to the music world, and doing my first real professional tour with an Irish dance band. We were based in the west of Ireland, but travelled every day, and most nights of the week played to towns and villages all over the country. To say that I was keen and enthusiastic would indeed be an understatement. When I wasn't practising the guitar, the bass, or the instrument I was booked to play, namely the drums, I talked about music endlessly, probably boring the socks off the more seasoned members of the party.

We arrived one night at a small country village hall 63

somewhere on the south-west coast. Carting my gear up towards the tiny stage, I listened to the familiar echoing sound of my heavy shoes on the slippery floor. Small though the place was, I saw that it sported a shining crystal ball. I also noticed, on this occasion, that immediately underneath it, in the centre of the floor, stood two large whitewood kitchen chairs.

I tried to work out what they might be doing there, but was baffled; they were not tall enough for anybody to have placed them there in an effort to reach the crystal ball, neither did they in any way match the other chairs around the walls.

When the dance finally got under way, I watched with interest to see if, and when, they would be removed by one of the organisers of the function, but nobody made such a move.

With each dance the floor got busier and, to all of us on the bandstand, the chairs appeared to be turning into quite a dangerous hazard. Couples in happy abandon went whizzing past them, missing by inches. By now, the music and singing had become quite secondary as far as we were concerned. The chairs were, without doubt, the stars of the evening.

The first half ended and we made our way to the refreshment room at the back of the hall, where local ladies served us tea and home-made sandwiches and cakes.

I mentioned the now infamous chairs to members of the organising committee, who just laughed, telling me not to worry about them. I even asked my boss if we should move them, but his reaction was, 'Oh, to hell with them, they've got nothing to do with us. If they want the things moved, let them do it themselves.'

The night was in full swing by now and the bandleader decided it was time to let loose with a good lively Irish dance. A great favourite, 'The Walls Of Limerick' was announced and all the laughing couples rushed on to the floor, holding hands and shuffling into position.

It was only then that my boss thought some action should be taken, fearing that, in the frenzy of the next few minutes, the dancers might find it impossible to avoid the obstacle in the centre of the dance floor.

'I'll go down and move them to one side,' I offered, wishing that the nagging worry of the chairs could be gone. An announcement was made asking the dancers to wait for just a minute.

I stepped off the bandstand and headed towards the middle of the floor, everybody moving aside to make way for me, at the same time greeting me with a few jeers and mock applause. I took a chair in each hand and at arm's length slid them to the side of the room. Back on the stand, the time was being stomped out by the boss's heavy boot, and at last, the Walls Of Limerick were scaled.

Suddenly, amid the happy laughing voices and dancing feet, there was an almighty crashing sound, the sound of women's screams brought the music to a halt and all eyes were turned in the direction of the commotion. The committee members rushed to the centre of the hall, where the dancers stood surrounding a gaping hole in the dance floor.

It turned out that, a couple of nights before, some workmen had damaged a few of the floorboards and had not been able to fix them in time. So what did they do? Like any decent workers they placed a foolproof warning sign and, as one of the patrons said, 'If that bloody fool of a drummer had left things alone, and minded his own business, everything would have been fine!'

Betty Driver Known and loved by all as Betty Turpin in *Coronation Street*, before that Betty Driver had a long and distinguished career in variety, musical comedy and recording. At the age of fourteen she was co-starring with Norman Evans in a revival of the Gracie Fields vehicle, *Mr Tower of London*. One night, at the Chiswick Empire, she swept down a staircase for her solo spot dressed beautifully in a full-length, tight-fitting French gown with a white fox cape around her shoulders. It all went wrong as she caught her foot on the bottom step and slid down the full length of the stage practically landing in the conductor's lap. She stood up to reveal that her dress was covered from top to bottom with the dark brown floor polish used on the stage. Shaken but not thrown, she ad-libbed with the conductor and carried on with her song. The audience loved her for it. The next day the local paper had headlines saying 'Betty Driver had a brilliant, most original entrance'. If only they'd known.

I collect sheet music and I found a copy of a song called 'You Don't Have To Tell Me, I Know' (a song, incidentally, a pal of mine always used to sing at auditions). On the front cover was a photograph of Betty. I sent her the copy and she thanked me. A few weeks later an episode of the *Street* opened with a shot of Betty, alone in the Rovers Return, polishing the glasses. She was softly singing to herself, 'You Don't Have To Tell Me, I Know'. I thought it was just for me.

Terry Duggan Terry and I first met on a TV series years ago. We've remained pals ever since. He has done the lot. Stunting, acting, and 'stag' stand-up. He is one of the best 'drunks' in the business and now does a superb solo routine as one.

In the days when he played clubs non-stop, Terry was approached by the manager of the place in his dressing-room. The manager told him: 'Tonight, please, no blue gags. No swearing. No wife or mother-in-law stories and no Irish, Scots, Welsh, Jewish, black or Chinese stuff. Please don't do 'em, we've had a lot of trouble here.'

Terry dumbly nodded and went on. Of course he had nothing left to talk about and came off to the sound of his own footsteps.

The club secretary was round in a flash. 'What was all that about?' he demanded. 'I saw you the other week doing some great material. That's why I booked you. What happened?'

'Well,' said Terry, 'the manager told me what not to do and I'd got no act left.'

'Manager?' said the secretary. 'What manager? Point him out to me.'

'Him,' said Terry. 'Him up at the bar.'

'He,' said the secretary, 'is the manager of the club down the road!'

T.E. Dunville A huge star in the music halls of the early twentieth century whose sad fading from fashion led to his taking his own life. In a theatrical club one night he overheard a fellow pro refer to him as a fallen star. He walked out and several days later his body was discovered in 'Suicide's Lock' near Reading.

In happier days he wrote his own story, *The Autobiography Of An Eccentric Comedian* and it is full of fascinating yarns. In one he refers to a rather perfumed tenor who had been a star in opera but whom time and a love of the bottle had reduced to knocking

it out round the halls where his 'over the top' style made him a popular, and well paid, performer. He was fond of country rambles but his Oscar Wilde-type appearance and behaviour always led to his being 'sent up' by the yokels he happened to meet.

T.E. remembered him facing a quintet of hecklers across a farm gate. 'How much do you men earn?' he enquired.

'I earn a pound a week,' answered the spokesman.

'How interesting,' said the irate flamboyant one. 'There are five of you, so that makes five pounds for the lot. Well, listen' – and here he gave them a snatch of a song, *Tra-la-la-la* – 'there's a month's wages for you!' Head in the air, he swept off.

Leslie Dwyer A well-known character actor on stage and in films, whose last role was the memorably miserable Punch and Judy man in *Hi De Hi!*

I did a play with Leslie and in the digs one night he said, 'Let me tell your fortune.' As it was free. I agreed. He merely held my hand and talked to me (I did have a chaperone). He scribbled something on a piece of paper and eventually said, 'You're going to get a big break, and it's something connected with these letters.' On the paper was written 'NSMAPMAWOL'. We tried every anagram we could think of but nothing worked. I kept the piece of paper, though, and about six months later I got my first chance in television in a show called *Not So Much A Programme More A Way Of Life.*

Kenneth Earle Born into a showbusiness family, Kenny has done the lot. He was the comedy half of the popular double act Earle and Vaughan and is now one of our most successful, and witty, agents and bookers of acts.

Kenny was staying in digs, while working the Theatre Royal, Accrington with a truly unique act. He thinks the chap was called 'The Unusual Jimmy'. Jimmy had no arms and did everything with his feet. Eating, drinking, painting, everything. He took a special chair with him wherever he went. One morning all the tenants were having breakfast together. After arousing initial interest, Jimmy's odd behaviour was now totally accepted. Suddenly he stretched out a foot and accidentally knocked over a bottle of HP sauce. 'Tsk! Tsk!' said one of the girls. 'Butter toes!'

The ubiquitous Alfred Marks remembers another armless wonder who, despite his lack of upper limbs, was constantly fondling the ladies he shared digs with. At the end of the week the landlady confided, 'I'm not having him here again – he's far too handy with his feet!'

Jimmy Edwards The handlebar-moustached larger-than-life (on and off) university-educated 'low' comedian who achieved national recognition through radio's *Take It From Here*. I worked in *Oliver!* with him. He played, brilliantly, Mr Bumble the beadle. We did six weeks in Toronto with the show, and that sanitised city really drove me crackers. Everything was so clean I longed to see just a scrap of litter. It got so bad that my agent sent me a parcel full of old fag ends and fluff just to stop me getting homesick. It was in Toronto that I first heard that inane expression, 'Have a nice day.' Terry Wogan swears someone in America said goodbye to him with, 'Have a nice life!' My fury at being constantly instructed to 'Have a nice day' amused Jim and one Sunday morning as we set out for a drive, on dropping a Catholic friend of ours at her church, he called after her, 'Have a nice pray!'

He had several highly publicised and aborted engagements to various ladies and June Whitfield remembered one, desperately trying to keep up with Jim's love of hunting, who fell off her horse into a pond. As she was going down for the third time she screamed, 'What shall I do?'

'Throw me the ring!' advised Jim.

The version of *Oliver!*, that Jim and I did together was directed by Peter Coe, who had directed the original version. All the company were looking forward to working with the great man. Alas, he was bored with the whole thing; didn't show up very often; and, when he did, he directed with little wit and destructive sarcasm. Just the thing to help people give a performance! One night when we'd opened he actually came along to watch the show and invited Jim and me for a drink. Jim paid, of course. The piece had gone well and the pair of us sat there waiting for just the odd word of encouragement. Nothing. Eventually he started asking Jim about an old polo pony he'd once owned. Jim, subtle as ever, answered by saying, 'You know, Peter, I'm a bit like an old polo pony. All I need to keep me going is a pat on the head and a lump of sugar.' Coe didn't even blink as he patted Jim on the head and put a knob of sugar in his mouth. What a sod!

Percy Edwards The legendary animal and bird impersonator (sound only of course!) began his radio career in the 1930s at Savoy Hill. He has appeared as an act or as the voices of animals in hundreds of broadcasts, television shows and films (the late Jim Henson was the only film maker to give him a credit).

His notoriety is summed up in the story of the old Suffolk farmer who was awakened, yet again, by the dawn chorus. He leapt out of bed to close his bedroom window and, as he did, shouted at his feathered friends: 'Why don't you shut up! Eff that wern't for Percy Edwards, you'd never have bin 'eard of.'

Percy's researches to get the voices of his animals and birds perfectly lead to this, my favourite, story. Percy says:

I was sitting under a hedge in a village in Suffolk watching   **69** for a tiny rodent known as the Bank Vole. Absolute stillness was essential as this small atom of life is so shy that the slightest movement, other than by surrounding plant life, would send it like quicksilver into hiding. I'd been there for about fifteen minutes when I heard voices and spotted two farm labourers on their weary way home from a day in the fields. As they passed, one nodded to me and I heard him say to his pal, 'Did you see who that was a-settin' in that hedge?'

'No,' said his mate.

'Why,' said the other, 'that was old Percy Edwards.'

'Percy Edwards,' came the reply, 'settin' under a hedge? Well blast me, bor. What's a grown man doin' a-settin' there?'

'I dunno,' said his friend, 'per'aps he's got a dozen eggs under him!'

Chris Emmett My sparring partner on *The News Huddlines* for the past eighteen years, Chris is, without dispute, the most versatile and in demand 'voices' man on radio but he is so much more. He is a talented writer, stage actor, a terrific dame in panto and a marvellous ad libber. Yes, in the words of Ian Dury, 'There ain't 'arf been some clever b******s.' Despite all this I like and admire him very much. I think you always do admire someone who achieves his effects in an entirely opposite way to you. He, totally unlike yours truly, is a very organised chap, a careful planner who, whenever possible, prepares well in advance for whatever he's going to do. For many years he appeared in and wrote lots of the sketches for the Ted Rogers TV quiz, *3, 2, 1*. I tell you this story at Chris's request. I had been booked for a Christmas edition of *3, 2, 1*. The sketches were all pantomime-based and Chris was writing them. He came round to my place to sort it all out.

In the middle of the meeting our agent, Morris Aza, rang and I told him Chris was with me. 'Why?' asked Morris.

'Sorting out the Christmas show,' I said. 'You know Chris – always leaves everything till the last minute.'

It was the fifth of April.

Everyone has stories of 'breaking up' on stage. I include just this one from Chris because his writing makes you 'see' the whole thing.

They say a panto audience is special; the children are, after all, the next generation of theatre-goers. I often wonder whether I was partly responsible for putting off a whole generation of potential theatre-goers.

It was a matinée and I was appearing as one of the three Broker's Men in *Cinderella* at the Queen's Theatre, Hornchurch. Anthony O'Donnell, Keith Morris and I arrived in the wings for our first entrance to see Buttons (Ian Talbot) and Prince Charming (Sheila Mathews) standing on stage, just staring at each other, with shoulders quietly shaking, for what seemed an eternity.

Eventually, Sheila turned and, without saying a word, walked off stage. As she passed us, her mascara running in black rivulets down her cheeks, she managed to gasp, 'Go on! Just . . . go on!' before fleeing to her dressing-room in a gale of laughter.

Ian managed enough self-control to peer out into the auditorium and say, 'No, not a Broker's Man in sight,' which was our cue. The band struck up with 'An Actor's Life for me' and we duly marched on stage to come to the usual percussive stop beside Ian and in the ensuing 'silence' that's when we heard it.

All that the cast had been told in advance was that the theatre had been booked out by all the children of the local supermarkets' staff. What became obvious during that infamous Scene Two was that they had all been issued with the same packed lunch with precise instructions as to how and when to consume it. By Prince Charming's first entrance they had finished their sandwiches and sausage rolls and made a collective start on their crisps.

Can you for a moment imagine the sound of about five hundred packets of crisps being eaten simultaneously?

The only way I can describe it is to liken it to the sound of rolling surf on a seashore. As tiny hands dipped into cellophane packets the rustling whisper swelled to a crackling roar and then subsided into a crunching, hissing sound, the cycle repeating in waves over and over again.

Well – I started to laugh. Quietly at first. Finding it impossible to speak, I turned to Tony behind me to see him quivering with silent laughter. A pleading look entered his huge, soulful eyes, then the tears started to roll down his cheeks, and that did it. My own silent mirth turned into an unsuccessfully repressed high-pitched squeal and that set us all off.

We roared, clutching our sides and each other, and the children munched on, oblivious to the effect they were having on us.

Eventually, Ian gave up on dialogue and simply followed Sheila's example. He walked off stage. His exit was normally the cue for our number and the M.D. quickly obliged. We were supposed to be singing and dancing, '*Hi, Diddly-Dee, We're Broker's Men, We Three,*' and so on, but five hundred children chose that moment to screw up their empty crisp packets (to the sound of a tidal wave crashing over Blackpool's North Pier) and none of us made it past the first '*Diddly*'.

We struggled to regain control and, I believe to this day, almost managed it when, as though at a precise signal from some mischievous deity, five hundred Coca-Cola cans were opened in rapid succession.

We howled. We hooted. We shrieked. The effect of this continuous laughter now reached the other members of the band – normally a po-faced lot – and the trumpet rapidly deteriorated into a vibrato farting sound and that finished us totally. We lay on the stage like beached whales, gasping for breath and mercy.

In the end, like Sheila, like Ian, we tco gave up. I signalled to the M.D. to wrap it up as decently as possible and the three of us crawled off stage.

The last thing I saw was row upon row of puzzled children noisily sucking on their straws, clearly wondering why these refugees from the funny farm had been let out for the day, just long enough to have a shameful nervous breakdown in the middle of Cinderella's forest.

Those children will now be in their mid to late twenties. Maybe they took it all in their stride; maybe the five of us did put them off theatre for life. We'll never know – unless they write in of course – in which case, my name is Helen Shapiro and I was in Plymouth at the time!

Fred Emney The famous son of a famous father (Fred senior was a music-hall top of the bill, his star turn being a sketch called 'A Sister to assist 'er' in which he played a midwife), Fred junior, with his vast frame, ever-present cigar and gruff, bemused throwaway style, had a highly successful career in musicals, farce, variety and films.

He once played, and stole the show with, the drunken photographer in J.B. Priestley's *When We Are Married*. One night the whisper went round that J.B. himself was in the audience with a group of friends. He was. At the end of the performance the company gathered together in the hope that the playwright would come backstage. He didn't. 'Oh well,' said one of the actors, 'perhaps he didn't like it.'

'Didn't like it?' growled Fred. 'If he didn't like it, he shouldn't have written it!'

'Wee' Georgie Wood was working in Brighton and Fred, who lived there, invited him to stay for the week. The fussy and pedantic 'Wee' Georgie, three feet nothing in height and completely unmistakable, was somewhat taken aback to hear Fred say to him on the phone, 'I'll meet you from the train. You'd better wear a buttonhole so I'll recognise you.'

Arthur English Another graduate of that toughest school of comedy, the Windmill Theatre, my brother Water Rat Arthur, as the huge-shouldered, kipper-tied, fast-talking post-war 'spiv', became a firm favourite on radio and in variety. His catch-phrases, 'Mum! Mum! They're laughing at me,' and 'Open the cage!' became part of everyone's vocabulary. When variety died, Arthur merely switched to other things. He, like so many excellent comedians, was a smashing actor. With his lethal combination of truth and attack he was soon equally admired by a new generation in theatre and television. The porter in *Are You Being Served?* was just one of his popular characterisations.

He shared many weeks in variety with the unforgettable 'Monsewer' Eddie Gray. Arthur was a huge top of the bill, and he always asked for the 'Monsewer' to be with him because Eddie made him laugh so much.

Arthur himself sent me just two examples of the 'Monsewer's' constant inventiveness – off-stage.

Arthur's first digs in Birmingham were at Mrs Coombs, 365 Hagley Road (you never forget the address of the good 'uns). He knocked at the front door. A lady opened it and Arthur enquired in a very loud voice, 'MRS COOMBS?'

'YES,' the lady replied – equally loudly.

'MY NAME IS ENGLISH,' roared Arthur. 'AR, AR-THUR ENG-LISH!'

'GOOD,' yelled Mrs C.

'HOW ARE YOU?' screamed Arthur.

'I'M FINE. NICE TO MEET YOU!' bellowed the landlady.

'This ludicrous conversation,' says Arthur, 'went on for some time until finally the almost voiceless Mrs Coombs croaked, "There's no need to shout. I'm not hard of hearing." "Neither am

73

I," I replied. There is, of course, no need to explain. Eddie had told me Mrs Coombs was stone deaf and Mrs Coombs that I was!'

Arthur's other story is about digs too. In Manchester this time. 'Our manager Dandy Page had booked Eddie and myself into accommodation that neither he, or us, had seen. There were some smashing digs in Manchester and some of the "how do we get out of this?" type too.' These were of the latter variety. The sight (and smell) of the place was quite enough for English and Gray so, without a word or a look to each other, they launched into a brilliant piece of invention. 'Where is the grand piano?' enquired Arthur. 'Can I see it please?'

The landlady's face fell. 'I know nothing about a grand piano,' she said.

'Oh yes,' Arthur explained, 'I must have a grand piano for my singing lessons. I practise one hour daily.'

'That's right,' added Eddie, 'I play for him. He's working on "Hold This While I Fetch a Copper" at the moment.'

Arthur started to shake. The landlady, thank heaven, had no piano, apologised profusely and quite understood why the two musical prodigies couldn't stay with her.

As Arthur said, 'Saved!'

Sid Field To those who saw him 'live', Sid was a comic genius. Sadly, his films do him no favours. Like all the great ones he needed a theatreful of people to be able to flower. Jack Tripp was his understudy during the days of his smash-hit West End revues. One night Jack saw him waiting in the wings at the Prince of Wales Theatre. One of the beautiful seven-feet-high showgirls passed him wearing, as Jack says, 'Just about one feather, two milk bottle tops and a five-foot-high jewelled head-dress.'

'Good evening, Mr Field,' she said.

'Hello,' said Sid. 'Working?'

Gracie Fields In my 'umble, she was the greatest female performer we have ever produced. She was an actress, a comedienne, a singer of comic and serious songs and a breaker of box office records from the London Palladium to the Batley Variety Club. She made over three hundred records, she was the first British film star and stayed at the top for over sixty years. She was, before the word had even been invented, a superstar.

In the 1920s the handsome matinée idol Sir Gerald du Maurier cast Gracie in his play *S.O.S.* at the St James Theatre. It was her first shot at a straight play and the rest of the West End cast didn't take too kindly to the importation of a music-hall singer and, at rehearsals, showed it by ignoring her. After two mornings' worth of cold-shouldering by the 'legits' she eventually won them over.

At rehearsals the next day she walked in and did cartwheels all round the room. 'Right,' she said, dusting herself down. 'Can any of you buggers do that?' From that moment on the cast, like everyone else, loved her.

In *S.O.S.* the character she played died in the first act, and the 75 rest of the cast found themselves playing to half a house at the beginning of Act Two. The audience had followed Gracie to the Alhambra where she was doing her variety act. Sir Gerald graciously said, 'I'd be over there with them, but I have to stay and finish the wretched play!'

He, the ageing matinée idol, always fell in love with his leading ladies and Gracie was no exception. After taking her to supper one night he kissed her, and she retorted, 'Don't be soft, lad, you're older than me dad!'

Her popularity was such that in 1939, according to Hansard, Sir Samuel Hoare prefaced a speech with, 'Gracie Fields is on the air tonight so it is obvious that the debate must end at an early hour.'

In 1978 she was made 'Dame Commander of The British Empire'. Her comment: 'So now I'm Dame – I just hope they don't call Boris (her husband) Buttons.'

Just after the Second World War, Gracie was to appear as top of the bill at the London Palladium. It was an enormously important engagement for her. All sorts of stories had been circulated about her behaviour during the war. People said she fled Great Britain when in fact she had simply got her second husband, the Italian film director Monty Banks, out of the country before he was interned. She actually spent the majority of the war entertaining the troops and raising both money in America and moral over here. But, as they say, throw enough mud and some will stick. Many people still believed she had deserted her country in its darkest hour so her Palladium gig was very much a hit or miss affair. Would the British public accept her again?

Her agent, Bert Aza, and his wife Lilian went over her act with a fine-tooth comb. The three of them discussed every song and sweated blood to get the balance just right. 'Now the opening song,' said Bert.

'I know what that'll be,' said Gracie.

'What?' asked Bert.

'I'm not going to tell you,' said Gracie.

'You must,' said the worried agent. 'Everything rests on that first impact.'

'No, it'll be a surprise!' She would tell no one except her pianist and he was sworn to secrecy.

Lilian Aza told me:

That opening night, Bert and I stood at the back of the Palladium holding hands and our breaths. She was so unpredictable. The number went up in the frame. The orchestra played 'Sally' and on she came! The audience seemed pleased to see her. She acknowledged the applause and went straight into the English version of 'La Vie en Rose'. The opening line was 'Take me to your heart again". The audience rose as one and she had them in the palm of her hand. Brilliant. Did she have her finger on the pulse!

Bud Flanagan The much-loved singer, with his partner Chesney Allen, of many much-loved songs was the unelected leader of the anarchic Crazy Gang. There are anecdotes about him scattered throughout this collection. Here's one for starters.

Bud, and indeed all the Crazy Gang, were great favourites of the Royal Family and were almost permanent fixtures in the annual Royal Variety Performances. During the line-up at the end of one of the shows, when the Royals 'chatted' to the artistes, Prince Philip asked Bud what he would be doing next.

'Well,' replied the Royal jester, 'I've got a crate of brown ale in the dressing-room. I thought we might all go back to your place.'

Florrie Forde Bud Flanagan remembered Florrie's golden pantomime rule. The greatest chorus singer the music hall ever produced always *had* to have the title of her latest song as the cue for the song itself; for instance: 'Have the Babes been found?' 'No.' 'Then we must find them, even if we have to go to Valencia.' Orchestra: Bell note into 'Valencia'. In *Cinderella* she came upon Bud, playing Buttons, while he was flirting with the heroine. 'How dare you!' she cried, and knocked him to the ground. 'That reminds me,' she announced. 'I've Got A Feeling I'm Falling.'

George Formby The ukulele-playing son of George Formby senior – a huge star in music-hall days – George junior started on the halls doing his Dad's songs billed as 'A Chip Off The Old Block'. His discovery of the ukulele, though, led to his flowering and he became a real 'one off'. Believe it or not, he was awarded the Order of Lenin – for being Russia's most popular film star.

George's wife, Beryl, has come in for a lot of stick over the years for never letting George kiss any of his leading ladies, keeping him short of cash and so on. Indeed, Gary Marsh, the well-known British actor who was in several films with George, 77 assured me Beryl allowed him just five bob a day spending money. But whatever she was really like, she did make her husband a star; and there was no fiercer advocate of his talent or his position in the business.

An old pal of mine, Peter Reeves, reminded me of this with a story that happened during the war. It was backstage at a special fund-raising variety show. As usual, the pros were all in the Green Room gossiping and a young female vocalist, who had made a name for herself with a handful of hit records, was holding forth. She was telling how she had been invited to entertain the Royal Family at Windsor Castle.

'Oh, they were so nice to me. It was wonderful. They sent a car for me and looked after me so well. They were so friendly, they knew all my songs and even sang along with me. They were so complimentary to me afterwards, we even had supper together ...' and so on and so forth.

Glowering in the corner throughout this sat Beryl. Eventually she could stand it no longer. 'That,' she said, 'is nothing. Nothing at all! Why George and I have been there that many times that the last time we went, just as we were leaving, the King says to us, 'Well now you know where we live, don't be strangers!'

Frank E. Franks A well-known Geordie comedian in the 1930s and 40s, he started as a 'lantern cooler', as they called the acts who appeared between films – to give the projectors a chance to cool down. Bob and Alf Pearson gave me this example of his, and their, sense of humour standing outside the stage door of the Sunderland Empire.

'We were standing in almost this exact spot,' said Bob, 'when round the corner came a vision of satorial elegance. Pearl-grey suit with a wide-brimmed hat to match. A yellow and red spotted bow tie, similar handkerchief and, wait for it, bright yellow spats! It was Frank E. Franks.' 'How are you Frank?' we asked. Frank shook his head and replied, 'Not so good. I've just been to bury the wife's mother!'

Patrick Fyffe For many years he appeared as Dame Hilda of the unique team Hinge and Bracket.

It was the ninetieth birthday of the great Dame Eva Turner and a special concert had been arranged at the Royal Opera House,

Covent Garden. Dame Eva had specially asked for Dame Hilda and Doctor Evadne to be part of the show. The two 'ladies' opened the second half and, unbeknown to them, the Maestro Tito Gobbi was waiting in the wings to introduce the next artiste. Their act was going well with everyone, except the Maestro. He was pacing up and down, glancing at the monitor and generally appearing extremely disaffected with the 'ladies'.

'What do you think of them?' asked a fireman.

'Rubbish!' was the reply. 'Their voices have all gone,' stormed Gobbi. 'They may have been good once upon a time. But it is very sad when women get to this age and do not know when to retire.' 'But they're not old ladies,' said the fireman, 'they're young men.'

'*Mamma mia!*' cried the Maestro. 'They are wonderful. I must meet them at once.'

He did, and much praise was heaped upon the Dame and the Doctor by Mr and Mrs Gobbi.

Will Fyffe, Junior The son of the great scots music-hall star and actor, Will is one of our most experienced accompanists and musical directors. During the 1960s he was in charge of Ronnie Hilton's musical requirements. Ronnie had had two or three Top 20 hits and so was constantly in demand for all sorts of charity functions. Will and Ronnie found themselves at a big Red Cross gathering at the Guildhall, Southampton where Ronnie was to present some prizes. They were greeted by the President of the Society, the Countess of Malmesbury. Shaking Ronnie by the hand she said, 'I've enjoyed listening to your gramophone recordings many times, Mr Hilton,' and turning to Will added, 'And of course I saw and admired your father, Will Fyffe, whenever I saw him at the London Palladium.' After the compulsory glass of sherry, the pair of them were introduced to the audience by her Ladyship: 'Ladies, here is that famous star of radio and television – Mr *Roland Hill*!' Ronnie, as is his wont, accepted this with good grace while Will, as is *his* wont, suppressed an evil snigger. His smile vanished however when the good lady continued, '. . . and with him is his friend and pianist, the son of the very famous Scottish comedian, Mr *Harry Lauder junior*!'

Will's mother used to tell the story of her son asking for a set of drums. She told him, 'You know Daddy doesn't like a lot of noise when he's at home.' Fyffe junior's reply was, 'But I'll only play them when he's asleep.' He got the drum kit.

Alan Gale A performer and producer of summer shows and pantos who, Bill Pertwee says, gave him more laughs on and off stage than anyone else he can remember. Alan was the last of the line, almost (see under 'Arthur Lane'), and apart from his many shows also produced an extremely talented son, Peter Duncan.

Bill recalls that whenever Alan forgot a song or sketch he would walk slowly into the wings and read the words, which he'd previously pasted on to a flat. Bill also remembers going backstage to visit Alan after a performance of his *Cinderella* at the Assembly Rooms, Tunbridge Wells. At the end of the first half Alan himself went out front to announce: 'And now something that is always a great moment in my pantomimes, ladies and gentlemen, the transformation scene. This scene . . .' He went on until someone backstage shouted 'Ready!' The reason for the delay was a sad one. The ponies accompanying Cinderella's cardboard cut-out coach were so old they had to be lifted on to the stage and held up by the cast and stage hands while the curtains were drawn backwards and forwards, twice, before they were lifted off again. Alan, of course, led the applause from the side of the stage with shouts of 'Beautiful! Beautiful!', while actual tears streamed down his face.

During his production of Old Time Music Hall at the West Pier, Brighton, Bill remembers him telling the audience in the interval that the second half would continue when the freezer was empty of ice cream.

Marion Pertwee (Bill's missus) worked for Alan under her own name, Marion Macleod. Marion was in an Alan Gale pantomime at the Theatre Royal, Middlesbrough in the early 1950s. He was a man who could put on a 'full scale' production with a cast of seven, and often did. He called all his productions 'full scale' with as many as 'twenty-five spectacular different scenes'. He would walk on with a chair or a plant pot and announce to the audience that it was a scene change.

The Middlesbrough pantomime was a 'lavish production'. Many of the artistes were playing two or three parts, and Gale himself played four different characters, all created by the judicious use of four different hats! His stage manager and partner did three different speciality acts. Fire eating, juggling and mind reading. The last was always popular in a Gale pantomime, with Gale: 'You can always spin it out with a duff audience,' he used to say.

The pantomime was billed as *Red Riding Hood* and was due to open on Boxing Day. Late on Christmas Eve it was discovered that the girl playing the title role had no costume (she'd forgotten to bring one with her). Never one to be thrown by such minor problems, Alan told his stage manager (who was in the middle of rehearsing his fire eating) to go into town and buy some red crepe paper. He returned, empty-handed, explaining that all the shops were closed. 'Never mind,' said Gale, 'we'll do *Dick Whittington*.'

Gertie Gitana A music-hall star, Gertie is remembered today as the singer of the ultimate boozer's ballad, 'Nellie Dean'. Whenever she and her husband, the impresario Don Ross, passed a pub through whose doors came wafting the mangled lay, she would say, 'Oh, listen to what they're doing to poor old Nellie.'

Gertie Gitana also played the saxophone in her act and the classic 'subtle' squeezing of a variety act into a pantomime is credited to her. Playing Cinderella, she sat friendless and cold in the kitchen of Hardup Hall – everyone else had gone to the Ball and she'd given Buttons the elbow – then sighed and said, 'Here I sit all alone, I think I'll play my saxophone!' She reached up the chimney, produced the instrument, and went into the act.

Glasgow Empire The 'graveyard of English comics'. Every English comic was terrified of working this particular hall. Only recently Des O'Connor admitted that, in his early days, he had to pretend to faint on stage rather than face a decision on his efforts from the Glaswegians.

An old pal of mine, the late Eddie Reindeer, told me whenever he had to work there he used to black up, call himself Eddie Reinhardt and do his patter in an American accent.

Two Irish comics came on very quickly in unison to their opening song: 'We are two Irish gentlemen – we've just come here to please you.' A voice from out front said, 'Bugger off!' Without missing a step they reversed and exited, never to return, singing, 'Right you are, bejabbers!'

A story of not too long ago, told by the man himself, concerns Bernie of Mike and Bernie Winters. Their act opened with Mike playing a clarinet solo. This *always* got their show off to a good start. Not at the Empire. The clarinet number finished to stony silence. Bernie then made his appearance by sticking his bowler-hatted head through the centre curtains. This always brought a laugh. Not at the Empire. It merely brought the observation from the gallery: 'Christ – there's two of 'em!'

Shaun Glenville A legendary dame in panto, and husband of our most famous principal boy, Dorothy Ward, Shaun is mentioned several times in these tales and every one concerning him is worth having. The master story teller Freddie Sales remembers Albert Burdon telling him this one.

Albert and Shaun were, together with Dorothy, in pantomime at Newcastle-upon-Tyne. Albert and Shaun were great friends and drinking partners and one evening, after a few jars in the theatre bar, decided that the night was young and they would continue their merry spree back in Albert's digs.

They duly made their way to Leazes Terrace where Albert, and most of the other pros, had their lodgings. All the houses had keys on string just inside the letter-box, and so the jolly pair quietly entered and sat themselves down in the front room. Shaun opened a cupboard and discovered a great assortment of booze while Albert found the glasses. The evening continued.

'I must say, these are very nice digs,' said Shaun.

'Why aye, man,' nodded Albert. 'I always stay here, 'cos the woman's a wonderful cook and has very good rooms.'

'They are lovely,' agreed Shaun. 'Look at that picture, for a start. What a beautiful painting!'

'You're right,' said Albert, squinting at the picture. 'It is beautiful, and do you know – I've never noticed it before.'

'And look at that furniture, Albert,' enthused Shaun. 'Not many digs have furniture like that.'

'True, true,' said Albert, trying to focus on the sideboard. 'Here, just a minute – Shaun, drink up quick and let's get out of here. We're in the wrong house!'

Tommy Godfrey One of the new 'Crazy Gang' in the musical version of Bud and Ches's story, *Underneath The Arches*. The show was devised and written for the Chichester Festival Theatre and really did take that place by storm. It later, thanks to the foresight of Lord Delfont, transferred for a year's run to the Prince of Wales Theatre in London. During its run at Chichester I was doing a Sunday morning Radio Two chat and record programme and one week I talked about Tommy. I told about him being called to an audition for a commercial, and explained that Tommy had just one tooth, in the middle of his grin.

He turned up at the audition, smiled and the entire room burst out laughing. Tommy, in his own inimitable manner said, 'What the bleedin' 'ell are you laughin' at?'

'Sorry, Tom,' said the director. 'Didn't anyone tell you?'

'Tell me bleedin' what?' said the ruffled Tom.

'This commercial is for the Colgate Ring of Confidence!'

During the telling of this tale, I referred to Tommy as the man who gives elocution lessons to Arthur Mullard.

Next day, just before curtain up in Chichester, I saw Tommy sitting in his dressing-room completely toothless!

'What happened, Tom?' I asked.

'You, you bastard!' said Tom. 'I heard your line about me and Arthur Mullard, and I laughed so much the bleedin' pickle stabber flew out and I've never seen it since!'

During the West End run of *Arches*, Peter Glaze, of *Crackerjack* fame, and a stalwart of the show, died. (Peter was invaluable as he had understudied the entire original Crazy Gang during their occupancy of the Victoria Palace and remembered all their best gags.) It was a sad company that made their way to the chapel for his funeral.

We all arrived at the cemetery in one coach. My son and I brought up the rear of the procession that made its way across the graveyard. It was like something from a Fellini film.

Heading the line were two six-foot showgirls, followed by the diminutive figure of Joe Black; then came more showgirls, Christopher Timothy and Don Smoothey. Eddie Gray's brother, Billy, came next, then several over emotional boy dancers, followed by the toothless Tommy smoking a huge cigar.

The entire cavalcade passed by two old ladies putting flowers on a grave. They looked up and, as my son and I passed them I heard one say to the other, 'They must be from a circus.' Peter would have loved that.

Rusty Goffe An excellent comic and musician, who just happens to be a dwarf. A Musical Rat of the GOWR famous for his witty ad libs – in music.

An opera company contacted Rusty and offered him a non-singing role in one of their productions. He agreed and attended rehearsals for a fortnight. He was never used until the director eventually said, 'This is you, Mr Goffe.'

'What do I do?'

'Well, you're just around in this court scene.'

'Doing what?' said Rusty.

'Oh, I don't know,' said the fraught director. 'Do what dwarfs usually do.'

'Right,' said Rusty, and sang, *'Hey ho, Hey ho, It's off to work we go!'*

Ken Goodwin *The Comedians* was the TV show that first pushed Ken into the limelight, and since then he has established himself as one of our most endearing comedians.

In the 1970s Ken was playing panto in Nottingham with the late Nat Jackley. One lunchtime the two repaired to Yates Wine Lodge. There they were greeted by a little old lady who recognised them both.

'Oh Ken,' she said, 'I love you on *The Comedians*, and you, Nat – well, you've been one of my favourites for years. You must let me buy both of you a drink.' She did and, almost telepathically, Nat and Ken looked at each other then at the old lady and together each took out a pound and slipped it, unknown to her of course, into the pocket of her rather threadbare overcoat. Their pious feelings vanished, however, when the lady informed them that she had just won several thousand pounds on the pools and was in the wine lodge having a farewell drink before she set off on a world cruise.

Peter Goodwright The 'ace' impressionist who has scored equally successfully in pantomime, straight plays and after-dinner speaking, Peter has this memory of Dickie Henderson.

One late September night, towards the end of a long variety summer season on the Wellington Pier in Great Yarmouth where Dickie was topping the bill, he and I had stayed behind after the show to share a cool bottle of Chablis.

Consequently when we came out of the stage door, the pier was deserted and all the bright lights extinguished. If any of the public were around at this time it was always to ask for Dickie's autograph. They usually ignored me. A cold sea mist was seeping through the wooden planking of the pier and, as we walked towards the promenade, the lone figure of an elderly man detached itself from the shuttered booths and came towards us. Dickie said quietly, 'Stand by for the star's autograph!' The man approached us and said, 'Could I have your autograph, please, Mr Goodwright?' I signed the book and looked around for Dickie. He had vanished. As the man walked away, the oh so familiar Henderson tones quietly floated through the shadows: 'Do you want to see a grown man cry?'

Leslie Grade Leslie was the famous agent brother of Lord Delfont and Lord Grade. He was Kenneth Earle and Malcolm Vaughan's agent and they toured the country for him when Bill Hayley was the bill-topper and the biggest attraction of the day. They opened at the Dominion in Tottenham Court Road and it was practically the birth of the blanket marketing side of popular music. The business was terrific and Leslie was over the moon. He even wore a Hayley badge on his Savile Row suit! After the first show, Kenny and Mal were in Bill's dressing-room when in came Leslie – 'Beside himself with gratitude.' He couldn't contain himself so, trying to get into the jargon of the times, he said with tears (and pound-note signs) in his eyes, 'Bill! Bill! you're a square!' Hayley never worked for him again.

Kenny and Mal had a problem with Leslie regarding pantomime, and decided to face him with their grievance. As was his wont he listened most attentively, thus encouraging the lads to go further and fall over each other to voice their complaints on every single aspect of the way Leslie was handling their careers. As they began to peter out, Leslie stopped them dead with: 'Do you want to go to the Palladium?'

There was a moment of silence, then a vigorous, humble nodding of heads. With a smile Grade pressed his intercom button and asked Myrna to come in. She did, and with an even bigger smile he said, 'Myrna, get the boys two tickets for the Palladium. Matinée will do.' Exit two crestfallen but laughing pros.

Lord Grade Bill Glaze, Peter's brother, told me this one about the great showman from Alec Fyne (the booker for ATV). Alec used to have a meeting with Lew, as he was then, to tell him who was on the bill for *Sunday Night At The Palladium*. The longer the show ran, the harder it was to get genuine variety top of the bills. They'd used all sorts of acts, including Topogigio, an Italian mouse puppet act.

Alec cast his net wider, and informed the governor one week that the headliner would be Tito Gobbi.

'Oh no!' said Lew. 'Not that bloody mouse again!'

'Monsewer' Eddie Gray A wonderful juggler and patterer, whose routines in fractured French were classics, Eddie was also, according to everyone who knew him, the funniest of them all – off-stage. There are dozens of stories about his exploits but here are just a few that I saw happen, plus some classics I've been told.

My own, sadly limited, time in his company was during a provincial run of *A Funny Thing Happened On The Way To The Forum*. Also in the show was Charlie Naughton, a pal of Eddie's from the Crazy Gang days. Charlie was over eighty at the time and Eddie made it his job to 'look after' the old boy. God help Charlie! They both stayed at a pub opposite the stage door and from my dressing-room I could see them crossing the road to work. Every time they would put on terribly crippled walks and stop all the traffic as they made their painfully slow progress; and every time, when they got half-way across they would jump up in the air and dance the second half of the journey to much effing and blinding from the drivers they had held up.

My agent came to visit me and Eddie insisted he take him, me and Charlie out to a little tea shop. I thought Eddie was behaving well, apart from juggling with the knives and forks on the table, as he chatted to my agent about the old days of variety. I *thought* he was behaving well, until I noticed that as he was chatting he was also buttering Charlie's bald head.

After the show one night I had a couple of local bigwigs in the dressing-room, with their wives, to discuss a fête or something I was to open. I'd just served them all a sweet sherry when into the room came Eddie, completely naked. 'Good evening,' he said to the banjacksed nobs, and proceeded to the handbasin where he relieved himself and walked out with a cheery 'Goodnight!' I could only splutter, 'I think he's senile.'

Whenever we had just an evening show I'd walk from my digs

and pick up Eddie from the betting shop. Those short journeys will stay with me for ever. He was always looking for trouble, and once steered me into Burtons, the tailors. Eddie was unrecognisable offstage. Without his top hat and moustache, no one knew him. He looked like a respectable old gentleman, and this was his great strength as a practical joker.

Once inside Burtons he gave me a bowler hat from a shelf. 'Try that on,' he said.

As I did, a young assistant came up and, because I was on telly at that time, said, 'Can I have your autograph, Mr Hudd?'

I obliged and graciously said, 'I'm sure you'd like Mr Gray's – original member of the Crazy Gang.'

'Yes, please,' said the lad.

Eddie signed and then put on an overcoat from the rack. 'What do you think?'

The assistant and I both agreed. 'Very nice.'

'Good,' said the master and grabbing me, still wearing the bowler hat, by the arm, propelled me out of the shop.

The lad followed us. 'Er, you haven't paid for the hat and coat.'

'What!' roared Eddie. 'Young man, you've got a lot to learn. You had two autographs. His' – pointing to me. 'Now, he's only just started so he gets a hat – and mine. Well, I've been in the business for many years so I always get a coat. Now be off with you!'

He kept this up all the way to the theatre, with the poor lad begging for the clothes back. He even carried it on into his dressing-room where he called all the other members of the company to witness the insult he had been subjected to. Mind you, he did give the lad a couple of 'comps' – eventually.

It was during one of our post-betting shop walks that he repeated one of his most famous gags, just for me. Approaching a pillar-box he suddenly shouted into the slot, 'Well, how did you get in there?'

I was a useless stooge for him because I always laughed, so this time I hid in a shop doorway to see what would happen. The brilliant conversation with the someone who was inside the pillar-box continued. 'You what?'

'I don't believe this,' he turned to address the small crowd that was gathering. 'There's a postman in there. He fell inside the box as he was collecting the letters and the door closed behind him.'

Then to the invisible prisoner: 'It's allright. Don't panic. Look, I'll nip round to the Post Office and get a key. Just hang on.'

The crowd had grown, and the Good Samaritan said, 'Look you keep him talking while I sort this out.' He strode away, leaving a clutch of people all shouting into the slot. 'Oh Gawd, I think he's fainted. He's not answering!' and so on. Weak-kneed, I followed the 'nice helpful gent' back to his true home, the theatre.

Here's a story told to me, and everyone else in the business, by Tommy Trinder. The last season Eddie did was in Brighton in Tommy's show. One night Eddie said to Tommy, 'You know, I think I've got a great idea for my act. If you'll help me out.'

'Course,' said Tom.

'Well, it would be marvellous if a big star like you would come on and do a gag with me.'

Tommy should have been the last person in the world to walk into a set up like this but even he, wily campaigner that he was, was taken in. 'What can I do?' he asked.

'Just walk on, for a start,' said the humble flatterer. 'The audience will be thrilled to see you. Then all you have to do is say, "Hello, Eddie." Yes, call me Eddie – the audience will think I know you. Then, "What did you have for breakfast today?" I'll say "haddock" you say "finnan?" and I say "No, thick 'un." I know it doesn't sound much, but I know it'll get a big laugh if it's you doing it.'

Tom, quite rightly, didn't think it sounded much but, to humour the ageing comic, he agreed to do it. 'Shall I do it tonight?' asked Tom.

'Oh no, I'll need to get it into my head first,' said Eddie. 'If we run through it every day I can put it in at the weekend.'

Thinking his old chum was, at last, past it, Tom agreed and Eddie, like the skilled angler he was, played Trinder along for a whole week.

'What did you have for breakfast today?'

'Haddock.'

'Finnan?'

'No, thick 'un.'

Finally, on the Saturday night, Eddie said, 'We've got a full house tonight, Tom, so I'd like to give the gag its best chance. Can we do it tonight?'

'Sure,' said the by now thoroughly bored Trinder.

That night he stood in the wings until Eddie gave him the loud stage whisper, 'Now!' On strolled Tom to a big round of applause. 'Hello, Eddie. What did you have for breakfast today?'

'Cornflakes,' said Eddie, and carried on juggling.

During the Second World War the entire Crazy Gang went to entertain at a big RAF camp. They arrived at the gates in two cars. The RAF police closely questioned the occupants of the first car, which included Flanagan and Allen, and were not con-

88 vinced. Suddenly Eddie stuck his head out of the following car.

Throwing up a Fascist salute he said, *'Ve haf cum for der plans of der Blenheim bomber.'*

The Chief of Police said, 'Let 'em in, they're The Crazy Gang.'

Larry Grayson
The comedian, sadly now practically retired, brought 'camp' to a fine art and, like so many originals, added a phrase to our language: 'Shut that door!'

Larry was abroad on holiday, sharing a table with a bunch of theatrical friends. As is usual in Larry's company, the table was in an uproar. He was in great form, holding court as only he can and a good time was being had by all.

Close by, a tableful of Germans (discussing just when after midnight they would put their towels on the sunbeds) started to send up the unsenduppable.

Larry held up a hand to quieten his crowd. He got up, slowly walked over to the Germans, placed his hands on their table and stopped them dead with just two words: 'Winston Churchill.'

These two stories are direct from the quaint quill of Larry:

Many years ago, I was appearing in *Babes in the Wood* at the Hippodrome, Goole. It wasn't a big pantomime by any means, but had a very talented cast. Now pantomimes, especially in those days, tended to have long runs and for certain members of the cast there wasn't a lot to relieve the seemingly endless routine of matinées and evening performances. But one of our number, the man who played the Woodcutter (and was usually very quiet and shy), got over this problem by being – to put it mildly – a friend of the bottle! But it seemed to make little difference, and unless you passed close by him on the stairs or had to share his dressing-room, you were really none the wiser.

But one matinée, just before curtain-up, he stumbled back through the stage door with a very strange expression, surrounded by a cloud of fumes which could have stripped the paint – or what was left of it – off the walls.

All went well, however, until we got to the scene where the Babes are all alone, lost and asleep, in the depths of the forest. Backstage, the wings were full of little fairies, waiting to go on to do a pretty dance number to the tune of 'Nymphs and Shepherds' when, all of a sudden, the Woodcutter came crashing down the back stairs, wielding his chopper, in a torrent of language which would have made a fireman blush!

The little fairies rushed cowering into the darkest corners, while in the pit, the orchestra – fearful for their lives – dived for cover. The audience sat riveted to their seats, thinking that this was all part of the plot, while the two Babes, who had wisely awoken pretty smartly from under their leaves, were being chased all around the scenery.

It was mayhem until my friend Flo Davenport, who was playing Fairy Godmother, took charge. Now Flo always had to work sideways, because she was as cross-eyed as Ben Turpin, that great stalwart of silent films. But despite all of that, she was an excellent performer with a beautiful voice and had been recommended to the producer by the famous north-country comedian Frank Randle. Without a moment's hesitation, she pirouetted on to the stage and, with a mere nod in the direction of the conductor, who had taken shelter under the drummer, calmed the situation by bursting into song with "Twas a Steamer, Coming Over', a well-known number of the day. How she did it, I'll never know, but as soon as she started singing, the Woodcutter was led calmly away, never to be seen again. That was one matinée I'll never forget.

Back in 1947, I was touring the West Country with H.V. Leslie's all-male revue, *Come Peep Through My Porthole*. Ours was a small company – there were only ten of us – with me as the leading lady, billed as 'The Yes Yes Girl with the No No Eyes'.

What a jolly little show it was, with songs, sketches and cross-overs! And with word of mouth preceding us into every venue, we had a great success with full houses all the way. To end the show on a high note, Mr Leslie had arranged a patriotic finale with Union Jacks, flags and bunting everywhere. Eight of the boys, in smart sailor suits, formed a pyramid before I made my entry, to loud applause, dressed as Britannia, complete with helmet, shield, trident – the lot! With as much dignity as possible, I was manhandled to the very top of the pyramid. How I didn't get a nose-bleed, I'll never know.

As soon as I was in position, we all began singing 'Rule Britannia' – which was always very stirring, with hardly a dry eye in the house. But one night when I thought things were going particularly well (we had just got to the bit about 'never, never, never shall be slaves') one of the boys in the bottom row – which as any ancient Egyptian will tell you, is very important when it comes to pyramids – began to have a coughing fit. (I think he'd been suffering the effects of damp beds for days.) Almost like slow motion, I felt the structure begin to sway and give and without more ado, the entire tableau collapsed in an undignified heap. Shield, helmet, trident and legs went flying in all directions and I landed up on someone's lap in the second row of the stalls, with my right ankle round the back of my neck.

By some miracle no one was hurt. But even now, if I walk too fast, I'm inclined to limp a little and whenever I watch *The Last Night of the Proms*, I always get a little twinge!

Joseph Grimaldi 'The King of the Clowns'; clowns are still called 'Joey' because of him. Grimaldi was the man who changed the whole face of pantomime. Well, he instigated its first big change – the elevation of the clown to the leading role. He, like so many great comedians, had a tough life. He began at the age of three and died, like Dan Leno, of exhaustion and 'over popularity'. The legend of the broken-hearted clown stems from his life.

The most telling story about him is a famous one. A man went to see his doctor complaining of depression. 'What you need to do,' said the doctor, 'is get out and about, enjoy yourself for a change. Cheer yourself up. Go along to Sadler's Wells and see Grimaldi.'

'Ah,' said the man, 'I am Grimaldi.'

Stanley Hall The legendary theatrical wig-maker. My son's godfather, the comic Eddie Reindeer, gave me this example of how people in showbusiness see only what they want to see. Eddie had just attended the first night of *My Fair Lady* at Drury Lane. The show, of course, was a triumph and the performances of Rex Harrison, Julie Andrews and Stanley Holloway brought standing ovations and ecstatic reactions. At curtain-down a totally bowled-over Eddie bumped into Stanley on the steps of the theatre.

'How about that show, Stanley!' gasped Eddie.

'Wonderful!' cried the expert 'syrup'-stitcher. 'Magnificent! You couldn't see a join.'

Another example of being aware only of what concerns us in showbiz. Two comics met. One asked the other how he was doing. 'How'm I doing?' he replied. 'Just terrific. I did the Des O'Connor Show two months back, and I paralysed 'em.'

'Oh,' said the other, 'I didn't hear about that.'

'And so,' continued the successful one, 'they gave me my own series. Number three last week. Fifteen and a half million viewers.'

'Well – I didn't hear about that.'

'And when the series finishes, I'm doing a new musical at Drury Lane.'

'I didn't hear about that.'

'Mind you, last week I had to do a working men's club. I was contracted, see. Do you know, I died on my feet!'

'Ah,' said his friend. 'I heard about that!'

Alec Halls Alec was a Water Rat, a genuine eccentric, a multi-instrumentalist whose bill matter was 'A Cavalcade of Junk', and a man with an odd sense of humour. Harold Taylor, the magician, told me of visiting Alec in his caravan. On one wall was an enormous photograph of Mick Jagger. It was inscribed in Alec's handwriting: 'Thank you, Alec, for introducing me to drugs.'

Tommy Handley Tommy started in variety, though he never achieved the fame there that he later did on radio. He was our favourite war, and post-war, radio comedian. His show *ITMA* (It's That Man Again) raised morale all through the war and, with its familiar characters, catch-phrases and terrific pace, paved the way for the brilliant *Goon Show*.

He was sharing digs with Arthur Askey, digs in which the inside loo was attached to the kitchen where the landlady and her family lived. On the Monday night Arthur and Tommy had just finished their supper, when Tommy said, 'It's no good. I've got to go!' The landlady and her family were still having their supper in the room right next to the loo. He made his way as surreptitiously as he could past their dining table into the lav. In his own words:

> I tried to be as quiet as possible. Then I pulled the chain. Nothing. I tried again. Nowt. I then tried all sorts of different combinations, you know, two shorts and a long. A pull and a hold-down, a savage jerk, the lot. Just as I was getting totally embarrassed (the landlady's family sitting outside could hear all my attempts), there was a banging on the door and the landlady shouted, 'Mr 'Andley! You have to surprise it!'

Michael Harvey An excellent straight man and 'feed' who was with me for ten years in panto, summer shows, clubs, legitimate theatre – anywhere where we'd be given a job, Michael had worked in practically every theatre in the country, and knew everyone in them – from managers to bar staff. On tour we always had the best dressing-room and the best 'digs'. Michael had been touring in the days when landladies would 'cater' for you, which meant that if you supplied the grub they would cook it for you. He kept for years a letter from a landlady that said: 'I note, Mr Harvey, you will be arriving on Sunday and I will be delighted to caper for you.'

The year 1964 saw the fiftieth anniversary of the RAF, and 93

Hughie Green put together a big charity show at the Victoria Palace to celebrate the event. I was on the bill and Michael, of course, was with me. All the cast were ex-RAF and one of the compères was Richard Burton. He was in the middle of one of his marriages to Elizabeth Taylor and, just before the show was to begin, they had a row and Mrs Burton swept out. Richard got stuck into the hooch but did his intro perfectly – held on to, out of shot, by two big RAF policemen. After curtain-down we all lined up to meet the Duke of Edinburgh, and Michael and I were next to the great Burton.

'Has anybody seen my wife?' roared Burton.

'I'm not sure,' said Michael. 'What does she look like?'

To give Burton his due he embraced Michael saying, 'You're my man!'

Just after the war Michael was involved, in an off-stage capacity, with the famous 'drag' show *Soldiers In Skirts*. He'd regale me with stories of the bizarre characters involved with that never-to-be-forgotten revue. All the cast had nicknames. There was 'Winnie The Witch', 'Isa Rex the Mystery Girl' (so called because he would do his make-up in a corner where no one could see how it was done!) and 'Selena the Horse'. On the show's last performance, at the Brixton Empress, all the cast received presents and flowers; but, for Selena, over the footlights came – a bale of hay.

Doug Hemmings The bass player on *The News Huddlines* from day one, Doug has the best musician's 'evil' sense of humour and so is great company as well as being terrific at the job. Doug tells this story, which he attributes to the saxophonist Don Honeywell. It really does sum up his fellow musicians' attitude to life and death.

Don was lying in hospital, dying of kidney failure. He knew he was. He was visited by another sax player who sat by the bed, burst into tears and said, 'Oh, Don, I'm so sorry.'

Don dragged himself up, looked him in the eye and said, *'You're ******* sorry!?'*

Another of Doug's stories concerns a Scots trumpeter who was with one of the BBC orchestras, who was having a rough time with his second wife, his first having died a few years earlier. He arrived home one night to find that the lady had left and taken all the contents of the flat – right down to the light bulbs – with

her. He phoned the BBC to say he wouldn't be into work that

day as he had a domestic problem. The kindly orchestral secretary expressed her sympathy and asked what was the nature of the problem.

'Well,' replied the dry Scot, 'it's like this. My first wife died and my second one won't!'

The dangers of late-night sessions – music and boozing – Doug illustrates with this story of yet another sax player, Bob Burns. Bob left the Elstree studios one night slightly the worse for wear and soon realised he shouldn't be behind the wheel of his car. He pulled into a layby and promptly fell asleep. A fellow musician was driving by and, spotting Bob's stationary vehicle, decided to stop and check if all was well. He pulled in in front of Bob and started reversing towards him. As he neared the car he was somewhat surprised to see Bob's car door open and the man hurl himself on to the road.

Bob later explained: 'I woke up to see tail lights coming towards me. I didn't realise I'd parked up – I thought *I* was the one that was moving. I threw myself out to prevent a crash!'

Dickie Henderson The suave, sophisticated and very funny master of visual comedy – remember his singer trying to be Frank Sinatra? – used to tell of himself, Bruce Forsyth and Sean Connery together in a taxi. They were going to a fight night, and Bruce was deputed to give instructions to the driver. The cabbie couldn't remember where he had seen Bruce before and kept on about it: 'I do know you, oh so well. I do know you, don't I? Come on, who are you?'

'I'm Bruce Forsyth,' said Bruce.

'Git aht of it,' said the driver, 'if you're Bruce Forsyth, I'm James Bond.'

'No,' said Sean, leaning forward. '*I'm* James Bond.'

Barry Cryer was sharing a table, at a big charity dinner, with Dickie when the organiser came over and committed the unforgivable. He asked Dickie if he would do a bit in the cabaret. It is an unforgivable thing to do because no performer likes being asked to perform off the cuff. They all, especially comics, like to have the chance to sort out and prepare what they think will suit that particular audience. But Dickie, being the affable fellow he was, merely muttered, 'Someone hasn't turned up,' and went off to do the job. Once he was on and getting a few laughs of course he started to enjoy himself. But not completely. Behind him, on the cabaret floor, were a row of microphones for the big American pop group who followed the compère. Suddenly, out on to the floor came an army of minders, sound checkers and general gophers. These sensitive souls then proceeded to adjust, re-arrange, count into and blow down the switched-on and very loud sound system. This went on all through some of Dickie's best gags.

Eventually, he stopped talking, turned and joined the audience in watching, and listening to, the chaos being perpetrated. After a Jack Benny pause he faced front again and said: 'I wouldn't mind, but it's a dog act!'

Joan Hinde 'Britain's premier lady trumpet player' is what her bill matter says, and Joan certainly is a superb instrumentalist. What her bill matter doesn't tell you is what terrific fun she is to be with and how the stories she tells against herself are little gems.

Joan works a lot with Ken Dodd, and during her act one night a friend of Ken's was standing in the wings, watching Joan. At the end of her spot he went back to Ken's dressing-room and said: 'That woman trumpet player! Do you know, my mother used to watch her on our old black and white set. Doesn't she tear up telephone directories any more?' (He was thinking of the strong woman, Joan Rhodes.)

Rehearsing for a show at the St David's Hall, Cardiff, Joan was approached by an old chap who came over and said, 'That sounded lovely. If you shut your eyes, it sounds just like Ivy Benson.' Ivy, of course, played the saxophone!

One night, after a show in Weymouth, Joan's husband Ken was packing their car ready for the off. As he stowed away her trumpet and evening dresses he overheard a man say to his wife, 'There you are, Edith, I told you that trumpet player was a man.'

My favourite story about Joan happened in Torquay and demonstrates just how quick she is with a one-liner. The musical backing on this occasion consisted of only a pianist and a drummer. During the afternoon rehearsal it became very apparent that the pianist was a highly nervous individual and had the most awful stutter. Joan, as always, did her best to relax him and assure him all would be well. At the end of the rehearsal she was putting her trumpet away when the pianist shouted to her: 'B.b.b.b.by the w.w.w.ay M.M.M.M.Miss Hinde – d.d.d.d.do I c.c.c.count you in?'

'Don't bother,' said Joan, 'I'll be on the second chorus by

then!'

Philip Hindin Provider of game shows for television and producer of the famous Hindin, Richard and Hicks revues, Phil put on the very first pantomime to be televised by the BBC and has a fund of panto stories. Here's a couple of my favourites.

Francis Laidler, the famous pantomime impresario, was presenting *Robinson Crusoe* in Birmingham starring his wife Gwladys Stanley in the title role. The scene was 'Outside the stockade'. 'Oh dear,' wailed Gwladys, 'I'm all alone on this island.' Suddenly, by magic, a theatrical hamper appeared next to her from which she removed a complete zouave uniform with folded-back jacket, képi, sword and a sequined top. She put it on and the orchestra started. Joining her came Francis Laidler's Tiny Little Tots dressed as French Legionnaires and sixteen Francis Laidler Ladies. Together, with much marching and countermarching, they stopped the show to 'The Marseilaise' and 'My Heart is Broken' from *White Horse Inn*.

Seven minutes later they all marched off, leaving Gwladys alone once more. She took off her outfit, threw it into the basket which she kicked into the wings and, with scarcely a pause, pointed to the ground and exclaimed: 'Look! A footprint!'

The totally bizarre has always appealed to Phil, and in one of his own productions he employed a white Jewish performer called Phil Rivers to play Man Friday. Naturally Phil had to 'black up' for the part. Apart from his black face he had a black leotard, black tights and black gloves. Phil was a *siffleur* (a whistler) and after the stockade scene used to do his speciality. This involved removing the index and middle fingers from his black glove and placing the two startlingly white digits in his mouth while he gave them 'In A Monastery Garden'. Having taken his applause, he then put the black fingers back on, looked out front and said, 'Massah! Massah! Come quick! A battleship! A battleship!'

One Christmas Philip couldn't find a theatre for his *Aladdin* pantomime, so he paid Issy Bonn rent to keep the production in his stores at the Atheneum for the whole year. The next Christmas same again: no date for the production, so in Issy's stores it stayed. Phil was cross – it was costing him money. Then, one night, while watching another of his shows up north he had a panic phone call from one of his assistants, Grace Clode. 'I've just heard on the radio that Issy Bonn's stores are on fire. What shall I do?'

The ever-resourceful Phil replied: 'Get down there in a taxi and fan the flames. It'll be the first time in two years *Aladdin* has shown a profit!'

Freddie Holmes Freddie was a founder member of the Radio Revellers, a four-handed close harmony singing group who, when rock and roll insisted that music was no longer essential, sadly disbanded.

I was doing my one-man show at the Churchill Theatre, Bromley. The cast consisted of (because I'm such a cheapskate) me in front of four musicians. After the performance I was washing off, and considering how much money I could save by only making up once a week, when a knock came at the door.

'Come in,' I cried inventively.

The door opened about a foot and Freddie's head popped in. 'I was in to see the show,' he smiled, 'and *I* spotted you.'

'An old one,' he said, 'but it fitted.'

Hope and Keen Mike and Albie (two cousins, the children of another famous double act, Sid and Max Harrison) have played their incredibly diverse act all over the world and are among the most talented and underrated performers in the business today.

Their partnership began in a Paul Raymond revue, and they could write a book about those days. For the moment you'll have to be content with just a few of Mike's memories. Their début was at the Chatham Empire where, as well as their acrobatic act, they had to take part in the dramatic 'scenas'. One was a Frankie and Johnny reconstruction. They were the only two blokes in a cast of naughty but nice Raymond-type birds. The story presented a problem. Mike played the man caught necking with the gangster's moll. Enter Albie, as the gangster who shoots him. Problem – who was to arrest Albie? Solved! Mike, in his violent death throes, used to choreographically roll off stage, don a policeman's hat and coat and 'nick' his own murderer.

The show was, of course, one of the first touring nude revues and Mike paints a vivid picture of the show's appearance at the infamous Glasgow Empire.

We naturally cut all our 'English' jokes. It was rough. Even the band took the precaution of putting chicken wire over the orchestra pit – to save them, and their instruments, from the expected projectiles that would descend towards the stage whenever the mood came upon the audience. One of the nudes did her posing (no movement allowed in those days), as usual finishing with two tableaus. The first, with a hobby horse between her legs, represented 'Boadicea in Full

Flight' and, for the big finish, she would place a small bowlful of paraffin on the floor, light it and appear as 'The Inca Fire Goddess'.

On the last night in Glasgow, as the blue flame flickered around her person, someone shouted from the gallery, 'Dinna burn it! – I'll hae it!'

Harry Houdini David Berglas told me this one about the legendary escapologist.

Houdini, Blackstone (America's foremost magician) and Dunninger (the world-famous mind reader) were sharing a meal. At the end of the evening, Blackstone offered to drive his friends home. Alas, when they got to the car its owner realised he'd mislaid his keys. Dunninger could not 'see' where they were, and Houdini was unable to pick the car door lock. Three very embarrassed magicians had to ask a policeman.

Hudd and Kay My first foray into the biz was as half of a double act with a school pal, Eddy Cunningham. We'd started together as amateurs in Boy's Club shows in Croydon, and got our first break as Redcoats at Butlin's. For an extra five bob more than the ordinary Redcoats, we were called Redcoat Entertainers. This simply meant we did shows as well as the ordinary duties. The Redcoat Show was the high spot of the week – for us! – and was a hectic hour-long revue in which Eddie and I were in everything – we insisted! On the first night of the show we did our double act, and then had a very quick change into a 'Singing In The Rain' scene. In the total blackness off stage we fought our way into two plastic macs and, almost immediately, reappeared. I wondered why the audience laughed and then clocked Eddy singing and moving in the most peculiar way. He looked like a chrysalis on legs. In the panic of the change, he had squeezed himself into a plastic suit cover.

Dickie Hurran The immaculate director of many spectacular revues from *The Folies Bergères* to Scotland's *Five Past Eight* shows directed a pantomime I appeared in in Bristol, and during a break in rehearsals the stage manager said, 'We've got Ken Dodd coming here after the panto. Will you send me the time sheets?' Dickie, well aware of Ken's reputation for going on far longer than he should, said, 'You won't need a time sheet. I'll send a diary!'

I saw Dickie at the end of a rather pretentious musical. 'What did you think?' I enquired.

'Nothing wrong with it that fifteen minutes of Jimmy Wheeler couldn't put right.'

Jimmy James Jimmy was a performer of brilliant sketches, featuring himself as the linchpin trying to make sense of the behaviour of his two stooges. The 'Lion in the box' was his most famous sketch, and Eli Woods became well known as his leading stooge. Roy Castle made his start in showbusiness as one of Jimmy James's team. Jimmy's son is James Casey who was the Head of Radio Light Entertainment in Manchester and whose credits include writing *The Clitheroe Kid* for over twenty years. He worked in his dad's act, too, and sent me this example of the way the James brain worked.

In the early days of television, my father was topping the bill in a programme from the North of England. Now you would expect that the studio manager, like everyone else in showbusiness, would have known the sort of act Dad did with Eli and myself. I don't mean the actual patter – Eli might be 'a wheel-tapper's listener,' or 'the last of the Mohicans – there'll be no more!' – but everyone knew the way we performed. Everyone but the studio manager.

'Ah, I've caught up with you at last, Mr James. Now what exactly do you do?' he asked. Another comic might have said 'juggle under water', but my father always preferred to take any foolish question on a ride into a fantasy world. 'I'm glad you've asked us that,' he said, 'because Eli's been worried about it. You see, when we open the act, hanging upside down on the trapeze in our Chinese costumes, singing 'By A Blue Lagoon She's Waiting' in three-part harmony, the camera can follow us I know. But it's the finish that's got Eli worried. When we hang upside down with the bowls of goldfish on the ends of the strings and we swing them round and round – it's what you call centrifugal, you know – our proud boast is "Twenty-five years and we've never spilt a drop." When we swing them, will the studio be wide enough? Still I'm sure you've got it all worked out. Oh, by the way, have the Chinese costumes arrived? We couldn't find them.'

The studio manager fled.

When Jim junior asked his dad why three Chinese would sing 'By A Blue Lagoon She's Waiting' he replied, 'It's a lovely tune.'

Eli's eccentric appearance and genuine stutter made him as popular as his governor, and today he has become a successful panto and character actor. But when the great Jimmy James died, Eli tried a solo act in the clubs. One of the most important things a club comic needs is a stock of razor-sharp heckler-stoppers, and one night, when the audience were saying more than Eli was, he held up his hand: 'I've g.g.g.g.ot s.s.s.ome gr.gr.gr.great hec.hec.hec.heckler st.o.p.p.pers – i.i.i.if y.y.you'll . . . wait!'

Rex Jamieson (Mrs Shufflewick) I think, in his own way, Rex was a genius. He created the unforgettable Mrs Shufflewick, the personification of all little old cockney ladies who sit in the corner of the snug behind a glass of gin or Guinness and regale all and sundry with lewd reminiscences – and always finish up crying into their liquor while reciting some maudlin mother-ridden ballad.

Alas, as the years went by it became more and more difficult to see where 'Shuff' began and Rex finished. But even in his cups he was gloriously funny. An eye-witness saw him entertaining in a gay pub one night as he unsteadily went into one of his famous stories, the one about the shoemaker who made a pair of boots for Queen Victoria and ever after displayed a sign in his window that read 'Cobblers to the Queen'. All the audience knew the tale by heart, which was more than Rex did, and they did their best to keep him on course. The tag was a beauty: 'And so he stuck a notice in his window saying – er what? What? Oh yes! – B******s *to the king!*'

'Jane' I remember seeing the lady who, supposedly, was the model for the famous *Daily Mirror* strip cartoon in a fly-blown nudie revue in Cambridge when I was doing National Service. Of course, my oppos and I had gone mob-handed. In the middle of her act, as she bent forward teasingly to remove a shoe, a pal

102

of mine tore a piece of calico right down the middle. It stopped the show and even the untouchable 'Jane' burst out laughing. We loved her even more for that.

Peter John Peter has carved a unique niche for himself in music hall. His character studies, from the genteel tramp to the ageing pantomime fairy, are the true stuff of the halls. He remembered working with a very popular lady electronic organist. She opened her spot with 'Happy Days Are Here Again', which she swung into as the curtains parted. On one particular night, however, the curtains opened and . . . nothing – no cascading chords, no coloured lights. The organ was mute. She desperately clicked switches and pulled stops, but nothing happened. Undaunted, she left her seat and stepped forward to address her apprehensive audience.

'Ladies and gentlemen,' she announced, 'owing to a loss of power, I am unable to entertain you with my organ onstage. However, in order not to cause you disappointment, I shall try to give you some alternative pleasure by coming in the pit.'

Ken Joy The multi-talented Ken is steeped in showbusiness and, like all 'born in a trunk' pros, he remembers and relishes the bizarre. Here are two of his favourite memories.

My father was, in the days of variety, a pit musician. He was offered a short season, playing solo violin, at one of our number three variety theatres – the Palace, Attercliffe! He took the job and, as a small boy, I accompanied him to the Monday band call. I was surprised to see, lying on the conductor's music stand, a pair of white gloves. A pair of white gloves in Attercliffe where some of the band didn't even wear bow ties! I was assured by one of the lads, though, that the conductor would wear them during the evening performance. That night the house lights dimmed and the conductor made his entrance – minus his white gloves. Throughout the first half, the gloves lay on the music stand. Came the interval, the house lights went up as the conductor grabbed the gloves, vaulted over the orchestra rail and disappeared up the centre aisle. Two minutes later he re-appeared wearing not only his white gloves but an ice cream tray round his neck. At the end of the interval off came the gloves and, once again, the vendor became the *chef d'orchestre.*

In the summer of 1973 I was appearing at the Cosy Nook Theatre, Newquay. Another gorgeous little venue, long gone. Like all summer shows of those days we had a speciality act. Ours was Johnny, the Musical Clown. Now Johnny had spent all his working life in the circus where, of course, one performs in the round. He wasn't used to the theatre's curtains, drapes and scenery. Came the first night of the show and on came Johnny in his clown costume, make-up and comedy top hat. Unbeknown to us he had a special finish. It was a closing bit which worked fine in the circus ring but . . .

This night Johnny's finish was almost the finish of our show. As he came to the end of his spot the lights dimmed and he began to play, on his saxophone, 'Keep The Home Fires Burning'. Suddenly he produced a box of matches and, still playing, set fire to his top hat. It was a beautiful picture. The lights were low, the band and Johnny playing Novello's immortal tune while the top hat doused in paraffin, blazed away – as did the curtains, drapes and scenery! Everywhere he moved he ignited another part of the theatre. Fortunately no real harm was done as we all rushed on stage with buckets of water and doused everything in sight, including Johnny. The audience, who thought it was all part of his act, gave him a standing ovation.

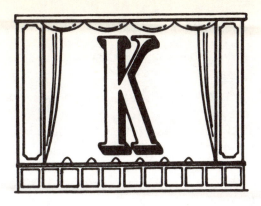

Fred Karno Originally an acrobat, he became a highly successful (and rich) impresario, producer, writer and director of knockabout music-hall sketches and revues. His name is immortalised in the World War One soldier's chorus:

> We are Fred Karno's Army,
> The ragtime infantry.
> We cannot shoot, we cannot fight –
> What bleedin' use are we?

His most famous revue was *Mumming Birds* or, when he took it to America, *A Night In An English Music Hall*. Charlie Chaplin played a drunk on the American tour and, for him, the rest was history.

Karno was an unpopular man and an example of his cruelty to pros was given me by Sandy Powell. Sandy understudied the principal comic in a Karno revue and one night, as a raw beginner, he was thrown into the deep end and shoved on. After the show Sandy, thinking he hadn't done too badly, sat in the dressing-room waiting for a few kind words from the 'guv'. Karno flung the door open, sniffed, said, 'Had your chance – missed it!' and strode off.

Davy Kaye The tiny Jewish comedian has done everything in showbusiness from tat revues to superb characterisations in films and entertaining Royalty. His one-man band routine is a variety classic.

Davy was working a week at the Liverpool Empire when the theatre's own Roman Catholic priest was making his backstage rounds. Davy had a cold and was blowing his nose when the priest tapped him on the shoulder, asking, 'Are you a Catholic?'

Davy put away his hankie to answer, and naturally revealed his nose.

'Oh, I beg your pardon,' said the priest, and walked away.

Gorden Kaye An excellent actor who after years of fine performances in the theatre, was catapulted to national fame as René in "'Ello, 'Ello'. He is so loved that the whole country held its breath when he was very seriously hurt in a freak storm accident. This story is one Gorden tells about himself.

Because he had promised to appear as René on Blackpool's North Pier, he went back to work earlier than he should have done. While Gorden was indisposed, his part was played by a lookalike. A few weeks into the run, one of the cast told him he'd overheard a middle-aged couple at the box office discussing the photographs of the company. The wife said, 'Look, Bert, it's 'im. They've managed to get 'im 'ere.'

Bert took out his glasses and after a careful inspection declared, 'No, luv. It looks a bit like 'im, I'll grant you, but that's not Gorden – 'e's 'ad 'is 'ead off!'

Harry Khan, 'The Mental Marvel' Charlie Chester told me, as only he can, about this incredible American brought to England by Jack Hylton. Charlie saw him at the 'Met', Edgware Road. Harry Khan would ask one of the punters to call out any huge number – say three million, four hundred thousand, seven hundred and ninety six – to be multiplied by another six figure number suggested by someone else in the audience. He would then give the total almost before the second person had finished talking! Charlie's description of his final stunt is mind-blowing. He would stand in front of a large blackboard, half the length of the stage. He would then have ropes attached to his ankles while he asked the audience to nominate *any* well-known poem, 'Gray's Elegy in a Country Churchyard', say, or 'The Charge of the Light Brigade'. He would then be hauled upside down with his back to the audience. In this position he would recite the poem out loud while reading a newspaper and writing, upside down so that the audience could read it, the piece he was reading. Too lazy to learn a comic song!

Charlie was out front one night when Khan asked the audience for any long word. Back came 'Saskatchewan!'

'Thank you,' said Harry, and proceeded to write it upside down and backwards while pronouncing it forwards. Round of applause.

'Another long word, please.'

'Mississippi!' Business as before.

'One more long word, please.'

Voice from the gallery: 'Rubber!'

Harry: 'I'd like it a bit longer, please.'

Voice: 'Well, stretch it!'

This got such a laugh that from that evening on 'The Mental Marvel' always employed a stooge to shout it out every night.

Neville King I think he's our funniest ventriloquist, not only a great technician but a total original. His 'Grandad' character is a living person, and a very objectionable one too.

Neville is just as funny off stage and to be in his company in any public place can be a riot. He really can 'throw' his voice, and I've seen a busload of passengers wild with frustration because neither they, nor the conductor, could find the dog that would not stop barking.

I was on a bill with him while I was in Liverpool to play pantomime. Every Christmas a local charity took the Philharmonic Hall in the city and talked a lot of pros into giving an afternoon performance for those who couldn't afford to pay for their seasonal entertainment, a job we all used to enjoy, believe me. In the dressing-room Neville asked if anyone would play the piano for him: nothing much, just a snatch of 'Mighty Like A Rose' at the end of his spot. The Police Band were on the bill and their pianist volunteered.

Neville went on, did a bit of the act and then introduced his accompanist. The copper entered and sat down at one end of the full-size grand piano. 'Grandad' noticed him and didn't like what he saw. Throughout the rest of the act he kept looking at the pianist and saying things like: 'He keeps staring at me,' and 'I don't like the look of him.' Neville tried to calm him but it was no good. 'If he looks at me once more, I'll 'ave 'im!' said Grandad.

He obviously did look at Grandad once more because suddenly the doll shot across the top of the piano, with Neville holding on. He landed on top of the copper and proceeded to ''ave 'im'. The policeman, years of training coming to the fore, automatically pulled out his truncheon and proceeded to belt the daylights out of Grandad – not Neville, Grandad.

The audience, including me, wept with mirth and, when I went round to congratulate the surprise treble act, Neville was crying with laughter too. Not so the guardian of the law who, when told by his helpless mates that he was marvellous, replied, 'Well, I didn't know the little bugger was going to go for me, did I?'

R.G. Knowles This Canadian music-hall comedian (there's a contradiction in terms), was a very popular contemporary of Dan Leno and Vesta Tilley. He was the man who invented the one-liner gag, such as, 'Take my wife – please!'

One night, half-way through his act, the theatre cat walked across the stage in front of him. He hardly paused as he commented, 'This is a monologue not a catalogue!'

The Krankies (Ian and Jeanette) A husband and wife comedy team, Ian and Jeanette have achieved enormous popularity via their inspired creation of Jimmy, the naughty schoolboy, and Ian, his minder.

Jeanette goes to great lengths not to let their young fans see her as herself, and always signs autographs as 'Jimmy'. However, during a panto run in Newcastle, she got caught. On being assured there were no more kids at the stage door she changed into herself and went shopping. A stray little boy suddenly appeared and asked, 'Are you Jimmy Krankie?'

'Yes,' owned up Jeanette.

'Then why are you dressed as a woman?'

'Ah,' said Jeanette, thinking on her feet, 'I'm so well known that when I walk down the street people keep stopping me so I disguise myself as a woman.'

He took this in and then said, 'Well, you're a *real* ponce. You've even got earrings and a handbag.'

Francis Laidler This story has been told by everyone, but it is a classic about the legendary presenter of pantos in the days when they would run till Easter.

Mr Laidler always gave his juveniles the names of flowers – Poppy, Daisy, Pansy and so on. It was the night of his final dress rehearsal and everyone was keyed up to please the governor. The overture went well, and up went the curtain. The chorus went into the opening. Enter the juveniles. But they didn't. 'What's wrong?' yelled Mr Laidler from his seat in the stalls.

A harassed children's chaperone appeared from the wings. 'I'm sorry, Mr Laidler,' she spluttered. 'Buttercup's shat herself!'

Arthur Lane Perhaps the last of the actor-managers, Arthur had a chequered career that would make a brilliant TV film. The stories of his keeping one jump ahead of his creditors are legion. John Inman, who worked for Arthur in 'rep', can do a whole evening of Arthur Lane stories – just ask him!

When Arthur ran the Wimbledon Theatre he always, if he had nothing booked in, would play *Sweeney Todd* with the smallest cast he could get away with. He loved playing the lead himself and it was the full bit – green sequins on the eyelids, the lot. One of his 'rep' companies had just finished a season at the seaside and Arthur, in trouble again, gathered them together for another bash at the Demon Barber. On the opening night, Arthur had placed a rather precious actor in the dreaded barber's chair and proceeded to cut his throat. With a wild cry he pulled the lever and the potential pie disappeared below. 'There!' said Arthur looking down the hole. 'No more will you mince along the front at Hastings.'

He booked me for panto one year. It really was a case, as *The Goon Show* so rightly put it, of 'Christmas Eve and not a tickle for pantomime.' When our small company gathered together there was no Arthur, no script and no one to tell us what the subject was. I phoned him and explained our dilemma.

'Is there any scenery there?' he asked.

I had noticed something vaguely in that line stacked outside the theatre. 'Yes.'

'Then see if there's a well in it.'

I went, saw there was, phoned again and told him.

'Ah well,' he said, 'then, it's *Puss In Boots*.'

'But, Arthur,' I said, 'there's no script.'

'Good God, man,' he roared, 'you know the story of *Puss In Boots*, don't you?' With Danny Purches and Freddie Foss, I stayed up all night and wrote it. It went very well.

Lew Lane Another producer in the old sense of the word: a deviser, planner and stage manager, he worked for years at the famous Churchill's night club in Bond Street.

Lew and I attended a preview of *Aspects of Love*. At the end of the show, which didn't do a lot for either of us, Lew asked a stage hand what the huge lorry outside the stage door was for. 'It's full of new scenery for tomorrow night.' Lew shrugged. 'Scenery you don't need – tunes you do!'

Sir Harry Lauder In 1919, he became the very first music-hall performer to be knighted. He was so honoured for his work in organising entertainments for the troops during the First World War. His tuneful, easy to remember songs have, like so many good ones, become folk music and their popularity made him a huge star in America and Canada as well as here. Quite a few Scots didn't approve of him because of his constant stressing the meanness of his fellow-countrymen. It was all done for a reason. He would arrive in a town to work a week's variety and almost his first action was to tip the porter who carried his cases one farthing. Within minutes it was all over town that the 'mean' Scot, Lauder, had arrived. He would say to his audiences: 'You can tell your friends I'm here this week – I've no intention of spending any money on advertising.'

John Lawson A music-hall sketch performer, he had a big hit with a piece called *Humanity*. The sketch would finish with a

terrific fight up and down a staircase, which eventually collapsed as Lawson and his adversary dropped dead. This violent climax always stopped the show. I found out from a lady who had worked in the sketch that John always employed an ex-boxer to play his part in the fight while he watched from the wings. As the curtain fell the boxer would collapse, while Lawson would come in front holding on to the proscenium arch for support and take the applause.

Benny Lee The Scottish-born singer and entertainer became a household name through his many radio series with Bernard Braden, and through his hosting of *Time For Old Time* on Radio Two. Benny is *the* memory man of popular music. If he doesn't know a song it hasn't been written!

This story originally appeared in the Grand Order of Water Rats centenary magazine, *The Trap*, and shows just how valued the artistes were in the days of variety. Benny writes:

One of London's most famous variety theatres was the Metropolitan Music Hall in the Edgware Road – now replaced by a fly-over! Like most theatres of its kind, it went into decline as the days of the music hall faded and when I was booked to appear there, in the mid-1950s, it was somewhat shabby and run down. I arrived on the Monday morning and, as I was top of the bill, made my way to the number one dressing-room. Suddenly the manager of the theatre appeared and asked if I wouldn't mind using number two dressing-room for the week. He explained that he had a troupe of performing chimpanzees on the bill, and as the number one room was the largest and on stage level it would help immensely in getting the animals on and off stage as well as storing them after their turn. I agreed and moved into number two upstairs.

On the Wednesday evening I came to work to discover the chimps, in their cages, outside number one dressing-room. The door was open and inside, I could see two men busily painting the room. New linoleum was on the floor and the whole place was bright and gleaming. I asked one of the men what was going on. He looked me up and down and said, 'Haven't you heard? We had the RSPCA inspector in last night and he said the room was unfit for animals!'

Dave Lee I worked with this jazz pianist and composer on *Not So Much A Programme More A Way Of Life* on television in the 1960s. Whether Dave was present on this occasion I don't know but he told me the story.

Tommy Kinsman was a society band leader whose posh gigs included dances at Buckingham Palace. He was stuck for a third trumpet player for one particular Royal 'do' and had to settle for a hairy jazzer. Tommy, as he always did, called the band together before the gig and instructed them carefully on the protocol for the evening. 'Now,' said the bandleader, 'if the Queen should speak to you, not that it's very likely, you call her "Your Majesty" at first and then, if the conversation warrants it, you call her "ma'am". You keep a distance of one yard between Her Majesty and yourself,' and so on.

The gig plodded on and at the first break the third trumpet player, tired, fed up and bored at having to play the polite 'dots' that the Kinsman sound required, went outside to smoke a cigarette that had no name on the side. He returned feeling much better, and the first person he saw was the Queen.

Unable to avoid him, she said, 'Good evening – are you enjoying yourself?'

From the back of his befuddled brain he tried to draw forward Kinsman's instructions. He failed and could only place a forefinger in the cleft of his chin, drop a curtsey and say, 'Yes, O Queen.'

Dan Leno Born in 1860, and only 44 when he died, he was probably the greatest comedian we ever produced and the idol of Victorian music hall and pantomime. For years after his death, whenever it rained, people, and my Gran was one of them, said, 'It's the angels crying with laughter at Dan.' His career, particularly towards the end, was dogged with mental problems and the last three years of his life were spent between theatres, convalescent homes and asylums. On being admitted to one he pointed to a clock and said to the nurse, 'Is that clock right?'

'Yes,' said the nurse.

'Then what's it doing here?' replied the sad little genius.

Claude Lester This is Jimmy Wheeler's version of a classic story (and if anyone should have known, he should). Jimmy wasn't averse to the odd drink or two – however, even he, the master, had to admit, 'Claude Lester was the greatest of all time.' Here's the story in Jimmy's own words:

His drinking got so bad that Parnell (Val Parnell who ran

the Palladium) and Cissy Williams (Parnell's assistant) had him up to the office and told him: 'It's got to stop.' He agreed and next week, Monday first house he was fine. Second house – murder again. But Claude was such a good performer they kept him on. Year after year they threatened to sack him for good but they never did.

Eventually they thought they'd cracked it. They paid his wages to his wife and banned him from getting booze on tick from all their theatre bars. They even got him barred from all the pubs *around* the theatre. In the end he had to go on a bus ride to get a drink! Then they wouldn't even let him out of the theatre.

Finally, after a Monday first house, his wife locked him in his dressing-room and went home till he was about to go on for the second show. He's going mad, shouting and screaming and banging on the door. They all thought, 'We've got him. He's got no money, no drink and he's locked in – perfect.'

Comes the second house, his wife unlocks the door and there he is – flat out on the floor, he can't even stand. How the hell did he get the drink?

Well, what he actually did – he banged on the door so hard the stage manager heard the row and came along. He didn't know the set-up at all and Claude says, 'Look, I'm putting a pound under the door.' (Where he'd hidden it, nobody knew.) 'Go and get half a bottle of Scotch and three of those straws you suck lemonade through.' The poor old stage manager goes off and comes back with the Scotch and the straws. 'Now,' says Claude, 'pass the straws under the door.' He does so. 'Now take the cork out of the bottle and hold it up against the keyhole.' He did that and Claude drank the lot, through a straw, through the keyhole. When they let him out for his second show he was paralytic. He was the greatest of all time!

Ian Liston The ebullient chairman and producer of the 'Hiss and Boo Music Hall', like anyone who is involved with music hall, has stacks of stories; and Ian has more than most. Here are a couple of my favourites.

He was chairing a show at a private function for the Effingham Rugby Club. Right up Liston's street, they'd be! They proved, under Ian's expert piloting, a terrific audience but the high spot of the evening (dare one say the climax?) came in the middle of

Michelle Summers's spot. I've worked with Michelle many times: she is a wonderful singer, but a trifle unknowing.

This particular night she sang a verse and a chorus of 'The Boy I Love Is Up In The Gallery'. She stopped after the third line of the second verse, 'For Johnny is a tradesman and works in the Borough', and asked politely, preparing for her audience participation bit. 'Do we have any Johnnies in the audience?' Uproar ensued. What a question to ask a rugby club! There *were* loads of Johnnies, in the audience and they landed at Michelle's feet singly and in packets of three! One even arrived, after being inflated, via an aerial tour of the room.

The biggest laugh of the night came when Michelle eventually turned to Ian and innocently enquired 'What did I say?'

Ian is constantly on the look-out for good new speciality acts, and he does find them. He's encouraged many kids he has spotted entertaining in the streets to become fully fledged professional performers. He was giving a try-out to two young jugglers at the Theatre Royal, Newcastle, whose act required the assistance of a volunteer from the audience. The volunteer duly appeared and was told to stand between the two lads with a carrot in his mouth. This, they explained, would be knocked from his teeth by a flying club. Upon hearing this the volunteer walked over to the chairman's table, took out his false teeth and promptly dropped them into Ian's tankard of beer.

'Listen,' he said, 'that lot have just cost me thirty quid on the bloody NHS and ahm boogered if these two fairies are going to bust 'em!'

Marie Lloyd 'The Queen of The Music Hall'; she was perhaps, until Gracie Fields came along, the greatest female performer we have produced. She was adored by the public and loved by her fellow pros – something very rare indeed. She had a touch of the Judy Garland tragedy about her. She was down-to-earth and outspoken on and off stage. When the first Royal Variety Performance was mounted, in 1912, she wasn't included on the bill. She was thought to be far too undainty a dish to set before the King. She was furious and threatened to have posters printed saying: '*Every performance by Marie Lloyd is a Command Performance – by Command of the British Public!*'

Even though she worked in America and France (indeed Sarah Bernhardt called her 'The only woman of genius on the English Stage') she was a Londoner born and bred, and there was her real home.

She played, and didn't do at all well, in Sheffield. At the end of her act on the opening night she faced the lukewarm audience and said: 'So this is Sheffield, is it? This is where you make all those knives, forks, spoons and circular saws, is it? Well, when you get to work tomorrow morning, I want you to take all those knives, forks, spoons and circular saws and shove 'em up your jackseys!' With which she swept off, saying, 'I'm back to London,' and disappeared into her dressing-room to pack.

No one knew what to do, but eventually the young assistant manager tapped on her door. 'Miss Lloyd,' he ventured.

'What do you want?' shouted Marie.

'I'm the assistant manager.'

'Well, bugger off,' said the lady.

'I will, Miss Lloyd, I will,' said the brave one. 'I only wanted to tell you the people of Sheffield have received your instructions and they are quite happy to accommodate the knives, forks and spoons but they beg to be spared the circular saws.'

Marie laughed, and stayed for the week.

David Lodge This popular actor has been featured in more than 150 films. His role in the magnificent war film *Cockleshell Heroes* has become legendary through Spike Milligan's constant sending up. Something, I must add, that David thoroughly approves of.

David began his career on the boards as half of a variety act. They were doing quite well until they worked a week at the notorious Grand Theatre, Bolton. They were booked to do twelve minutes but came off after eight to the sound of their own footsteps. But, with all the confidence of youth, they went back and took a bow to even more deafening silence – for a week – twice nightly. On Thursday night the local police club were in the audience and their chief confided to the theatre manager, 'Bring that act back and I'll have them arrested.' Luckily for us, and for him and his partner, David decided to become an actor.

Jimmy Logan The Scottish comedian, actor and impresario told me this lovely story of an accident turning into a triumph – all due to his own quick thinking.

The pantomime was *Sinbad The Sailor* with Jimmy and David Hughes at the Alhambra, Glasgow. The theatre's fire curtain was held up by water pressure, and one night Jimmy felt an ominous drip hit his head. The drip multiplied and the safety curtain started descending, very slowly. A pipe had burst and it was soon obvious that the curtain would reach the stage well before the end of the first half. Jimmy came right downstage and started ad-libbing to the audience of about two thousand. This was fine for a while, but the realisation that it would take a long time to hoist the curtain back up (no electric motors in the Alhambra, just a manual system of chains) made Jimmy think even harder.

It so happened that the theatre carpenter, who'd worked there all his life, was about to retire. Jimmy asked one of the orchestra to find him. He did and the bemused old man suddenly found himself being beckoned on to the stage. Once there, Jimmy proceeded to do a 'This Is Your Life' on him. For more than half an hour the carpenter, who'd never faced an audience before, held the punters, the entire company and the orchestra spellbound with his memories of the Alhambra and of the stars he'd carpentered for. The curtain was finally raised, and our hero exited to tumultuous applause. I should think that was more pleasing to him than any gold watch the management might have presented.

The opening of the next scene was 'The deck of the good ship *Mary-Ann*' with the chorus doing a dance routine with mops. On this occasion they abandoned the choreography and simply cleared up the flooded stage.

Len Lowe Just about everybody has employed the expertise (at making comics funny!) of Len Lowe, the ultimate straight man and feed.

He was working with a famous star who invited him into his dressing-room to meet a lady – yes, the touring version of the wife! The star had a problem. How could he smuggle the lady into his digs that night without the puritanical landlady knowing? He had a great idea (the one that didn't work for someone else – see under Norman Teal). He would give his girlfriend a piggy-back up the stairs so that the dragon would only hear one pair of footsteps. It worked, and a pleasant time was had by both parties.

Alas, the crafty Casanova hadn't counted on the landlady bringing him his breakfast in bed the next morning. She entered, saw the two of them and went berserk. 'How dare you!' she shrieked. 'This is a respectable house!'

The star, thinking on his back, looked terribly hurt and

remonstrated, 'Just a minute! Just a minute. Don't you realise that this young lady is a fully paid up member of the VAF?' (Variety Artistes Federation – the forerunner, for variety folk, of Equity.)

'Oh!' responded the landlady. 'I'm awfully sorry. Does she want one egg or two?'

No wonder the lad was a star.

Len was 'feed' to Billy Dainty for quite a time, and their adventures in clubland deserve a book to themselves. They arrived at one club to be told that there were no musicians, not even a drummer – Very annoying, as a major part of Billy's act was eccentric dancing. That night, however, the resourceful Len sang Billy's opening routine and filled the drummer's chair by playing the drum part on his own body!

Macdermott G.H. (The Great Macdermott) 1845–1933

An actor/singer who, like so many before and since, put a word, 'jingoism', into the English language. It came from a song by G.W. Hunt with the line: 'We don't want to fight but, by Jingo! if we do'.

In 1877 Russia declared war on Turkey. For reasons too complicated to go into here opinions in Britain were split as to which side we should support. Then the problem was solved. Someone brought Macdermott the Jingo song and he sang it to a packed house at the London Pavilion (where most top-hatted Tories were found). The impact on that pro-Turkey audience is described by Macdermott himself:

As the music struck up for my song, I advanced slowly down towards the footlights, assuming at the same time an aggressive warlike character. I had hardly sung the first line of the verse –

The dogs of war are loose, and the rugged Russian Bear,
Full bent on blood and robbery, has crawled out of his lair

when every face was turned in my direction. The second line had them on their feet –

It seems a thrashing now and then will never help to tame
That brute, and so he's bent upon the same old game.
The Lion did his best to find him some excuse
To crawl back to his den again. All efforts were no use.

By the time I got to the chorus they were standing on the tables and cheering.

We don't want to fight, but by Jingo! if we do,
We've got the ships, we've got the men, we've got the money too!
We've fought the Bear before, and while we're Britons true!
The Russians shall not have Constantinople!

The audience went bananas and, at the end of the song, rushed round to Gladstone's house and broke all his windows. It was said that a music-hall song had changed history. The man who wrote the song, G.W. Hunt, was declared a hero and 'The Great Macdermott' gave him a guinea for it.

The other side of a wonderful reception for a patriotic song is in a story Chesney Allen told me while we were rehearsing *Underneath The Arches*. In the golden days of the music hall there was a little comic who never seemed to be able to find the right material to please his audiences. With the outbreak of the Boer War he thought he'd cracked it. He found a sensational patriotic song which was, like all of them, saying what swine the Boers were and how lovely we were. He tried it out. He entered in front of a Britannia backcloth dressed as John Bull leading on a bulldog draped with a Union Jack and proceeded to give the enemy hell. At the end of the song he, as usual, got the bird. Picking up the dog he made his weary way to the wings, pausing only to shout over his shoulder, 'And I hope the bloody Boers win!'

Cameron Macintosh The wonder-boy producer who indeed was only a boy when he presented his first West End hit. He had been an assistant stage manager on the original tour of *Oliver!* He also worked on stage, playing in the crowd scenes. One scene called for a boy to be in charge of a barrowful of meat pies. This was Cameron's part. Folk who worked on that tour have confided, 'He was the worst pie-boy we ever had!' Still, he did graduate to presenting *Miss Saigon*, *Phantom Of The Opera* and *Cats*. He so loved *Oliver!* that he swore, when he was still a rotten pie-boy, he would re-present the show in the West End one day. He did. It began as a four-week Christmas fill-in and stayed for five years. I played Fagin for one year and the bane of my life were my 'gang', the boys who were Fagin's pickpockets. Licensing laws meant a constant turn-over of the unpredictable little barnstormers and some, who I had to rehearse with every week, weren't quite right for the job. One extremely well fed (the gang were supposed to be starving urchins), very posh boy turned up. He wasn't a natural. Whenever he was supposed to be moving he wasn't. When he was required to be still he couldn't. After an hour of this I observed, 'You, my son, are like a fart in a colander!'

The rehearsal finished and I forgot my colourful note. The boy didn't and told his mother what I'd said. She in turn phoned Cameron and complained. 'I must object. Mr Hudd referred to my son as being like a fart in a colander.'

'Oh dear,' was his reply. 'Well, I'm inclined to believe him – he's a very truthful man.' We never saw Little Lord Fauntleroy again. Thanks, Cam.

Don Maclean The highly successful comedian and ex-host of TV's *Crackerjack* has amazed everyone by becoming the host of BBC Radio Two's *Good Morning Sunday*, and so bringing much-needed genuine humour to religious broadcasting. Don, like all real pros, relishes the stories of the nights he had a hard time. He cut his showbusiness teeth in the working men's clubs.

> While doing a summer season at Skegness in the 1960s I supplemented my meagre earnings by working a Grimsby club on Sunday nights. On my début there, as I finished my spot to rather mediocre applause, the Entertainments Secretary leapt on to the stage and threw an arm round my shoulder. 'What is he doing,' I thought. 'I've not gone that well.'
>
> He began to speak into the mike. 'It has been brought to my notice that several members in this club have been saying I've been fiddling the artistes' money, so from now on it will be my policy to pay out all the artistes on stage. Hold out yer 'and, son.' Thereupon, in front of a stunned crowd, he proceeded to count six £1 notes into my *hand*.

One club Don played insisted on all the artistes lining the stage at the end of the 'do' for a finale. Their closing chorus was followed by the Club Chairman who confided to the audience, 'Interesting show we've had tonight. That magician, he were good. We like a bit of magic here.' Applause. 'The contralto – well, she sang all the usual: "Bless This House", "Ave Maria" and "The Wedding", but we like a good singer and she were.' More applause. Just Don left. 'Now the comedian, he weren't quite our cuppa tea, was he?' Exit Maclean on all fours.

He went particularly badly, he says, at one South Yorkshire club but as he came off the Entertainments Secretary said, 'Very nice, son, very nice.'

With all the anger that only a comic who has suffered can muster he demanded, 'What do you mean, "very nice"? Nobody laughed.'

'Nay, lad,' said his comforter, 'tek no notice of that. If Frank Sinatra came here, they wouldn't laff!'

The Great Marvo This story was one of Bud Flanagan's favourites. Early in his career he worked on the bill with a magician, The Great Marvo. Business during the week in question was bad. Something had to be done so on the Wednesday, the town was flooded with handbills that proclaimed 'Cannibalism in the Twentieth Century! – I, The Great Marvo, will give £5000 to the Wallasey Maternity Hospital if I fail to eat a man at the theatre both houses on Friday.' The handbills caused a sensation.

The first house on Friday was packed. None of the other acts meant a light, everyone was waiting for The Great Marvo. On he came, did a few tricks and then, joined by his wife dressed as a nurse, announced: 'And now, cannibalism in the twentieth century. The moment in the show when I will eat a man.' The entire house sat forward. 'Any volunteers?' The house sat back but no one volunteered. The Great Marvo shrugged and said, 'Well, I definitely have a volunteer for the second house.'

The second house came and, once again, the place was heaving at the seams. 'Any volunteers?' asked Marvo and this time, to a thunderous round of applause, a giggling local lad came up on to the stage. Marvo produced a contract and enquired of the volunteer, 'Are your parents still alive?'

'Yes.'

'Then, if anything should go wrong, I, The Great Marvo, promise to pay them fifteen pounds a week for life.'

The 'nurse' removed the lad's shirt and laid him down on a trolley while Marvo cleaned his teeth! He had a little bowl by the trolley and, surreptitiously taking out a knife, nicked the lad's arm. He then rubbed some Lysol from the bowl into the cut. The volunteer gave an enormous roar, shot off the trolley, leapt over the footlights, over the orchestra pit and, to catcalls and boos, ran out of the theatre. The Great Marvo shrugged, went to the front of the stage and, through gleaming teeth, asked, 'Any other volunteers?'

Max Miller 'The Cheeky Chappie', 'The Pure Gold of the Music Hall', Max was the greatest front cloth comic I have ever seen or will see. His 'working' of an audience – taking them into his confidence, blaming them for the innuendos his act was sprinkled with, was a joy to behold. His outrageous floral plus-fours and 'Jack the lad' image made him a folk hero. He was the eternal commercial traveller, the great 'puller' of birds with a fund of smutty stories; he could sing you a song and could never be out-talked or outwitted. He was the bloke everyone wanted to be. Off-stage, he was a mystery. He wasn't a mixer, except on the golf course (he was a scratch golfer) and was famous for never buying a drink. He became very wealthy and was rumoured to own half of his beloved Brighton. One evening he was in a pub after a show, and telling everyone how many houses he owned, when Ted Ray chipped in: 'Why don't you sell one and buy us a drink!'

My own experience of his behaviour in a bar goes back to 1959 when my partner Eddy Kay and I were on the bill with him at the Finsbury Park Empire. It was an unbelievable week for me. I watched him, and his co-stars G. H. Elliott, 'The Chocolate-Coloured Coon', and Hetty King, 'All The Nice Girls Love A Sailor', every single performance. One night, during our rather shaky seven-minute routine, I noticed Max himself watching us from the wings. As we came off to our usual round of indifference, Max grabbed me and said, 'I liked the Shakespeare bit at the end' (it was supposed to be two Noel Cowards talking). 'Come upstairs and we'll have a drink.'

Well this was it, wasn't it? Gather round, my dear little grandchildren, and I'll tell you about the night Max Miller bought me a drink. Eddy and I looked at each other, blinked in disbelief, but followed Max up to the circle bar.

There was no one in there, as the first half of the show was still on. Max sat us down and proceeded to talk about the business, what we hoped to do, did we have an agent? He asked us every question except 'What'll you have?'

Eddy and I looked at each other again, I nodded and Eddy got up. 'Would you like a drink Mr Miller?'

'What are you on about?' demanded Max. 'Sit down.' He carried on giving us all sorts of hints about our act till a silence descended.

I sighed and rose. 'How about a drink, Mr Miller?'

'Sit down! I asked you for one, didn't I?'

I sat down, but still there was no move of the Miller hand towards the pocket, just more general chit-chat. Suddenly the doors of the bar burst open and the audience came in. It was the interval.

Almost the first man in spotted Max. 'Cor blimey! It's ole Max! What will you have?'

With a speed that made his on-stage delivery sound like Clement Freud's, he replied, 'I'll have a large gin and tonic and what will you have, Roy? Eddy?'

He kept his promise: he did get us a drink!

122   The most well-known story about Max concerns his appearance

in the 1950 Royal Variety Performance. Jack Benny was on the bill, too, and Val Parnell, who was producing that year's show, had given him twenty minutes, with an agreement he could go on longer if he wanted. Max was told, 'Six minutes, as rehearsed.'

Came the night, and Max abandoned his rehearsed routine and did well over his allotted time. Charles Henry, the stage director, could be heard out front shouting: 'Come off, Maxie!'

Max turned to the wings and said, 'No, the others have had their chance. Let me have mine. The Americans do.'

He went marvellously well with the audience but, when he did come off, Parnell – white with rage – told him, 'You'll never work for me again!'

'You're twenty five thousand pounds too late!' retorted Max. (This figure gets bigger with every telling of the tale.) A huge row blew up encouraged, naturally, by the press.

Within two years, though, after a procession of not too successful American stars had topped the bill at Val Parnell's Palladium, Max was asked back and, of course, the place was again the world's number one variety theatre.

A threat is one thing, but showbusiness is business.

Laurence Olivier is supposed to have based his famous performance as the broken-down music-hall comedian, Archie Rice, in *The Entertainer* on Max. Max's comment was: 'I consider it a compliment to be insulted by Sir Laurence Olivier.' After the great comedian's death, Olivier said, sadly, 'Max could do it to perfection – Archie, all the time, just missed.'

Howard Leader, the BBC TV *That's Life!* presenter, told me this fascinating little tale. During the war Howard's uncle was captured at Dunkirk and spent four years as a P.O.W. The Germans insisted that every appearance by one of their officers should be acknowledged by a 'Heil Hitler!' from the prisoners. This, of course, didn't sit too well with the lads, but they managed for four years to swallow the pill by answering every German shout of 'Heil Hitler!' with 'Max Miller!'

Their captors were never any the wiser, putting it down to, 'Ze strange Eengleash cockerknee accent.' Howard, like me, feels it is a delightful tribute to Max that, even in their darkest hour, the mere mention of his name brought the chaps a giggle. Wouldn't the patriotic Max have loved that?

Spike Milligan The most inventive writer and performer of the last fifty years (I am an unashamed Milligan junkie) loves music hall and variety, which makes me love him that much more. I wish I knew him better. Any man who can walk into an undertaker's, throw himself on the floor and shout out, 'Shop!' is OK with me.

I did share a dressing-room with him, and about a dozen others, at a Royal Variety Performance and I heard his comment to the Prince of Wales as that gentleman took his leave of the great Goon. 'Farewell, Milligoon,' said the Prince.' Ta-ta, Trainee King,' answered the Spike.

At another RVP I shared a dressing-room with a very popular singer (who had better remain nameless, to protect his romantic image). As on all these occasions the lavatory was constantly occupied by sweating, twitching, gibbering participants in the annual 'do'. After his eighth visit to the toilet he commented, 'I never realised adrenalin was brown.'

Albert Modley Mike Craig is Albert's number one fan and writes of him:

Albert was my childhood hero. The man responsible for my love of comedy. He introduced me to laughter. It was 1941 at the Dewsbury Empire. I was six years of age. Albert came on to that stage and did something that I would get a clout for. He acted daft! His catch-phrase advertised the fact ... 'Eeeh, intit grand when you're daft?'

Thirty years later I produced a radio programme on which he topped the bill. That was probably the most satisfying night of my life.

I have never met anyone in the business who didn't love Albert. Eric Morecambe, Ken Dodd, Sandy Powell, Max Wall, Tommy Trinder, Arthur Askey, they all just adored him. Arthur never tired of telling a story about Albert which took place in 1955 at the first Royal Variety Show held in the North, at the Opera House, Blackpool. Arthur always prefaced the story with a memory of the three 'famous' wives of three of the northern artistes taking part ... Beryl Formby, Mabel Pickles and Doris Modley. Arthur said ... 'It was the middle of August but there were Beryl, Mabel and Doris all wearing their full length mink coats!'

The Albert story revolves round the fact that the Opera House didn't have a Royal Box. Just two blank walls, as people who remember those days will testify. So, a Royal Box was built on one side of the theatre only. Obviously, all the artistes made their 'bows' very proudly to the posh new box and its

BILLY 'UKE' SCOTT – trying to look like his photograph.

BINNIE HALE: '...and I've got to call you Mother.'

TED RAY: 'Sell one and buy us a drink.'

DANNY PURCHES – 'he hypnotises chickens.'

(*Above left*) IVOR NOVELLO: ' "Keep the Home Fires Burning" backwards.'

(*Above*) ANNE SHELTON: 'Saint Tom Trinder.'

JOHN STYLES — 'half an hour in the broom cupboard.'

(*Above*) JACK TRIPP: 'How humiliating.'

(*Above right*) MAX WALL: 'You're the cause of it all.'

TOMMY TRINDER: 'Is this a proposal?'

JACK TRAIN – 'he got in at Doncaster.'

LAUREL and HARDY: 'Did they really appear here?'

ELSIE and DORIS WATERS – 'Have you ever heard of Gert 'n' Daisy?'

CILLA BLACK: 'Sing to it!'

DOROTHY WARD: 'Look what the Good Fairy keeps giving me.'

'WEE' GEORGIE WOOD — 'In 1923 Fanny Brice said: "You're a little shit!"'

ALBERT WHELAN: 'At last, my hat, gloves and scarf.'

R. P. WESTON and BERT LEE: 'Did he like it?'

JIMMY WHEELER: 'I think it's the polo at Hurlingham.'

THE WATER RATS: the Centenary Show at the London Palladium in 1989 – the author is still trying to collect stories.

inhabitants – Her Majesty the Queen and the Duke of Edinburgh. All, that is, except Albert. On he came, to the strains of 'On Ilkley Moor Bah't 'at', bowed to the blank wall, looked up and said, 'Oh 'eck, 'ave they gone 'ome?'

John Moffatt John is a smashing actor whose knowledge of music-hall artistes, especially their gramophone recordings, is encyclopedic. He remembered Binnie Hale playing pantomime with Shaun Glenville as Dame. One lunchtime Shaun arrived at the theatre twenty-five minutes late for the matinée – he had over-imbibed. The totally professional Binnie collared Shaun and said, 'Really, Shaun, it's too bad. You come in here twenty-five minutes late, stumbling about in a drunken stupor, smelling like a brewery, slurring your words with your flies undone – and I've got to call you Mother!'

Cedric Monarch 'Cedric' was the founder of the Three Monarchs harmonica group. The act has long disbanded and Cedric is now one of the very few comedians who tears 'em up whatever audience he is working to – dustman or duke.

For more years than he cares to remember, Cedric and the Monarchs were part of *The Black and White Minstrel Show* at the Victoria Palace. One of Cedric's bits was a ventriloquial burlesque where he would ask himself a question then put on an enormous ginger beard to cover his lips before he answered. This giant ginger thing, of course, covered his real beard – the famous tiny black one. When he met HRH Prince Philip, after a Royal Show the Duke pointed to the little black one and asked,

'Is that a real beard?'

'No, sir,' said Cedric, pulling the false one from his pocket, 'but this is.'

Pat Mooney One of the most successful and enduring Irish stand-up comics, Pat learnt his expertise and professionalism through the toughest school of all; yes – once again – the working-men's clubs. Here's one of his favourite horror stories.

In the late 1960s he was engaged to appear at a really rough club in Sunderland. His fee was £22, which was a fair old whack in those days. He was preceded by a singer attired in a blazer with an RAF badge, grey flannels and collar and tie, totally wrong for such a place. His first song was 'At The End Of The Day', followed by 'How Soon?' By his third song he was dying on his feet and the audience was pelting him with beer mats and coasters. He came off to a terrified Pat quaking in the wings and commented, 'They're a little bit on the hard side.'

Pat's costume was, to say the least, a little bit over the top: emerald green suit and shoes, green bowler hat and, just in case there was any doubt as to his nationality, he carried a shillelagh. The chairman got up and introduced Pat:

'Well, I know you didn't like that last fella. I must admit I thought he was a load of crap myself, but you've got a canny turn coming on now. I know how good he is – he's on £22, and that's £2 more than we paid Bobby Pattinson' (one of the local heroes) last week. Here he is: Pat Mooney.'

From that moment, Pat knew he had no chance. Sure enough, as he walked on, he could see the look of hatred spread over the faces. He was getting more on that one night than they were earning for a week's hard graft down the pit. Pat flogged himself to death for the next few minutes – nothing! The audience had run out of beer mats to throw, so one hurled a heavy ashtray which landed at our hero's feet.

Pat admits that if he'd had any sense he'd have walked off there and then, but a rush of blood made him pick up the ashtray and throw it back! To his horror, he saw it had caught a bloke on the temple and the claret was flowing.

At this the audience went berserk and started clambering on to the stage after Pat's blood. Pat, wielding his shillelagh like a good 'un, eventually managed to get back to his dressing-room where he locked and bolted himself in. For what seemed a lifetime he sat there, quivering, until order was restored.

A knock came on his door.

'Go away,' shouted Pat. 'I'm not opening this door until the police come. I've got to get out of this club right away.'

'This is the Concert Secretary,' said a voice. 'You can't go yet, Pat. You've still got your second spot to do!'

Morton Fraser Harmonica Gang The British equivalent of the American vaudeville act, Bora Minovitch's Harmonica Rascals, were a bunch of zany harmonica players who complemented their first-class musicianship with slapstick comedy. The dwarf 'Tiny' Ross was the butt of most of their humour. Dave King, one of the first television comedians and now a smashing 'legit' actor, started his career with them. It is always a struggle to keep a 'mob-handed' act together, and by the late 1950s, when Hippodromes, Palaces and Empires were closing by the hundred, it was practically impossible. For a short while it did seem that the big working-men's clubs would take over from the theatres and most of the established acts headed for them. Tony Vincent, who ran the Gang for the last years of its existence, told me the exact moment when he knew the time had come to jack it in. It was the night when the act that had played the Palladium, and every number one theatre in the British Isles, was introduced, by one 'Wheeltappers and Shunters' type of concert chairman, as 'The Morphy Richards Harmony Bomb!'

'I knew it was the end of the road,' says Tony. 'Not one word right!'

Peter Moss Though he spends most of his time in recording studios these days, the arranger, composer (he wrote the *Grange Hill* theme) and musical director for *The News Huddlines* has been and still is, on occasion, in charge of the music for solo performers in theatre and cabaret – for Faith Brown, for instance, and Dana and Freddie Starr.

In his early days he spent a week working for David Whitfield. It was towards the end of David's career and the majority of his audience were female fans from the old days. In a bid to liven them up, David would stop in the middle of a ballad, pull out a starting pistol and fire it willy-nilly. When the panic had subsided he'd comment, 'Nobody sleeps when David's on.'

One night, after this terrifying exhibition, a very irate old lady stormed her way backstage and hammered on the star's dressing-room door.

Full of charm, David opened the door and enquired: 'And what can I do for such a lovely lady?'

'You're so clever at firing guns and frightening the life out of people,' shrieked the shaking pensioner, 'you can be just as clever with my laundry!' And with that she thrust into his welcoming hand a pair of once-white drawers and exited into the night.

Tom Moss Bill Martin, an absolute cornucopia of Water Rat stories, told me this one about the much-loved Tom. They were discussing how success hadn't changed many of their friends in the profession. With a few exceptions! 'If I see any sign of it beginning to happen I warn them,' said Tom. 'I say to them "Remember – the higher the monkey climbs up the tree, the more he shows his arse!"'

As Bill commented, 'What a gentle piece of philosophy.'

Jacinta Mulcahy An Irish girl with a stunning voice, Jacinta played her first pantomime principal boy with yours truly at the Theatre Royal, Plymouth.

Now one of the great pleasures of panto is the freedom it affords the comics to ad-lib. There are always chances to throw in lines that are not in the script. Often an inspired ad-lib can stop the show and the following year you'll find it's printed in the script. One night, at the half-hour call, she collared my missus and said, 'Debbie, will you ask Roy to tell me before the show when he's going to ad lib.'

Chic Murray The off-beat patter of this Scottish comedian made him a folk hero of his brother artistes.

There was a well-known agent in Scotland whose office, naturally, was at the top of a flight of stairs. For anyone looking for work the ritual never varied. The artiste would knock on a wooden flap which would be raised by the agent's secretary. 'Yes?' she would enquire.

'Mr So and So to see Mr Robertson.'

'One moment' – down would come the flap – pause – up flap. 'Mr Robertson says you're a nice wee act, but there's nothing for you today.' Descent of flap. Exit down stairs.

One morning Chic went through the ritual but, after the usual brush-off, knocked again. The totally bewildered secretary raised the flap. This had never happened before.

'Yes?' she said.

'Nothing,' said Chic. 'I just wanted to take a bow!'

Charlie Naughton The tiny bald butt of all the Crazy Gang's gags, on and off stage, Charlie enjoyed drinking, especially after the show. As a familiar and much-loved figure, he was always safe. Wherever he finished up in London, a friendly cabbie would always pick him up and deliver him safely to his home in Streatham. They'd call round to the stage door of the Victoria Palace for their money the next night.

Charlie had a medical check-up and the doctor warned him that he must stop drinking, have early nights and take some exercise. 'You live right next door to Streatham Common,' counselled the doc. 'Get up early and have a stroll round there.'

Charlie dutifully did this, but gave up the whole idea when, on the third morning, a cab stopped and the driver, bundling him into the back, said, 'Don't worry, Charlie, I'll get you home.'

When 'Monsewer' Eddie Gray died I asked Charlie if he'd like to come to the funeral with me. He said he would, so I laid on a car to take us down to Brighton and bring us back. Off we went, and I said to Charlie: 'We're a bit early, so we can stop for a drink on the way.'

'Not for me, thank you, son,' he replied. 'I'm on the wagon.' A totally unexpected comment!

We got as far as Purley, and Charlie tapped the driver on the shoulder. 'Let's pull into this pub.'

'I thought you were on the wagon?'

'I am, I am,' he said, 'but there's no need to be ridiculous about it.'

The gags the Crazy Gang got up to during their many successful years together were legion, and Peter Glaze saw and told me about a classic example of how just one small move can create chaos concerning a lady called Edna Squires-Brown.

Edna had an act with doves and was the speciality in a Crazy Gang revue. She had two types of birds. One sort that she kept on-stage with her had their wings clipped so they couldn't fly, and these would pose all over her. The second eleven could fly like the clappers and were released from a basket in the gallery to swoop down over the heads of the audience and join their pals on Miss Squires-Brown.

One night Charlie and Eddie Gray simply swopped the baskets. As she opened the basket on-stage the birds were off! Some of them are probably still raising families in the Victoria district. The basket in the gallery was opened, the birds waddled out and immediately posed all over the startled customers.

Another story from Chesney Allen. During the war, while the Crazy Gang were in residence at the London Palladium, a bomb fell on the place and lodged in the roof. George Black, the governor, took a chance, put canvas underneath the hole and said: 'We carry on.'

The band, full of trepidation, made their way into the pit, set up their music and nervously settled down to play. Suddenly a shower of grit landed on the drummer's head and drums and with a wild cry he ran out of the theatre, followed by the rest of the orchestra. Only George Black had the courage to look up towards the roof and discover, in the topmost box, Charlie Naughton with a bagful of gravel.

For many years, in the Westminster Bridge Road, there was a post-box with a slot that faced into the road, which meant that you diced with death if you wanted to post a letter. Its position was down to two inhabitants of the Victoria Palace. Of course: Eddie and Charlie. Coming to work one afternoon, they noticed workmen preparing to put the post-box in situ. Eddie, who without make-up looked every inch a respectable gent, walked over to the Post Office gang.

'Good afternoon,' he said, showing them his Variety Artistes Federation membership card, 'Mr Shankers, Post Office Pillar-Box Siting Officer. Just checking the plans, if I may.' The guy who thought he was in charge produced the street map and showed 'Mr Shankers' where they'd been instructed to position the pillar-box. 'Yes, this is right,' he said. 'But it has to be this way round. You see, it's very difficult for the scrimpsen scrayvile to undulate the cordwinder unless it is. Do you see?' – the Emperor's new clothes.

'Oh yus, course.'

'See to it, then, and we'll check once we've instigated the trafficfill at the junction box.'

And that is why, for many years, to post a letter in the pillarbox near the Victoria Palace meant taking your life in your hands.

Max and Harry Nesbitt There are many tales of this comedy duo of the 1930s and 1940s. This one, apocryphal or not, was told me by Freddie Sales. I hope it is true.

Max and Harry were in digs in some grey Northern town and sharing the accommodation with a troupe of midgets. After supper one night the usual relaxing chat and booze session was under way. As the evening wore on, Max and Harry learned much of the trials and tribulations of life as a little person. How difficult it is even to get up on to a normal-sized chair and try and eat at a tall table.

As the drink disappeared, and the tales became more horrendous, the brothers started to become maudlin and were almost in tears as the difficulties of the tiny troupers were listed. They both determined to right a few of these wrongs. When the midgets had gone to bed they found a saw and proceeded to cut all the legs off the chairs and tables.

What the landlady thought and said the next morning when she discovered her furniture almost on the floor, and the legs neatly piled in the grate for firewood, is not recorded.

Walter Niblo A legendary number two front cloth comedian, he (according to Bill Martin) spent many years playing the number two variety of theatres. Eventually he got a decent date: the Metropolitan Theatre, Edgware Road. At the band call, the rehearsal with the band on Monday morning, Walter handed his music to the conductor – another legendary variety character, Ivan Dozin. The band parts were in a terrible state: torn, beerstained and just about held together with horrible bits of sticky brown paper.

Ivan picked them up with his baton. He obviously didn't want to handle them. He looked up at Walter and said, 'Are these actually your band parts?'

'Yes, they are,' answered Walter.

'Well,' said Ivan, 'they are disgusting, filthy and deplorable!'

'Really!' said Walter. 'Wait till you see the act!'

131

Peter Noone The original Herman of Herman and the Hermits, Peter, as he's proved in shows like *The Pirates of Penzance*, has developed into a good actor/singer. He is excellent in pantomime, too, and I shared *Dick Whittington* with him a few years back. He has a very beautiful French wife, who wasn't too good with the English then. Both I and a dressing-room full of people were quite surprised one night after the show when Mrs Noone came in from a side room carrying a large cardboard box full of mail from her home, and asked, 'Peter what shall I do with all these French letters?'

Tom O'Connor A school-teacher turned comedian, sadly, he – like so many others – has had to bury his talent in sterile television game shows. They surely are the killers of creative comedy. Tom is a good pantomime performer and tells this tale of playing pantomime in his home town Liverpool.

At this particular matinée the front two rows of the stalls were, surprisingly, occupied by a party from a rather posh boys' school. Tom was in the middle of the 'ghost gag'. This is the bit where the actor says to the audience: 'If you see the ghost/gorilla/rat, you will tell me won't you?' The 'ghost' then appears, while the actor, instructed by the audience, looks everywhere except where they tell him. This always results in chaos and that afternoon was no exception.

'He's behind you!' screamed two thousand juveniles.

'Over here?'

'No.'

'Over here?'

'No, *behind* you!' In the middle of this thunderous reaction there was a short silence, and a piping treble from the posh school was heard to say, 'Don't shout any more, Charles, the man's obviously an idiot!'

Whenever I do panto, I always insist that the kitchen slapstick scene is included. My version is a pale shadow of the great Charlie Caroli's, but the kids love it and it gets big laughs.

Almost without exception stage managers try to keep it out. It does involve a lot of mess and so slows down the essential panto quick changes of scene. I fight slosh and pail to keep it in.

One Christmas our director was adamant. 'No slosh scene!' He and I, alas, had never got on, but he was an important and respected putter-on of pantomime so I usually had to fall in with his ideas. But not this one. I dug my heels in and won. Or so I thought!

With a typical shake of the head he said, 'All right, but it'll have to go in here.' The spot he'd proposed was followed by a song from the principal girl and then I was back on again. I had about a minute to remove the mashed-up soap that covered me from the waist down. I pleaded for longer but: 'No – can't be done!'

'He thinks I'll cut it,' I confided to my pals, 'but I won't – I'll do it.'

It was bloody horrible having to go back on with the dried soap still clinging to my nether regions, but I did it. In the wings I removed every stitch of clothing, jock strap and all, and literally scraped the gunge off the bottom half while a dresser got me ready, working from the top down, for the next entrance. All went reasonably well till the night the principal girl looked off into the wings during her song. She saw me, stark naked, bending over while I towelled between my legs. We looked at each other and she spluttered to a standstill. So did I. I hadn't realised before that the song she was singing was 'Love Is Where You Find It'.

Alf Pearson The smaller of the top of the bill singing duo, Bob and Alf Pearson, Bob played the piano while Alf stood and sang. Their gentle humour and immaculate harmonies made them enormously popular on stage, on record and, most memorably, on radio. Their signature tune 'We bring you melody from out of the sky – my brother and I' evokes sweet memories for any fans of Ted Ray's *Ray's A Laugh*. Bob and Alf also brought some famous characters to that show – the schoolgirl Jennifer and the lady who admired 'young Doctor Hardcastle' so much and was constantly told by Ted, 'He's lovely, Mrs Hoskins!'.

Sadly Bob is no longer with us but Alf, with his razor-sharp mind and quirky sense of the ridiculous, remains one of the Water Rats' very best storytellers. Here's a couple straight from the horse's mouth. The first echoes, yet again, that golden rule, 'Never book into unknown digs.'

Probably the worst digs and landlady we came across, we encountered on our first visit to Wigan. Arriving early Sunday afternoon at Wigan station we were approached by a youth about seventeen years old, who stated that if we hadn't fixed accommodation, his mother had rooms, and because she wouldn't tip the stage manager, he in turn wouldn't recommend her, so her rooms were often empty. We thought it was a pretty sad state of affairs and decided to accompany the boy home and stay with his mother. He assured us there was a sitting room with a piano where we could rehearse and two bedrooms. Actually the rooms weren't too bad except that the lounge was papered with black wallpaper covered in yellow roses. It was quite large with plenty of chairs but nowhere to sit down – if you know what I mean.

We were having a chat with the landlady when we heard a funny noise coming along the passage towards our room. 'Oh!' said she, 'this'll be Polly.' Into the room clumped a parrot. Now it was the middle of the moulting season and the parrot's head was as bald as a coot's and just one solitary feather was in the place where her tail should have been. Poor Polly looked the picture of abject misery. The landlady looked at Polly and asked her, 'Polly – what's pros?' 'Pros,' answered the parrot, 'is buggers!'

'And Polly,' she then enquired, 'what's your mother?'

'Me mother's an old cow!' replied Polly and so, having done her act, turned and clumped out of the room, presumably back to the kitchen.

'Isn't it funny the way parrots swear?' said the landlady – not realising she and the parrot had exactly the same accent.

In the middle of the week we took in a head of celery, some mature Cheddar cheese and some tomatoes saying we would like these for our tea with some thin bread and butter. We couldn't believe it when she brought the tea in. The celery was just the green tops. She said, 'I cut all the roots off. I knew you wouldn't be wanting them.'

On the Saturday lunchtime she called me into the kitchen. 'Will you taste the gravy in that bowl and see what you think?' I took a sip from a spoon and it was awful. I rushed to the sink and spat it out. The inside of my mouth was on fire. 'What on earth was that?' I gasped.

'Ah,' she said, 'I thought it were funny. You see my son has been cleaning his motor-bike chain wi' paraffin in that bowl and I knew he hadn't cleaned it out properly.'

You can be sure, from that moment on, whenever we were going to a town for the first time we never fixed digs on spec. Only if they had been highly recommended by trustworthy pals did we take them.

Bob and Alf were always in demand for private functions and this next story is one we all wish had happened to us. Alf says:

Bob and I were booked for the Annual Ball of the Licensed Hoteliers and Victuallers at the Savoy Hotel. We arrived on the night and presented ourselves to that doyen of toast-masters, Mr John Mills, whom we knew quite well, and told him we were in the cabaret. 'Oh my goodness,' said John, 'they're all drunk! They don't see each other for twelve months but when they do, they really let their hair down. You won't get any attention from this lot.'

'Well,' we said, 'we have to see a Mr Whittaker.'

'Whittaker!' said John. 'He's the worst of them all. That's him standing over there.'

We walked over and said, 'Mr Whittaker. We are Bob and Alf Pearson.'

'Bob and Alf,' he cried, and flung his arms round us, 'what a lovely act. There's your money and I want you for next year!' We took it, looked at John Mills who cast his eyes towards heaven and shrugged. Well ... what would you have done, chums?

Leaving the stage door of the Sunderland Empire, the brothers were accosted by a local. 'Yer booger!' he said to Bob. 'Ye've changed, but a would know ye anywhere.'

'What do you mean I've changed?' asked Bob.

'Why man,' said Bob's friend. 'Ye've put on a bit a weight, an' ye've changed your hairstyle, but I would have known ye anywhere, man – Charlie Chester.' Said Bob, 'I'm not Charlie Chester. My name's Bob Pearson.'

'Ye booger,' said the gent. 'Ye've changed yer name an' all!'

Jimmy Perry The comedy writer and ex-actor (they are always the best), together with David Croft, created the yardstick by which all situation comedies should be measured: *Dad's Army*. The series, and more importantly its characters, are loved by the British, young and old. Jimmy's careful observation of human beings with all their strengths and weaknesses is captured in this touching little story.

When David Croft and I first created the television series *Hi-De-Hi* in 1980, the chief character was the holiday camp comic, Ted Bovis, played so truthfully by Paul Shane. He represented all the bottom-of-the-bill comics I had ever known. When he worked outside the holiday camp, to use an old-fashioned showbusiness saying, he couldn't get arrested, but inside the camp he was King. The holiday-makers loved him. They lapped up his terrible old routines, and he bathed in their applause. His great act was 'Famous people on the Toilet'.

The character of Ted Bovis was drawn from my experience of working with a camp comic at Butlin's in Filey in 1951. I was his feed and it was right at the start of my career. I was in my twenties, very brash and thought I knew it all. The comic would have been in his fifties, tired and worn out with a life-time of

137

failure, but he was safe performing in the holiday camp. The fly-blown old routines we did were greeted with laughter and applause every night.

Towards the end of the season we were asked to appear in a charity show at Scarborough. My partner was over the moon. 'This is our big chance, Jim,' he said. 'We'll knock 'em cold.' And in my innocence I was swept away by his enthusiasm.

The show was a midnight matinée and all the stars who were appearing in the summer shows in Scarborough and Bridlington were on the bill. The theatre was packed. The mayor and the local dignitaries were in the front row and everyone was in evening dress, as was the custom for a civic function some forty years ago.

We were on about half-way through the first half. The show started well. We stood in the wings, listening to the laughter and applause. Then the orchestra played our music and on we went. Our first gag got a polite titter and then the rot set in. We were dying but we ploughed on.

Suddenly my partner turned up stage, and I can still see his tired old face today. He was wearing heavy old-fashioned make-up and his eyes had the look of a hunted animal. 'I've lost 'em. They're not laughing,' he whispered. 'They don't think I'm funny any more.'

Somehow we got through the rest of the act and came off. The comic slumped down on a chair and the other artistes who were standing in the wings drew away from us as if we were lepers.

I looked down at the crumpled figure in his loud check suit and thought, 'You stupid old fool, you may have had it but *I* am going places.' How cruel the young can be! We got back to the dressing-room and the comic started to wipe off his make-up.

Then it dawned on my youthful arrogance that the glamorous profession I had come into had another side. 'Don't worry, old man,' I said. 'They love you in the holiday camp.' Suddenly his whole mood changed. 'You're right, Jim,' he said. 'They *do* love me in the camp, don't they?'

Jon Pertwee Yet another stand-up comic, he has graduated from variety through being one of our top voices men on radio to the 'legit', notably as Doctor Who and Worzel Gummidge.

Coming out of the Shepherd's Bush Empire one night, Jon saw a very big man leaning against the stage door wall. The man whistled at him, turned his head, shoved a piece of paper into his face and muttered, ''Ere, sign this.'

As only Jon can, he smiled and said, 'How can I resist such a charming invitation,' and signed his name.

The man, still leaning against the wall, took it, read it, crumpled it up and threw it away.

Another autograph hunter, a small boy with a dirty scrap of paper, accosted Jon outside the Finsbury Park Empire. 'Who am I?' asked Jon.

'Buggered if I know,' replied the lad.

'Then you don't want my autograph,' said Jon grandly and swept into the theatre.

A few minutes later an upside-down face appeared in the window of his semi-basement dressing-room. ''Ere, mister, can I have a photograph?' said the face.

To get rid of him, Jon signed a photograph and passed it to the boy with, 'There you are, now you *know* who I am.'

'No I don't,' said the lad. 'I can't read!'

Again coming out of a dressing-room, this time with a very beautiful girl he had just met and was trying to impress, Jon was confronted by a huge, obese, drunken reveller.

'Out of my way, you big ponce,' requested the large one, 'and take that poxy whore with you.'

Returning the girl to the shelter of the stage door portico, Jon bravely returned to his assailant and demanded: 'I beg your pardon. *What* did you say?'

The big man steadied himself, and a few inches from Jon's face replied, 'I said – out of my way, you big ponce, and take that poxy whore with you.'

'Thank you,' said Jon. 'That's what I thought you said, but don't say it again.' He turned away and, on trembling legs, returned to where he had left the beautiful nymphette. She had gone. So much for old world chivalry.

Sandy Powell One of my all-time favourite comedians was a huge star in the 1930s through radio and records (selling literally millions, in the days when nobody bothered to count them). He was a wonderful burlesque performer. His incompetent ventriloquist and diabolical magician were masterpieces. He evolved the dreadful 'vent' through being on a variety bill with *three* real ventriloquists. 'Brilliant booking that was,' said Sandy. But he thought it might get a laugh if he came on, in the star spot, carrying a doll. It did and he developed the act from there.

One evening he was with some pals in a pub discussing where they'd be working the next week. One, a ventriloquist notorious for his lack of lip control, said he'd be in Sheffield. 'You'll do well there,' said Sandy, 'the lighting's terrible.'

When the big clubs came into being everybody had to play them. There was no other work. To see some of the great theatre acts struggling in those plastic palaces against drinking, talking and heckling was a sad spectacle. It was a case of horses for courses – some wonderful club acts died the death when they played variety halls.

Sandy would wipe his brow and tell of his first experience of them.

I went to my home town to do my first club. To get backstage you had to walk through the audience. I did, and was greeted by all sorts of folk who shouted, 'Can you hear me, mother?', slapped me on the back and explained to their friends, 'Of course we're related you know.'

I went behind the curtain and got changed. The preceding acts, and especially the compère, were being given a terrible time. The compère was a local favourite but every time he went on they howled him off. He said 'I'm not going out there again.'

I said, 'You must. I can't just walk on. You have to introduce me.'

'All right,' sighed the lad. He stuck his head through the curtains and just said, 'Here's another one!'

I went on, did the vent and died the most terrible death. My second spot was the 'cod' conjuror and that went down the Swanee as well. I had to run the gauntlet through the audience to go home. This time no one looked my way, but I did hear them saying, 'Well not *really* related – only by marriage.'

Danny Purches The gypsy singer who had a big hit with a song called 'Golden Earrings' is an interesting bloke. He's a full-blooded Romany and told me once he could hypnotise chicken. This, he explained, could be achieved by running a forefinger and thumb downwards from the top of the beak. They followed the movement and went cross-eyed in the process.

Whether he could control chicken I never found out, but I

witnessed something amazing which he did to a baby seal. It had been washed up on the beach just outside the theatre we were working. The poor creature was so terrified it bit anyone who came near. Danny approached it, sat down on his haunches and quietly chatted to it. After about ten minutes he picked it up, carried it to the harbour's edge and dropped it into the sea. Perhaps he wasn't the kidder everyone thought he was.

Alan Randall Alan is a brilliant musician, whose jazz-orientated talents have rather tended to be shoved into the background because of the success of his George Formby-inspired singing and ukulele playing. Being associated in any way with a performer of yesteryear can have its drawbacks. Alan remembers working a summer season in Clacton; in the bar after the show two eighty-year-old ladies approached him.

'I hope you don't mind me asking, but when was it you made all those films?' Alan assured her it wasn't him, but she insisted, 'I'm sure it was. You used to ride a motor-bike in the T.T. races and fly upside down in an aeroplane.'

He carefully explained that that was George Formby, he was just doing an impression and that his name was Alan Randall.

She pressed on: 'Well, we thought it was funny when we saw your name was Randall on the poster, but we thought you used to be George Formby.'

Her friend then took over and proceeded to explain that she had heard lots of people in showbusiness don't use their own names or, if they're not doing very well, they change them.

Says Alan, 'They honestly believed I'd changed my name from George Formby to Alan Randall. As they left, looking puzzled, I overheard one, of them say, "I'm sure it *was* him. He sang all the same songs!"'

Frank Randle The tattily-made films (originally almost exclusively shown in the North) of this strange, brilliant, wayward comedian are still worth seeing today. He was a true eccentric, a great boozer with a mercurial temper, who hired and fired his staff and stooges as the mood took him.

George Melly, the jazz singer and writer, told me this story
which he heard while he was on tour with Mick Mulligan's Jazz

Band. Mick was a great chatter to stage door keepers and once asked one of that vanished breed if he'd ever known Frank Randle.

'Aye, I knew the daft bugger,' said the stage door man. 'While he was here he put an advert in the paper. It read "Wanted Immediately. Chauffeur/Bricklayer". When he came in to work that night, I asked him why the hell he wanted a chauffeur stroke bricklayer. He said, "Well, he'll only work six days a week as a chauffeur so, on his day off, I'll have to drive myself and I get so pissed I always knock our front wall down when I get home." He was a daft bugger!'

Albert and Les Ward remembered seeing him in pantomime flanked by two stooges. As the three of them stepped down to the footlights Frank, to the great delight of the children, broke wind, *very* loudly. He accusingly asked the stooge on his right 'Did you do that?'

'No,' replied that gent.

'Was it you?' he enquired of the other.

'Certainly not!' stooge two answered.

'By 'eck!' said the culprit. 'It must have bin me!'

Steve Rawlings A sensational young juggler, he has succeeded on both the 'alternative' circuit and in traditional music hall. He paralysed West End audiences in *Sugar Babies* with Mickey Rooney and Ann Miller, too.

The big finish of Steve's act is an incredible feat of balancing involving a bottle, a tray, several glasses, a set of flaming torches and some juggling balls.

A volunteer from the audience is essential to this routine and Steve's handling of the punters was always second to none – until one night.

At a company function all was going well; the trick was half-way through with the props balanced on Steve's chin when he asked his volunteer, as is his wont, to 'Grab my balls!' Alas, it was the lady volunteer's birthday and she had celebrated it in an extremely liquid fashion. She was 'kaylied' and, as every good drunk always does, took her instructions literally.

As Steve says, 'It wasn't so much that she did indeed grab my personals, but the way she did it. I'd made her an offer she couldn't refuse. Her face lit up and her Russian shot putter's body trembled with excitement. She gave me a whack in the nuts that still makes me wince today. The bottles, glasses and contents went everywhere. The audience were crying with laughter almost as loudly as I was with pain. I did put together some sort of finish, but what amazed me were the number of people who came up afterwards and said how much they'd enjoyed it, and how did I manage to do that every night!'

Dick Ray A brother Water Rat, a producer and impresario, he is the man who runs the Opera House in Jersey.

At one time Dick looked after a band who toured the country playing for hunt balls, dinners and so on. Posh dos. At one very sophisticated 'gig' (musicians' talk for a job) the tenor sax player whispered to the bandleader, 'Jimmy, I've got to go to the loo.'

'You can't,' said the governor, 'you can't leave the stand until the official break.'

Two numbers later: 'Please let me off. I'm dying here.'

'Shut up! You will leave the stand at the end of this set.'

One number later the sax player put down his instrument, stood up and said, 'It's no good. I've *got* to go!'

'Sit down!' hissed the leader. 'You *can't* go now. You've known about this gig for six weeks.'

Dick's wife, Peggy, was originally a 'turn' – and a very good one. Dick was driving her to a BBC TV audition and he wasn't sure where the studios actually were. They stopped at some traffic lights, next to a huge truck. Dick called to the driver: 'Shepherd's Bush?'

The driver stuck his head out of the cab. 'Eh?'

'Shepherd's Bush?' repeated Dick. The trucker sighed, switched off his engine, climbed down and walked to the back of his truck. Suddenly the Rays' Mini started to move forward.

'What *are* you doing?' shouted Dick. 'Shepherd's Bush?'

'Oh **** it!' said the helpful trucker. 'I thought you said "give us a push!"'

Charles Reardon Charles, the one stage door keeper I got to know very well, was in charge of the artistes' entrance at the Palace, Shaftesbury Avenue – from the days of Novello through to *Jesus Christ Superstar*. I did a Danny La Rue revue there for a year and my dressing-room was right next door to Charles's cubbyhole. He was brilliant at speaking gobbledegook, a combination of backslang, camp and wild invention. Charlie

Naughton of the Crazy Gang was terrific at it too. I'd often hide out of sight, giggling and helpless, as visitors to the stage door were questioned by Charles in his own language.

'Ah, good evening, sir – is it wharpled on the escafu perhaps?'

'Pardon?'

'I'd like to be a little more gratified, but it was the colour of the ansifkay that did it mostly.'

'What?'

'I'm sorry – he's left!'

A well-known American impresario, Lee Ephraim, was presenting a show at the Palace, and the leader of the orchestra complained to Charles that whenever he tried to tackle Mr Ephraim about an increase in pay for the band Ephraim always got in first with some criticism of the music.

'Well, all you have to do,' advised Charles, 'is give him a burst of the gobbledegook. He'll say "What?" you say "It's about the money for the band" and you're in!'

'Great,' said the muso and learnt, parrot-fashion, a chunk of Charlespeak.

'Well?' asked Charles the next day. 'What happened?'

'I went in,' said the distraught leader, 'did that chat and the old sod held up his hand and said, "That's exactly what I wanted to talk to you about!"'

It was Charles who told me that when Ivor Novello left the stage at the end of a performance every night, he would stop about twenty feet from the stage door entrance in exactly the same position and hold a discussion with an imaginary person. This was to enable his 'groupies' waiting in the street to see the Novello profile. He even had a small spotlight strategically placed for the fans to get the full effect.

Another legendary stage door keeper was Wally at the City Varieties, Leeds, during the run of television's *The Good Old Days*. When I knew him he did nothing but sit in a collapsing horse-hair armchair and expostulate about how the business had never been the same since Dan Leno died, but in his earlier days he'd been the stage manager at the Varieties. Terry Cantor, who presented umpteen pantomimes at the famous little theatre, said at one dress rehearsal that the tabs didn't come in at the end of the first half. Wally, whose job it was to do just that, was nowhere to be seen. Eventually, in answer to Terry's frantic shouts, he put his head round the wings and said, 'Sorry I missed that one, Terry – I was drowning some kittens.'

Peter Regan The ex-bandleader who became a very popular toast-master. Toast-masters, who are of course performers too, have their own favourite and unfavourite venues. Peter has had more mishaps at one place than any other.

Every time I enter this particular banqueting suite I shudder. The place is a jinx to me. Each time I've attended a function there something has happened. At the height of one banquet I banged my gavel on the centre of the top table, which promptly caved in. A large anniversary cake did the same as I supervised the cutting of it. Yet another gavel banging on a tablecloth-covered side table heralded a ghastly cracking sound – underneath the tablecloth was a glass top!

But worse was to follow. I was supervising a grocers' convention. The reception was warm. The meal was excellent and the flowing wine created just the right mood for the chairman's speech. I banged the gavel and nothing went wrong. I had beaten the jinx!

The chairman rose, notes in hand. Suddenly the double entrance doors at the end of the room burst open and there, framed in the doorway, stood a tall auburn-haired woman carrying a rolled umbrella and bristling with rage.

She glared around the room and made towards a large man sitting with a blonde partner. Walloping him around the head with her brolly she screamed, 'You deceitful b*****d. While I'm left at home, looking after the kids, you're out with your fancy bit!'

With the help of the errant husband and under a hail of umbrella blows I managed to escort the injured party into the entrance hall where, as one wag put it, 'The cabaret ended.'

The venue, called the Horseshoe, had been unlucky for me once again.

I follow that classic with another example of Peter's painstaking preparations to amuse. Ken Dodd replied for the Guests at the Centenary Water Rats Ball. The Ball was held just after Ken had been found innocent of income tax charges. It was a touchy subject and nobody wanted to be the first to refer to the trouble and, in the preceding speeches, nobody had. Ken stood up to speak and, as he did, what seemed like three thousand fake five-pound notes fluttered down from above him. The moment's silence was broken by a roar from fifteen hundred throats. The laugh grew and grew as Ken picked up every single one, and insisted on counting and pocketing the lot before he said a word.

I glanced upward to see a grinning face looking over the balcony as the last few fivers were emptied from a huge briefcase. The case and the evil grin both belonged to Regan!

Eddie Reindeer A brother Water Rat, a comic, he had for his signature tune 'Jingle Bells'! We did panto in Belfast together and I had been going on about how clever the new *That Was The Week That Was* wave of comedians were. That night in the middle of the slosh scene, dressed in long black wig, bra, corset and drawers, he fell backwards into a huge bathful of gunge and said, 'Could David Frost do this?'

Freddie Sales Freddie, a brilliant visual comedian who, after years of knocking it out round the variety theatres in the UK, went to America where he became extremely popular, is, alas, now retired. He sent me this wonderful story which I reproduce exactly as Freddie wrote it.

The expression 'They were rolling in the aisles' is often used as a metaphor to describe an audience truly helpless with laughter. To create such a state of shrieking, rib-aching, convulsive laughter is the ambition of every comedy entertainer. Such a moment is rare, yet I did witness such a phenomenon, one I shall never forget, and I regret that my humble efforts to relate the incident in the written word may lose some of its impact.

It occurred in Melbourne. The Tivoli Theatre. The show? A new concept entitled 'Ladies, Lions and Laughter'. Something very different for Australian audiences.

The stage converted into a circus ring, but a proscenium jutting out into the audience permitted dancers, variety acts and comedians to present their talents. The problems of accommodating the lions, and shoring up the stage for the elephants, had all been overcome and I was invited to the preview matinée performance.

The show was excellent. Long-legged dancers pirouetted with feathers all a-quiver, comedians comedied and jugglers juggled. In between the lions leapt through rings and the sea lions balanced beach balls on their noses.

Then came the *big* act. The elephants. Three ponderous pachyderms plodded on to the stage. It was obvious they were still nervous about the stage. They stood, three abreast, facing the audience. The trainer, a small man armed with the traditional stick, shouted orders to them. They gazed at the audience, swaying gently from side to side in perfect rhythm. And then, keeping up the rhythm, the middle elephant slowly turned. Still slowly swaying in tempo with the other two, he stood broadside on to the audience. The audience assumed it was a part of the act, but then – the elephant peed.

Please believe me, this is quite a sight. One must have the same feeling of wonderment at the first sighting of Niagara Falls. This roar, this cascade of thundering water. Steam rose from it as it hit the sawdust. The trainer was confused. He could not continue with the act. He walked up and down in the corner of the stage looking at the audience and shrugging his shoulders. The audience? They were laughing.

The flow of pee ceased. There was a look of great relief on the elephant's face. He – yes, this was definitely a 'he' – got back into the swaying rhythm of the other two and returned to his central position. The swaying continued, side to side, never stopped. The trainer leapt back to take control. He yelled. He waved his stick. Forget it, oh brave trainer. The elephant on the right – keeping up the rhythm – slowly turned. Again, was this part of the act? But one could see the trainer was puzzled. The elephant turned until its back was to the audience. And then the tail went up – and it was not exactly a pleasant sight, but it was very interesting for its . . . backside? Bottom? (How can one describe this in a genteel manner?) Its very large rectum slowly opened, and there appeared the biggest, brown bowling bowl you have ever seen. Trust me, it was big! This rotund mass of excretion then fell to the floor with a very big thud. If that little trainer had stood underneath, it would have killed him. This brown cannon-ball was followed by yet another, each one appearing as if by sleight of hand (or in this case sleight of arse). About four of these vast by-products of pachyderm digestive system thudded to the floor. The moment of relief completed, the elephant took up the rhythm again, and turned, swaying gently to face the audience once more. The audience were screaming with laughter. Women were dabbing their eyes as mascara streamed down their faces. The auditorium reverberated with the sound of their laughter.

Perhaps the elephants were competing against each other that day? Perhaps they heard the laughter and decided each could better the other? Every part of this incident appeared choreographed, for from the wings minced – and I do mean minced – a tiny little man wearing a black Russian-type blouse buttoned to the neck, black evening dress pants. He was bald but had been in the sun and his bald head gleamed like a red beacon. In one hand was the largest dust-pan I have ever seen, and the smallest hand brush! As he ran there was the hint of a 'plié' (as in ballet) as he commenced to roll (it was the only way!) these loads of elephant excretion on to the large dust-pan. It was obvious these articles were heavy. He had to strain to lift them. But as he was doing this, the impossible happened.

The elephant on the left – still swaying – he or she – slowly began to turn. This very slow turn presaged what was to come. The trainer had given up any idea of control. He still paced to and fro, looking at the audience and shrugging. The audience sensed the elephant's next move. It is a psychological trick in comedy production to 'telegraph' to an audience the next hilarious bit. This was exactly what happened when that elephant began to turn. The audience knew what it was going to do. They were waiting for it! There was a slight hiatus as the audience were laughing in subdued tones, but the next scream of laughter would erupt as that elephant executed his or her massive bowel movement. Remember, the elephants are still swaying – side to side – the rhythm never stopped. The elephant turned. The back was to the audience. The tail went up like a signal – and another consignment of large brown bowling balls arrived.

As the first ball appeared, it was as though the theatre would be buried beneath the avalanche of sound that greeted this moment. Screams, yells, roars, ear-splitting laughter as the audience rocked – quite helpless with laughter. Surely nothing could top this? How wrong can you get? All this happened whilst the little man with the red head and the outsize dust-pan was rolling the first lot of bowling balls into his pan. He looked at this other elephant as it turned. The expression on his face was one of sheer disbelief. Now he was confused. What should he do? Wait for this new delivery of elephant poo? He moved toward the elephant but realised his pan was pretty full, so looked at the audience, smiled and shrugged and, still mincing but struggling beneath the weight, he staggered to the wings. He returned almost immediately and waited and watched the steady 'thud – thud – thud' of the next load. Another mincing walk and he began rolling, rolling, rolling the next lot into his large dust-pan.

Then came the 'tag' – the knock-out punch. I would stress at this juncture every word describing this event is true. It is a moment I will never forget. For now the middle elephant, he of the long pee, was not to be outdone. He would not be upstaged by his two friends. He started it and he would finish it!

He slowly turned. Still swaying. The little man with the pan looked up. He realised what was going to happen. He threw down his brush in anger and he stamped his foot in temper. Slowly, swaying the middle elephant presented his backside to the audience and, once more, the horrendous sight of a big grey wrinkled behind contorted, went into spasm and lo, there did appear more of these gigantic spheres. Huge! Heavy! The thuds echoed as they hit the stage.

It was then I witnessed the phenomena all comedy entertainers want to achieve. The audience were literally out of their seats and were on their hands and knees, rolling in the aisles!! Some banging the floor with their hands – rolling onto their backs, screaming with laughter – they were helpless. I have never seen the like of it since. I too was convulsed with laughter. Nobody knew what to do. The trainer had given up. The little man with the giant dust-pan was gesticulating in anger at all the crap he had to clear up. The elephants never stopped swaying – side to side – gazing so solemnly at the audience. I am sure they must have known what they were doing. The front of house curtain was lowered on this scene. The show could not continue. But no one complained. That moment is branded on my memory. If only I could get laughs like that? I wonder where I can buy three elephants?

Leslie Sarony Dancer, comedian, actor, singer and recording star, he made over a hundred and fifty records under his own name and hundreds more under assumed ones – even he didn't know how many. He twice sold a million copies of a recording. I apologise for going on about Leslie, but I feel it is important to get down exactly what he achieved in his long, highly productive, lifetime in the 'biz'. He was Victorian man. He wasn't a specialist but interested in every aspect of our game and good at everything he attempted, too.

He began as a dancer and singer as part of a juvenile act, Parks Eton Boys, and graduated to principal dancer in the original *Show Boat* at Drury Lane with Paul Robeson.

He was a songwriter supreme. It was during the run of *Show* 151

Boat that he wrote, after hearing two chorus girls arguing, 'I Lift Up My Finger and I Say Tweet Tweet', an enormous hit.

He could write songs to order and, almost, at the drop of a hat. He did loads of records with Jack Hylton and told me about recording in the 1920s and 1930s.

> Hylton would ring me around midnight and say, 'We're doing four titles tomorrow – be there!' I'd sit down, write the songs, Hylton would have them orchestrated and we'd do them the next day. They were recorded straight on to the wax. If you got it wrong you had to do the whole thing from the beginning. No editing in those days. You were very popular if you made a mistake.

He wrote some huge hits: 'When The Guards Are On Parade' (which is still played by the Guards bands today) and the million-seller that put a new phrase into the English language, 'Ain't It Grand To Be Bloomin' Well Dead' as well as 'Jollity Farm', 'Rhymes', 'Wheezy Anna' and one of Sir Edward Elgar's favourite songs, 'Muckin' About In The Garden' (written under the name Q. Kumber). To go through the titles of a handful of his songs brings, rushing back, the Britain of the 1920s and 1930s – 'Strolling Down The Strand', 'Tune In', 'Teas, Light Refreshments and Minerals', 'A Game of Darts' and 'I Like Riding on A Choo Choo Choo'.

In the 1930s, with Leslie Holmes, he created the top-of-the-bill variety act of The Two Leslies. The act broke up at the end of the War and Leslie Sarony while still doing his solo variety turn, found himself in the legitimate theatre gleaning smash notices in drama from Beckett to Shakespeare.

He wrote hundreds of parodies and original songs for the Vaudeville Golfing Society (an all-male set-up whose annual dinner is a must for everyone who likes honest vulgarity). Leslie's rabelaisian contributions had titles like 'Piddling Pete', 'The Snake Song', 'A Brewer's Best Friend', 'Easy Anna', and the masterpiece, 'Phartology'. They're still quoted today. When accused of going too far, he replied, 'If they're funny, they're not filthy.'

He was a ball of fire. at well over eighty he entertained the residents of Brinsworth House (the residential home for old pros in Twickenham) with a medley of his songs. One of the audience, Annie Augustin (an ex-barrel jumper who was over a hundred years old at the time) said after his performance, 'Wasn't Leslie Sarony's son marvellous? I remember all those songs when they first came out!'

His last television appearance was in 1984 on a variety bill from Manchester. I compèred the show and he wasn't very well at all. During the show he sat on a chair in the wings, looking very old and frail, but, as the band played 'I Lift Up My Finger', he jumped up, pulled the front of his blazer down, strode on and proceeded to paralyse them with an eight-minute medley of his hits. When he came off I could see he'd had enough.

He went to sit down but the floor assistant grabbed him and said, 'I'm afraid we missed a couple of shots, will you do it again?'

'No he won't,' I said, but he pushed me aside and did the whole spot again with, if possible, even more energy than the first time.

He came off and I apologised to him for *them* making him do it twice. He said, 'Listen they wanted it again and that's that. I've kept them sweet. Very important.' He added with a twinkle, 'You never know what it'll lead to.' He was eighty-five.

He was a tiny little man who made up for his lack of height with his volatile and highly opinionated views on showbusiness, life, politics – everything! I used to love him phoning me. He'd never start with 'Hallo' but would immediately launch into a great tirade about something that had got up his nose. I remember him doing ten minutes on Arthur Scargill without once repeating himself. But he would always finish, like the true pro he was, with a gag. I once managed to get in that I had just bought a dog and he, without drawing breath, said, 'I had a dog with an ingrowing tail. You had to look up its arse to see if it was pleased. Ta-ta!'

He told me once he'd been in a big London store during the run-up to Christmas. A man and his granddaughter were waiting for the Magic Grotto to open. Leaning against a counter was Father Christmas, smoking and chatting up one of the lady assistants. The little girl spotted Santa, ran up to him, tugged at his sleeve and said, 'Hello, Father Christmas.'

The merry old bringer of seasonal joy looked down and said, 'Bugger off. I'm not on till eleven!'

'So much for the bleedin' Christmas spirit,' was Leslie's comment. 'Ta-ta.'

Billy 'Uke' Scott Forget George Formby, Billy is *the* genius of the ukulele. As he said so often on radio, 'I will now prove to you that it is possible to play melody on the ukulele.' And he did. He is a clever songwriter and a witty observer of the showbusiness scene: 'What is the hardest part of a hard   153 profession?' 'Trying to look like your photographs!' and 'When are you going to give up?' 'When I've used *them* up.'

Billy did a week's variety with Jack Train (the immortal Colonel Chinstrap in radio's *ITMA*). Jack gave Billy a lift back to London at the end of the week. The Sunday morning drive was a pleasant one until Jack, spotting a fly inside the car, suddenly whipped off his trilby and desperately tried to drive the insect out of a window. The visitor wouldn't leave so Jack pulled into a layby and, opening the car door, ejected the fly.

'What on earth was all that about?' said Billy. 'It was only a fly. Did you think it was a wasp?'

'No,' said Jack, totally seriously, 'but he got in at Doncaster. He'll have a wife and kids waiting for him somewhere. If he'd stayed with us he wouldn't have been able to get out until Hendon and he wouldn't have known where the hell he was. At least he's in with a chance now!'

Billy, like most of the good-hearted variety acts, would, if the landlady had been a helpful one, give her a couple of 'comps' for the first house on Friday. (Even in the golden days, the thinnest house of the week!) His landlady in Birmingham qualified, and on his return to the digs he asked her if she'd enjoyed the show, 'Oh yes,' she replied, 'but I couldn't get over how strange it is – your *name's* "Uke" and you *play* the uke!'

Daphne Shadwell She is a television producer who loves showbusiness. There's a contradiction! Daphne's father was the popular musical director, Charles Shadwell, whose marvellous laugh on radio was appreciated by listeners and, even more by the comics. Daphne's sister, Joan Winters, did a double act in variety with Guy Fielding and while working a week up North heard a man say to a small boy who was looking at a photograph of George Formby, 'Aye, that's George Formby, lad, and you think on – you'll look like that one day if you keep playing with yourself!'

Charlie Shadwell was a lovable eccentric and, during his stint as musical director at the Coventry Hippodrome, travelled everywhere by bike. He was always late and once Md'd an entire variety bill wearing his hat. He'd arrived just in time for the show and had forgotten to take it off. On one occasion he, late again, was pedalling furiously down side streets to avoid the traffic. He turned into the main street to find it completely clear of traffic and lined with people. He had forgotten it was the day of a visit from King George the Fifth and Queen Mary. He'd arrived in the main street just before the procession. His reception from the crowds was tumultuous, rivalling even that of the pair who followed him.

Jimmy Shand The world-famous Scottish accordionist and bandleader was having breakfast in his hotel room one morning when he found he'd used all the marmalade and preserves but still had a piece of toast. This could not be wasted so he phoned down to room service for some honey. The girl arrived with just one individual portion, packaged in what he called 'one of those plastic thimble jobs'. Jimmy looked at it suspiciously and declared, 'Oh, I see you keep a bee!'

Don Shearman The best variety musical director of them all, Don reminded me of a disastrous charity night we shared at the Theatre Royal, Windsor. Don was, as on so many occasions, my accompanist. He says:

> The variety show was being staged in the presence of HRH (and Companion Water Rat) Prince Philip a few weeks before the much publicised wedding of Prince Charles and Lady Diana Spencer. Now the Theatre Royal is a playhouse and the resident crew, used to the leisurely pace of a straight play, found a fast-moving variety show somewhat difficult to cope with. Technically everything went wrong.
>
> The first disaster occurred after only ten minutes and involved the pianist Walter Landauer. Walter finished his first item and, as was his custom, rose from the piano, stepped downstage and took a bow. At this point the crew closed the tabs behind him and removed his piano thus bringing his spot to a premature end and causing Walter great distress.
>
> From then on things went from a brightly lit Hinge and Bracket being seen creeping on with their props to no lights at all on the band's music stands. Finally Roy took the stage thinking 'nothing more can happen now'. Wrong!
>
> After just three minutes of his act, in the middle of a joke, in came the tabs between Roy and myself; in came more tabs between me and the band; on came the stage crew, who lowered the piano lid, thereby squashing Roy's prized top hat and proceeded to remove the piano. I was sitting there

155

ready to play and literally had to fight them off – with words quite inappropriate to a Royal occasion.

While all this was going on, yet another of this ill-starred gang repeatedly walked onstage and tried to take away Roy's microphone – while he was speaking into it! After about the third attempt, Roy's patience finally gave out and, looking up to HRH, he said, 'Gawd – it's a good job this lot aren't organising your do on July the 29th. You'd have no chance!'

A trend Don, and most 'proper' musicians, regret is the proliferation of electric keyboards in place of real pianos. He says:

While they're very effective in many types of work (for instance in recording, in a rock band, or enhancing the sound of a small theatre orchestra) I personally think no keyboard can match an acoustic piano for accompanying, especially solo accompanying. With electric instruments there is always the risk of a breakdown. One of my most embarrassing moments was caused by just such a breakdown.

I went to accompany Don Estelle at the opening of a very up-market bingo hall somewhere down the M3, and took a keyboard. In setting up, a wire in the mains lead of the instrument worked loose and caused a short-circuit, blowing several fuses and delaying the start of Don's act. With the help of the house electrician we found some sockets still live and got things working, but with wires trailing all over the stage. However, all went well until Don managed to catch his foot under a lead, thereby dislodging the plug and silencing the keyboard in the middle of a song. I dived forward and pushed the plug back in. There was a blinding flash, and all the stage lights went out. Quite unperturbed, Don carried on singing unaccompanied while the electrician, the bingo caller and I were crawling around trying to put things right. The final blow was the appearance of a front-of-house man loudly complaining that I had put his fridge out of action and what was I going to do about all his ice cream that was melting? Mr Steinway got it right the first time.

The Simmons Brothers Keith and Alan are perhaps our most underrated comedy team, though their early days in the business were spent being out of work more often than in and they were, like all of us, regular habitués of the dole office. Out of the blue there came an offer playing cabaret on a three-week cruise around the West Indies for P and O. Unfortunately the paperwork for their passports was carried out in the same place, and the faces of their fellow unemployed were a picture when the clerk called out, 'Who are the two who are going on a cruise to the West Indies?'

The Simmons Brothers are original, highly likeable and extremely creative. The hazards of being half of a double act were pointed out to me by Alan who came out of a stage door and was greeted by a woman: 'I know you . . . you're one half of the other one!'

Stage door encounters are great 'bringer downers', and after a performance of Danny La Rue's *Mother Goose* the lads were met by a lady taking photographs. 'Could I take one of you two together, please? Only I want to finish the film.' We've all had that one!

Their fate, in panto, is that of all double acts – the Robbers, the Chinese policemen or the Broker's men. In 1977–78 they were giving their Robbers to Nat Jackley's Nurse at the New Theatre, Hull. Keith says:

> The nursery scene used to end with Nat waking up in bed and discovering us in the room; we would do a panic run-around and finish up jumping into bed with Nat. At this point a huge maroon (one of those loud bangs that makes everyone jump out of their skin) would be fired, the bed would collapse and the scene would finish with a blackout. It never failed and always got a big laugh and prolonged applause. One particular matinée, though, all did not go according to plan.
>
> Nat woke up and 'discovered' us. We chased around and leapt into the bed. The maroon didn't go off. We looked at Nat and Nat looked at us. Suddenly he broke wind, and certainly not in the delicate fashion of a nurse. This was something else. In theatrical terms – it was a complete Sunday Concert! Now aware that the expected proper explosion was not going to happen, Nat spoke the immortal line: 'Well – that will have to do!'

Keith is also a highly successful writer of comedy, mainly for Brian Conley. While he was working on a sketch about country music, he decided he needed some inside information. He phoned a magazine called *Country Music News* whose head office was in Orpington in Kent. An oldish lady answered the phone.

'Hallo,' said Keith,' is that *Country Music News*?'

'Well, it is,' she replied, 'but he's gone down the shops!'

Tod Slaughter He was the king of the melodrama, whose colourful productions of spine chillers like *Sweeney Todd* and *The Grip of Iron* were popular as alternatives to variety in the golden days. Fred and Frank, the Cox Twins, were in the audience one night at the Bedford, Camden Town, as Tod gave his villain in *Maria Marten.*

> He was a great 'baddie'. He would ham it up outrageously, whipping the audience into a frenzy of booing and hissing. This particular night he had just killed the girl, who was lying dead on stage. Suddenly the sound of police whistles came from the wings. Tod threw himself into a wild panic and cried, 'The police are coming! What can I do? What shall I do with the girl?'
>
> A voice from the gallery advised him, 'Give her one while she's still warm!'

I remember seeing Tod at the Croydon Empire, where he would always go to the pub opposite the theatre between his appearances on stage fully dressed as the Demon Barber, blood-stained apron – the lot.

In his production of *Sweeney Todd* (where hot meat pies were on sale during the interval) Tod, as Sweeney, ran down the centre aisle chasing a victim. He, in turn, was pursued by a posse of Bow Street Runners. One night when I was there, some smart-arse stuck out a foot as the company ran down towards the stage. The victim tripped and fell, bringing down the Demon Barber and several guardians of the law into an undignified heap.

Tod was furious. He got up wild-eyed and roared, 'Who did that?' The culprit was pointed out. Tod seized him, marched him up the aisle to the back of the theatre, and threw him out. He returned, to enormous cheers, wiping his hands on his apron and declared, 'Now – on with the play.'

Don Smoothey A cockney comedian who has done everything in the business, from concert party to the Palladium, Don was a tower of strength in *Underneath The Arches.*

One Christmas Don, playing Dame in panto, had the usual bunch of kids up onstage and asked them all to sing a nursery rhyme or tell a joke. He said to one tiny girl, 'Have you ever done anything on the stage before?' 'Yes,' she said, 'wee-wees.'

Paul Squire A vastly underrated comedian and impressionist, who stopped the Royal Variety Performance in 1980, told this story during a get-together after a charity show.

> The pantomime was *Snow White And The Seven Real Dwarfs*. The director was in the stalls arranging the first entrance of the little men. 'You three come on stage right, wave and exit stage left. Good. You three enter stage left, wave and exit stage right. Excellent. And you' (to the one remaining) 'now you're Dopey, so you come on stage right, stop, wave and then do a cartwheel off, stage left.'
>
> 'I'm sorry,' said Dopey, 'I can't do a cartwheel.'
>
> 'Oh, Gawd!' exploded the director. 'What's the point in being a dwarf if you can't do a cartwheel!'
>
> Within a split second he realised what he'd said and apologised.

On the same subject, in one rather tatty version of *Snow White*, the management could only afford three dwarfs and one of them was a lady with a crepe hair beard! The other four were concrete gnomes pulled on on a plank with wheels!

Which brings us to the ultimate saving of money in panto, with one line in *Ali Baba and the Forty Thieves*. The villain enters with a couple of the thieves. 'Right,' he cries, 'you two come with me,' and holding up a masterful hand to the wings, 'the other thirty eight of you – stay there!'

Rosemary Squires I believe she is one of our most underestimated singers. Her phrasing, 'thinking through a song', and masterly musicianship are her great talents. Perhaps, in these odd times, they hold her back!

Rosie's musical arrangements are commensurate with her ability – in other words, very hard to play – and she remembers a band call when the musicians were having a very hard time trying to get them right. The drummer in particular was suffering, twitching and jerking all the way through the   159 rehearsal. Eventually he put down his sticks and said to the conductor, 'What time is it?'

'I don't know,' said the harassed M.D. 'about one o'clock, I think. What do you want to know for?'

'Because,' said the drummer, climbing out of the orchestra pit, 'I've got an appointment with my psychiatrist!'

'Nobody was too surprised,' said Rosemary, 'least of all me!'

Nick Staverson Nick is a former children's television host who has developed into a first-class panto performer.

Nick was playing Buttons in *Cinderella* in Canterbury. Two real characters were playing the Ugly Sisters, Tommy Osbourne and Chubby Oates. It was Nick's first panto appearance and he was madly keen to impress. One night during the trying-on of the slipper scene, the stage was suddenly plunged into darkness. Eventually, after what seemed an eternity, Nick decided he'd better go on and do something. Miraculously, as he walked on, the lights came back on. 'Don't worry, everyone,' said Nick, 'I've just put 50 p in the meter.' This got such a response from the audience that he, drunk with power, totally forgot what he had to say next.

After a suitable wait, Tommy Osbourne said, 'I just wish you'd put your money where your mouth is!'

Jerry Stevens Comedian, compère, after-dinner speaker and golf tournament organiser extraordinaire, Jerry sent me this cheery tale, which makes all the bad days in showbusiness seem nothing.

Some years ago American singer Jack Jones and I were appearing at the Alhambra Theatre, Bradford, which was one of the venues on his UK concert tour. Shortly after completing the sound and lighting rehearsals, the stage manager asked if I'd mind popping down to his office for a minute as there was something he wanted to show me.

The 'office', which was below stage level, was really a large cupboard, and the walls were totally covered with hundreds of photos of many of the acts who had played the theatre over the years.

One of the larger pictures was of Laurel and Hardy. 'Did they really appear here?' I asked.

'They certainly did, about 1950 it was,' he said. 'Anyway, that's not what I wanted to show you. Just have a look at this photo, here, and tell me – is that your dad?' He pointed to a postcard-size photo among the sea of faces covering the wall.

'No,' I said, 'it's me.'

With a look of disbelief, he said, 'It can't be you, that photo's been up there for donkeys' years!'

'That's right,' I said, 'it was 1962 or 63, when I did a week's variety in The Hoover-Daz Show.' (This was an early attempt at sponsorship, which sadly failed to delay the death of the variety theatres.)

'But was your dad in showbusiness?'

'No, he was in a steelworks,' I told him.

'But you're talking about nearly twenty years ago with that photo,' he said, 'so it can't be you, surely? You hardly look any older.'

'Well, I can assure you that it definitely is me.' I could see he wasn't truly convinced, but he certainly had made me feel good, and with a spring in my steps I bounced back up the stairs like I might have done twenty years before!

About half an hour later, the stage manager knocked on my dressing-room door to ask if I'd mind speaking to an old lady at the stage door. He explained that she wanted to see Jack Jones, but as he was resting back at the hotel before the show, she wondered if I could help her.

At the stage door I was introduced to this very shy lady, no more than five feet tall, probably about eighty years old and very well dressed in her Sunday-best coat and matching hat. With gloved hands she was holding a gramophone record in its very old sleeve, and told me that it was a copy of 'Donkey Serenade' by Jack's father, Allan Jones. She said she had always been an ardent fan of Allan Jones, and though she knew that she would never get the opportunity to have him autograph the record sleeve, she would be so grateful to have it signed by his son Jack.

I asked her to leave the record with me, and told her I would have it signed ready for her to collect after the show. At this suggestion, she begged my forgiveness, but said she couldn't possibly let her precious possession out of her sight, even for a moment. I then suggested she bring it back to be signed after the show. She explained that she wouldn't be at the show because she had to catch the last bus to her village in the Yorkshire Dales at 7 p.m. She asked what time Jack would be arriving back at the Theatre, and I advised her to return at 6 o'clock. While saying this, I was quietly hoping to myself that Jack and his dad would be back in time to see her.

As you read this, I can almost hear you saying, 'Jack and his dad?'

Let me explain. Back in the 1930s, Allan Jones had become firmly established in America, as a true showbiz superstar. His recording of 'Donkey Serenade' was a worldwide hit. He had his own radio show, appeared in Broadway musicals, and in a series of films with the Marx Brothers, which made him into a Hollywood movie star.

Almost fifty years later, now well into his seventies, he was still working, and having just finished a three-month tour of America, starring in *Man of La Mancha*, he'd come over to England for a holiday, and to spend some time with his son during Jack's UK tour. He was wonderful company, and I spent many a happy hour with him during the tour.

Before we ended our spell on the road, he even appeared in the show during the last week of concerts. With a flowing cape and wooden staff hired from a theatrical costumier's, he walked on stage following Jack's introduction and, re-enacting his role in *Man of La Mancha*, sang 'The Impossible Dream'. His vocal power, considering his age, was quite incredible. He brought the house down every night, and I'm convinced that Jack almost envied the wonderful stage presence and dramatic qualities so naturally displayed by his father.

With the knowledge that there was in store possibly the most fantastic surprise for this lovely old lady at the stage door, I was concerned by her reluctance to consider returning later, for fear of missing her bus. At that moment, of course, she wasn't aware that what she might be missing was a once-in-a-lifetime chance of meeting her idol.

I had to be sure she came back, so I told her. I explained that she must come back because she was going to get a wonderful surprise. I said, 'Not only will you get Jack Jones to sign your record, but you'll also get it signed by Allan Jones, because he's going to be here too.' As I was saying this, I was already anticipating her surprise and excitement at the news. However, I hadn't expected the degree of surprise I might cause and, bearing in mind her age, I was, for the next few moments, deeply concerned by her reaction.

The news appeared to create a shock to her whole system. She took two steps back, went almost rigid, and at the same time threw up one hand in a jerking motion, and clasped her forehead. This sudden movement dislodged her hat and exposed a beautiful thick mane of silver-grey hair which fell to her shoulders. As I quickly retrieved the hat, I was aware that she had begun to shake uncontrollably from head to toe. The loss of her hat was an added embarrassment to her composure, and she was desperately trying to replace it, and tuck her hair beneath it, while still holding on to the gramophone record. I tried to assist but, still trembling, she was forced to give up the attempt to replace her hat.

She didn't know which way to turn, and though she was trying to say something, her quivering lips would only allow her to make a sort of high-pitched moan. I gently took hold of her hand in an effort to calm her nervousness, and asked if she was all right. Still visibly shaken, she eventually managed to speak, and asked if what I had said was actually true. I assured her it was, and that when she returned, Allan Jones would definitely be there. This confirmation only succeeded in causing her to catch her breath, and with a loud gasp, she again began to shake violently.

The stage door keeper, who had been standing close by during the whole incident, quickly produced a chair. As we sat her down I just kept talking, saying anything that came into my head which might help to relieve her anxiety. I told her what a very nice man Allan Jones was, that he was a real gentleman, and that I was sure he would be more than happy to sign her record, and even say hello. Her emotions still in turmoil, she now expressed concern at causing further inconvenience by returning later. I realised this was a reaction to her own embarrassment, and reassured her that it would be no problem at all. I said it would be such a shame to have come all this way and then miss the chance to get something she really wanted so much.

I think she realised at this point that what I'd said made sense, and it was a relief to see signs of her recovering from her state of bewilderment. She thanked me over and over again as she was leaving, promising that she would be back at 6 o'clock for sure.

I'm delighted to say she did return, and she did meet Jack and Allan Jones, and they both signed her record.

It was a wonderful moment, and I think it was almost as big a thrill for me. After all, I'd had a great day, what with the stage manager paying me that earlier compliment, and the fact that I had played a small part in making an old lady happy.

Clive Stock Gwen Overton and Clive Stock are the last of the romantic duettists, and wonderfully popular. Alas for those of us who don't live there, they are now almost permanently based in Wales where they run their highly successful medieval banquets.

In 1943 Clive was in Ivor Novello's *Arc de Triomphe*. It looked as if France would be liberated soon, so Ivor decided to write a new scene for the show. In the middle of rehearsals an official-looking man in bowler hat and pinstriped suit, and carrying a briefcase, bustled in.

Ignoring the bustle around him he approached the great man. 'Mr Novello,' he said. 'You've let us down. We haven't received your composition.' Apparently, British composers had organised a competition to write a march for the underground movement in France. Vaughan Williams, Sir Arthur Bliss and Vivian Ellis had all contributed but Novello, being the busiest of men, hadn't.

'Just let me finish this rehearsal, and I'll be with you,' said Ivor. The official, tutting and clucking, retired to a chair and waited. The rehearsal over, Ivor went over to the piano and, without playing it, dotted down something on a piece of manuscript paper and handed it to the cross little man. He was delighted and left.

The company gathered around the 'guv'. 'What did you write?' one asked. 'How does it go?' asked another.

'I've no idea,' said Novello. 'I just copied down the first sixteen bars of "Keep The Home Fires Burning" backwards!'

It won the competition, was recorded by Olive Gilbert with full choir and orchestra at the Royal Albert Hall and was used by the underground in France as a signature tune to put the wind up the Germans.

Clive was in a production of *No, No, Nanette*. Two comics were playing the scene prior to Nanette's entrance. They finished the scene but she didn't appear. They carried on, ad-libbing till dry, but still no sign of the heroine. The desperate call-boy finally located her in the toilet. 'Miss! Miss!' he commanded. 'Come off – you're on!'

Sir Oswald Stoll He is generally thought to be the man who sired variety. Many people say he took away the red-blooded subversive anarchy that was the very heart of music hall, too. He seems an odd chap to be involved in the biz being, from what I'm told, a rather prissy, puritanical Mrs Grundy sort of man. His roots were certainly OK, though. He had been in charge of his family's music hall, the Pantheon in Liverpool, at the age of fourteen.

He became the managing director of the famous Moss Empires group, built variety theatres all over the country *and* the London Coliseum. How he picked the site for the Coliseum is typical of his painstaking methods. He stood at various places all over London and made notes as to how many people passed the spot. He found that St Martin's in the Fields was the busiest place around show time, and so bought the nearest bit of land to it.

He was a shrewd businessman, and even put his mother in charge of the Coliseum box office for a while.

He had a notice in every one of the dressing-rooms of his theatres: *'Do not ask for complimentary tickets. If your friends won't pay to see you, who will?'*

An example of his acerbic wit was in his sending of telegrams. The classic story concerns the dancer Espinosa. He hadn't been in the country very long when he was booked by Stoll to appear at the Shepherd's Bush Empire as the final turn on the bill.

Espinosa lived some distance from the theatre and so complained that he would have great difficulty in getting home after the show. He even sent a telegram to Sir Oswald:

'Will you kindly alter my time. I am last act on and live eighteen miles from the theatre. How can I do it?'

Stoll's answer was a one-word telegram: 'Move'.

John Styles John is the number one Punch and Judy man in the business as well as being a top children's entertainer and an excellent stand-up comic for grown-ups!

To plug a Punch and Judy Festival in Covent Garden, John was interviewed by Michael Aspel on the telly. After demonstrating the age-old playlet John emerged from his booth to chat to Michael. He gave a quick history, then got on to the 'swozzle' – the small instrument, about an inch square, that has to be held against the roof of the mouth to produce Punch's voice. To work a swozzle properly is not easy. It has to be moved around by the tongue to accommodate the other voices, and all this time the puppets are being operated.

'Have you ever swallowed it?' asked Michael.

'Oh yes,' said John.

'What happened?'

'I had to eat a lot of plum pudding, and leave the rest to nature,' John told him.

'Could I try?' ventured Michael. 'Certainly,' agreed John, and offered him a selection of swozzles. Michael had a go and, after coughing, spluttering and nearly choking in the attempt, asked, 'And you say you actually swallowed one of these?' 'Yes,' said John. 'That one!'

John was compèring a one-night variety bill at what is laughingly referred to as an 'all purpose venue'. This, in fact, means it's not much use for anything. The stages are usually too low, the auditoriums are too wide, the dressing-rooms miles away from the stage and often there are no wings to get on and off from. John's venue was of just this type. The only way to get on and off the stage was via a row of steps at the front of the platform. John introduced the next act and then, blinded by the lights, negotiated the steps. He headed for a set of double doors which, he assumed, would lead into a corridor and then backstage. He went through them to find himself in a cleaner's cupboard. Being the perfect pro, John stayed there in pitch darkness surrounded by brooms, hoovers and polish until the act had finished. It lasted half an hour.

Success This is one of my favourite stories of how success can affect a performer. Whether it's factual or not doesn't matter. There are more than several grains of truth in the tale.

Two comics met in Charing Cross Road, in variety days the home of all the agents. One was working, the other wasn't. The unemployed one went into a tale of woe: no money for the rent or for food for his wife and kids. His flush friend pressed a tenner on him and left for work with the recipient's grateful thank-yous echoing in his ears.

The showbiz wheel spins and their positions are reversed. The former unemployed one was now, following a successful television series, topping the bill at the London Palladium while his generous friend couldn't get a job.

Seeing his pal's name in lights, he remembered the tenner and he called at the Palladium stage door. 'Charlie Cheesecake,' he advised the stage door keeper, 'to see my top of the bill friend.'

'One moment, sir,' cautioned the janitor and disappeared into Mr Big's room. He returned with 'I'm sorry, he doesn't know you – kindly leave the stage door!' Disgusted and broke, Charlie Cheesecake shuffled away.

The wheel spins again; Mr Big was down on his uppers and bumped into Charlie Cheesecake. 'You swine!' said Charlie. 'I called at the Palladium for that tenner, and I needed it, and you didn't even have the courtesy to invite me into your dressing-room!'

'I know,' said the almost weeping Mr Big. 'I was a bastard. I believed everything people told me. The agents, the bookers, the hangers-on. I thought I was God's gift. I deserted every one of my old pals – I left the wife and kids. I've got my come-uppance now, though. I put all my money into a revue and I've lost the lot. No, don't say a word. I know I was a complete and utter bastard!'

'Well,' muttered Charlie, 'it does happen. I just hope you've learned your lesson.'

'Don't worry,' said the fallen star. 'I know now – believe me!'

They parted. Another year went by and Mr Big was back on top, bigger than ever with his own show at The Prince of Wales.

'Now I'll get my tenner back,' thought Charlie and called at the stage door. The keeper rang through, said, 'Certainly sir,' put the phone down and pointed along the corridor: 'Last dressing-room on the left.'

Charlie, full of bonhomie, tapped smartly on the star's dressing-room door. It opened four inches, Mr Big's face appeared and said, 'Sorry, Charlie – I'm a bastard again!' and slammed the door.

John Randolph Sutton John's grandfather was the immaculate light comedian Randolph Sutton, who made 'On Mother Kelly's Doorstep' his very own.

John was playing a club in Plaistow and signing records after the show. A man came up to him and said, 'I've seen your grandfather's grave in Brighton.'

'I don't think so,' said John. 'He was cremated and his ashes buried in Mortlake.'

'No,' said the know-all. 'I've seen the grave. It's in Brighton.'

'Look,' said John, 'I was at my grandad's funeral in 1969. He was cremated in Mortlake.'

'You're wrong!' insisted the bloke. 'I've seen the gravestone. It says on it "Randolph Sutton – The Chocolate-Coloured Coon".'

It seemed too difficult to explain that 'The Chocolate-Coloured Coon' was how G.H. Elliot was known on stage!

Harry Tate A sketch comedian whose 'Motoring' became a classic, Harry Tate's catch-phrase was 'Good-bye-ee', and he was the first to sing that famous song. Here are two stories about him, told to me by Wee Georgie Wood.

Georgie, a great thirster after knowledge, used to attend debates in the House of Commons and once took Harry Tate along with him. Bonar Law was haranguing his opposite number with fire and brimstone when, during a slight pause, Harry said, in his enormous stage whisper, 'They think it's all real!' The incident is reported in Hansard: 'A stranger was ejected from the public gallery.'

One night, at the infamous Glasgow Empire, a member of the audience shouted at Harry: 'Harry Tate you're pissed!'

Harry blinked, looked at the gent and enquired, 'I beg your pardon.'

Once again the erudite Glaswegian advised, 'Harry Tate you're pissed!'

Harry turned to his son Ronnie who was in the sketch and said, 'You see, *you* weren't sure. I told you I was!'

Harry lived, at one time, in the Beverly Hills of English music hall – Brixton. One afternoon he was walking home when he found a chauffeur scratching his head over a broken-down Rolls-Royce. He looked in the back and there was the famous stage beauty Gladys Cooper.

'Ah, Miss Cooper,' said Harry. 'You won't know me.'

'Indeed I do,' replied the gracious Glad. 'Mr Tate. You are a wonderful comedian.' 'Thank you,' said Harry. 'I was only going to say that while your man is sorting out the vehicle, would you care to rest at my chambers? Just around the corner.'

'Thank you. I'd be delighted,' accepted the lady.

Harry led her to his house, put his key in the lock and ushered Miss Cooper inside. He called out, 'Darling I'm home.'

From 'er upstairs came, 'About time, too, you drunken old sod.'

The imperturbable Tate waved an airy hand and explained: 'The little woman.'

Bud Flanagan told of spending Christmas Day with Harry and his family. When the crackers were pulled, Harry got two interlocking nails. 'What's this?' asked Harry.

'A puzzle,' said Bud.

'Really?' said a fascinated Tate.

'He spent the next three hours trying to get the two pieces of metal apart,' said Bud. 'Eventually with a great snort of disgust, he held up the two separated pieces and roared, "Ridiculous, it isn't a puzzle at all."'

Jack Taylor The well known Blackpool putter on of shows. Alfred Marks remembered the story of Jack 'lashing out' and employing the famous West End director Robert Nesbitt to produce one of his revues. Robert produced very spectacular, and very expensive, shows and didn't change his methods when employed by Jack. On being asked how the show was shaping up Jack answered, 'Don't ask. Every time he says "let's not spoil the ship for an 'apporthof tar" it costs me five grand!' Robert Nesbitt, because of his love of 'moody' lighting was nicknamed, by Eric Morecambe, 'The Prince of Darkness'.

Norman Teal One of the most respected bookers of acts in the Blackpool area, Norman has had a fantastic journey to 'respectability'. He was, of course, a turn. He was company manager for the infamous Frank Randle and he did a double act with Roy Castle.

This classic happening, Norman assures me, was witnessed by him and Roy while working a week in Portsmouth. Sharing their digs was a female impersonator from the other theatre. Having supper with the landlady one night, they heard two pairs of footsteps on the stairs. The landlady investigated, and discovered the female impersonator taking a sailor aloft. 'No, you don't,' she said. 'Oi, Barnacle Bill, out you go! I'm not having any of that in my house.'

The next night exactly the same thing happened, but on the third night they heard just one pair of footsteps ascending.

'That's OK,' thought Norman and Roy, but the landlady was no mug.

Throwing open the door she saw the resourceful drag act giving a sailor a piggy-back up the stairs. 'I don't believe it,' she cried. 'Bloody cripples now!'

Many people have quoted this next story, especially Roy Castle. The town was Salford and one particular Christmas there were two pantomimes there, *Goldilocks* at the Hippodrome and *Snow White and the Seven 'real' Dwarfs* at the Palace. Most of the casts of both shows were staying in the same digs as Roy and Norman. One afternoon, having tea in the lodgings, they heard a continual 'Thud! Thud!' from the floor above.

'What's that?' enquired the lads.

'It's all right,' said the landlord. 'It's the dwarfs in the toilet jumping up and down to reach the chain.'

This is my favourite of all Norman's stories, and it was told to him by an act he'd worked with on tour in his early days. It was the days of cine-variety (a programme of films interspersed with 'live' acts).

The act had arrived at the cinema, found his dressing-room, laid out his make-up and props when a knock came on the door. 'Hallo there,' said the manager, for it was he.

'Am I on?' asked the act. 'Not yet,' said the governor. 'There's the news and a couple of shorts first. You'll be on in about twenty-five minutes.' This information was accompanied by a sniffle and a constant dabbing of the eyes.

'Has something upset you?' enquired the turn.

'It's the main feature,' said the manager, lips a-tremble. 'It's one of those parables that just gets you, and makes you realise there's a lot of goodness and kindness in people. What a story! It's all about a little boy, from a poverty-stricken home, who is struck blind and whose parents can't afford the special treatment he needs. Eventually, after a lot of national publicity, he is befriended by a millionaire who takes him all round Europe and finally, in Zurich, he finds a specialist who can cure the lad.'

Another wracking sob, and he continued, 'Oh, and when you see the child's face! He can see! The blue skies, the flowers, and the beautiful countryside. Wonderful! But then there's a twist to the story. While the millionaire is taking the lad on this tour of Europe they have a car crash and, of all things, the boy is thrown clear but the millionaire is seriously hurt. Now *he's* in danger of losing his sight! The final scene is, well—'

The tears were now streaming down the manager's face. 'The boy's at his benefactor's bedside and says, "You have been very good to me, sir. Can I donate one of my eyes back to you?" I'm sorry but it really is heartrending. The millionaire says, "No, my dear. I am old and you have all your life before you. I know it will be a good life because I have made provision for you and your parents. You will never want again." It really does make you realise what good there is in the world.'

'It sounds a marvellous film,' said the act. 'By the way, can I have a sub?'

'F*** off!' replied the manager.

Bobby Thompson Known as 'The Little Waster', he was a great Geordie comic who rarely played outside his home territory, and a total original. His humour was based on the Geordie world of the 1920s and 30s: the world of debt, the club and his love/hate relationship with his missus – 'wor lass'. Once more people understood that beautiful accent he could have worked further afield, but he didn't want to.

He was at his very best on his home patch yet he filled the Wimbledon Theatre with ex-pat Geordies and those who love genuine funny men. Joe Ging who was, after me and a gentleman called Stan Heatlie, Bobby's greatest fan, told me this story which illustrates how protective his admirers were.

Stan Heatlie was the chairman of Northern Arts and he had to look after Sir John Betjeman, the late Poet Laureate, when he came to open a transplanted railway station at the Beamish Open Air Museum.

'Tell me, who is your best local comedian?' enquired the bard.

'Bobby Thompson,' said Stan.

'Never heard of him,' snorted Betjeman.

'Really?' said Stan. 'Well, he doesn't read your poetry!'

Tommy Trinder The legendary great ad-libber once said to me, 'If the audience don't heckle me, I haven't got an act.' He was an 'alternative' comic before that phrase was thought of.

His most quoted retort concerns his catch-phrase, 'Trinder's the name.' He was resident comedian at the Latin Quarter nightspot in the West End and one night, very much the worse for wear, Orson Welles sat at a ringside table with his wife of the day, Rita Hayworth.

Trinder entered. 'Trinder's the name!'

'Why don't you change it?' roared Welles. Like lightning Trinder came back: 'Is that a proposal?'

He was, like The Crazy Gang, a great favourite of the Royals. As an approved Royal jester he could get away with murder. When he was just a beginner, he entertained the Duke and Duchess of York and years later he entertained them again. The venue was the Royal Variety Performance and the Duke and Duchess were now King and Queen. At the end of the show handshaking, King George said to Tommy, 'You've come a long way since we first met.'

Trinder replied, 'You haven't done so bad yourself, sir!'

Jack Seaton, one of Tom's great pals and the man who runs the British Music Hall Society, remembers Tom at a Water Rats dinner to honour HRH Prince Philip. During his speech, Trinder apologised for having to rush off in time to catch a boat for South Africa. 'Surely you mean a ship?' interjected the brave Prince.

'I don't know about that, sir,' replied Tom. 'But this morning the wife caught the boat train.'

Tommy had a great feel for publicity and people still remember the huge posters he had all around London during one of his long residencies at the Palladium. They simply proclaimed: 'If It's Laughter You're After – Trinder's the Name!' He even took a poster site outside Aldgate Bus Station. As it was a well-known Jewish quarter, he thought he'd have the message in Hebrew. The *Jewish Chronicle* sent him an old man to translate. The old boy did the job and Tom asked him how much he owed him.

'Five shillings,' he said. 'That's what I get in the Police Court as an interpreter.'

Tom gave him a fiver and the old chap couldn't do enough for him, even asking, 'Do you have any Jewish friend you'd like to write to in Hebrew?'

Tom said he had, and a letter, in Hebrew, was dispatched to every agent in town.

Tommy used to tell this story against himself.

The most notorious of all the variety musical directors was a man called Sydney Kaplan. His great gag was, on a Monday morning when you gave him your music to rehearse with the band, to declare that your 'parts' were impossible to play. Why didn't you get him to do you a nice clean set? If this didn't work, he'd try and sell you leatherette covers for your music with the name of the act embossed in 'gold' on the front. He was the world's worst audience for a comic – even more so if you hadn't bought his music covers – and I remember one night at the Finsbury Park Empire he started to laugh during my act. I panicked, what had happened? He merely waved his baton towards my groin and I saw I'd forgotten to do my flies up. What a sense of humour he had!

Tommy, in his early days, found himself working two or three different variety theatres the same evening. He'd dash from one to the other. For a comic this was dodgy, as you didn't know what gags had been already cracked before you arrived. Tommy ('flash little git I was') used to take a musical director's frock coat with him, which he insisted the MD should wear while he, Tom, was on. On the back of the coat, in large letters, it said 'TOMMY TRINDER'. As all the audience saw of the MD was his back they were reminded of who was on all through his act. This was OK for the first conductor but by the time he'd got to his third theatre the coat was a bit damp and smelly.

Sydney Kaplan, in his usual helpful manner, donned the evil garment and Tom went on. He told one of his best gags. Silence. 'Someone's cracked it already,' thought Tom. 'Here Sydney,' he said to that, by now smirking, musician. 'Did someone tell that gag before me?'

'Yes,' shouted back Kaplan,' Dan Leno.'

Kenneth Earle remembers him and his partner Malcolm Vaughan sharing a week's variety in Blackpool with the singer, Ronnie Carroll. Tommy was the star of the show and acted as compère. He always called Ronnie 'The Singing Skull', and introduced him to the audience as such. Ronnie was a gambler and not a very good one. (There are many stories of him having to play extra weeks at clubs for nothing in order to pay off his poker debts.) He, Malcolm and Kenny decided to do the pools and Ronnie thought that they could get a better perm if they had another person in the syndicate. Off they went to Tommy's dressing-room and put the idea to him.

'How much will it cost me?' asked Tom.

'It's a fiver a head,' said Ronnie.

'A fiver!' said the well-known director of Fulham Football Club.

'For that I could fix a result!'

Syd Wright, the xylophonist and original 'Sammy Finkelfeffer' in Issy Bonn's variety act, remembers Tommy being interested in buying a house. The owner was asking quite a price so Tom, 173 being a persuasive talker, rang him up to see what he could do in the way of haggling. The vendor obviously didn't recognise the Trinder voice, as his answer to Tom's enquiry as to why the price was so high was: 'Well, the house has great historical value. Tommy Trinder was born here.'

Tom, suspecting a wind-up, pressed on. 'Oh, really? Is there a plaque on the wall saying "Tommy Trinder was born here"?'

'No,' said the seller. 'You can't do that until the person's dead.'

'Well,' said Tom. 'Why don't you put up a plaque saying "Watch This Space"?'

Tom did a summer season with Anne Shelton, who was very fond of collecting medallions of the saints. At the end of the season he gave her a medallion with his face on. It was inscribed 'Saint Tom'.

Jack Tripp The immaculate, ebullient, brilliant dancing and sketch comedian, for many years with the famous 'Fol-de-Rols' summer show. He is today's top pantomime dame. Jack played panto one year with Basil Brush, whose 'minder' is Ivan Owen. As is usual, after a day off, the company met at the half hour call to discuss what they'd been up to. Poor Ivan said, 'Well I had an awful weekend. I got home to discover we'd had burglars. They'd ransacked the entire house but do you know they didn't take a thing.' Commented Jack, 'How humiliating.'

Jack is the son of a Plymouth baker, and in the days 'B.T.' (before television), when radio was the only evening leisure activity, showbusiness was a mysterious world to his relations. He'd just done his first professional job and an aunt asked him if he'd liked it.

'Oh yes,' said Jack. 'It was wonderful.'

'Well,' replied auntie in her lovely West Country drawl, 'you've always got somewhere to go at night.'

Janet Brown was in a Derek Salberg pantomime with Jack at Wolverhampton. Jack was a great favourite of Derek's and the Black Country audiences, and for many years he played dame in that part of the world, often in Wolverhampton. One morning Janet watched two women inspecting the front-of-house photographs.

'Oh look!' said one, 'they've got Jack Tripp again.'

'Jack Tripp?' said the other. 'Who's that?'

'You know,' said her friend. 'We've seen him before – she's marvellous!'

Stanley Unwin Master of the totally misunderstood word, Stanley's highly original talent made him a household name. He recalls being out-'Unwinised', via Ted Ray.

Stanley had been advised, by Ted, to take up golf. 'It's a leisurely pursuit,' said Ted, but you will have to concentrate. It will take your mind off work, and relax you ready for your evening's labours.' It certainly did the trick for Ted. 'But,' he warned, 'you must take lessons from a pro. He'll get you into the correct swing and give you the proper approach to the game. Without this you'll never be any good at it.'

Stanley had an engagement in Glasgow; what better place to find a helpful pro than at the home of the game? He duly appeared at one of the nine clubs around Glasgow and the pro asked him about the shots he found most awkward. His accent was so broad, 'even Stanley had trouble understanding him; and he was completely mystified when he kept referring to a club called a 'yarras'. Stanley told him that the 'yarras' was a new one to him.

'Noo,' said the pro. 'I mean, when ye're in the boonker, get yarass reet doon in the sand!' The biter bit, but it did improve Stanley's bunker shots.

To really appreciate the next story you have to picture four people: Stanley himself, Cardew Robinson, Gerry Campion (TV's Billy Bunter) and Tommy Cooper. Gerry ran a little drinking club in Shaftesbury Avenue which is worth a book in itself.

(I remember sitting there alone one lunchtime when down the stairs came Tony Hancock and Sidney James. Sid took a stool at the bar while Hancock poured about ten quid's worth of tanners into the fruit machine. He didn't win once, so retired 'hurt' to the bar. Sid took over on the machine and his first sixpence yielded the jackpot! Hancock didn't even look round but, as the noise of tumbling coins echoed round the room, his face was beautiful. Galton and Simpson captured Sid and Tony perfectly.)

It was in Gerry's Club that Cardew introduced the then-unknown Stanley to Tommy. Gerry, always one to enjoy a 'situation', said to Cardew: 'Get Stanley to tell Tommy about his early magic researches in Egypt.'

'Tommy,' said the Cad, 'I want you to meet Stanley Forthuscady who's just back from his magic researches in the East.'

Tommy shook hands and seemed interested, so off went Stanley regaling him with a story of how the Farouga twins (both fez'd tasslode which each lifted reveal small rabbi under the hat) had shown him the original scarab coffinal with the mummy-swathe bandage – still lid stuck and the bomes passed throom without conceal or hingey.

Tommy's unique face turned towards each of the participants in turn as Stanley went on. 'A great cry went up as the crowl all shot up on their boves! Then came the miraculous sphynx-smile as the gypty waved his wand from the pyramiddle, and someone tickled its bottom. It was terrific.'

The little 'Cooper-cough' punctuated the tale until the last full stop. Then came a pause as Tommy gave all three one final glance before he gave his decision. 'E's bleedin' barmy!'

Dick Vosburgh An American who has become one of our top comedy writers Dick's track record is fantastic. He has a stack of kids and when I first knew him he wrote all his stuff on the Underground! He would stay on an Inner Circle train until he'd finished. It was quieter than at home, he said.

Max Wall The surreal humour of this unforgettable eccentric comedian had always been a favourite with his fellow pros and discerning variety fans. Late in life he was 'discovered' by yuppies and his creativity diminished – as it always does when a comic talent is worshipped by the wrong people. He was as eccentric off as he was on.

Bill Pertwee worked with him in a panto, *Little Bo Peep and her Live Sheep*! The first half finale had Max surrounded by half a dozen live sheep. The animals were kept in boxes at the side of the stage. At the appropriate moment the fronts were opened and the sheep ran out to gather round Max. The combination of bright lights and sudden activity frightened them and they, every night, demonstrated how scared they were by defecating as soon as the audience saw them. This regular occurrence forced Bill to systematically pay attention at this moment – just to hear what cue lines Max would deliver. He remembers two: 'Hello! Ad-libbing again!' and 'Well, that's their opinion of the show!'

Max's association with the opposite sex always gave him trouble and I remember standing next to him in the Gents in Grosvenor House. Looking down he muttered, in that unmistakable voice, to no one in particular: 'You, you little swine – you're the cause of it all!'

Dorothy Ward The legendary pantomime principal boy was still showing her legs at seventy. One Christmas she was playing Colin, the miller's son, in *Puss In Boots* for Emile Littler. At the dress rehearsal she made her first entrance in her 'poor boy' costume but wearing a positive fistful of diamond rings. She was very proud of how well she'd done, and wanted everyone else to know too. At the end of the run-through, Emile Littler said, 'Dorothy, darling, you're supposed to be the poor miller's son. I think we should dispense with the diamond rings.' Dorothy said nothing, but on the opening night she came on with her hands behind her back and said, 'Here am I, Colin the poor miller's son.' She then waved her bejewelled hands at the audience and added, 'And look what the Good Fairy keeps giving me!'

Shaun Glenville, the dame comedian, was the husband of Dorothy Ward and Alf Pearson told me what happened when she bought a Rolls-Royce. Shaun rang his pal, Robb Wilton. 'The car's a beauty,' said Shaun. 'How do you fancy a spin in the country?' Robb liked the sound of this idea, and the two of them set out for a drive. They passed several pubs, and didn't pass several more, until eventually they decided it would be safer to spend the night at an hotel. Early the next morning Robb awoke to the sound of breaking glass. He looked out of the window, and there was Shaun taking a sledgehammer to the headlights of the Rolls.

'What are you doing?' shouted Robb.

'My boy,' said Shaun, thinking of his wife's reaction to his night away from home, 'we're having the accident now!'

Jack Warman Charlie Chester gave me this memory of a first-spot variety comic. Charlie, as we all did when young, used to stand in the wings every night watching everyone's act, hoping to learn. It was while watching Jack that Charlie witnessed the biggest laugh and round of applause he's ever heard. Jack, who was painfully thin and getting on a bit, used to open his act with 'Hallo, workmates.' This particular night he had a bad cold, and his opening greeting was accompanied by a violent cough. Disaster. His false teeth flew out towards the orchestra. Miracle. Jack's reflexes were so good that at the same time his arm shot out and he brilliantly caught the choppers in mid-air. In one movement he turned his back on the audience, replaced the errant 'Hampsteads' and carried on talking. He couldn't continue. He'd stopped the show.

Elsie and Doris Waters (Gert and Daisy) At the height of their fame on radio, variety and in films the two sisters were driving themselves to an engagement in a remote part of the country. They got lost and decided to ask directions from a group of children. As they explained their problem, Doris 179 became aware of one boy who was studying them closely. 'We've been recognised,' thought Doris. 'Have you ever heard of Gert 'n' Daisy?' she asked the lad.

'Oh yes,' said the boy. 'I've heard of it, but I don't know where it is.'

Bob Webb A stand-up comedian and singer who should be better known than he is, Bob, like me, started his career at Butlin's. Bob has lots of stories of strange acts and this is my favourite.

A young man had begged to be given a 'live' audition and the nice Frank Mansell, who was in charge of booking for the camps, gave him a chance.

He turned up and his mate approached Bob, who was compèring the showcase. The mate said, 'I'm his manager. Just read what's on the card.'

Bob did: 'Ladies and gentlemen, once in a lifetime a man is born whose talents defy description. Meet the man of mystery – the Great Mandu!'

On came the enigma and proceeded to walk up and down on a pile of broken glass. He cut his feet to pieces. But before Bob could hustle him off, he was into the next miracle – pushing hatpins into his body. Bleeding from every pinhole, he entered the Twilight Zone for the third time – fire-eating! Even he made a noise as he pulled the flaming torches from his black and blistered mouth. 'Aaargh!' he went. He was in agony. His manager looked worried. Frank Mansell was hurrying towards the stage to get the battered and bleeding fakir out of sight while Bob, a great help, was crying with laughter.

'Into the finish!' commanded the manager. Dragging himself to his feet, the Great Mandu grabbed the mike and sang, 'Oh the good life – full of fun – the ideal!'

Bob takes twenty minutes to tell this story (thirty with laughs) and it's a masterpiece.

Bert Weedon The legendary 'king of the guitar', after years as a session guitarist, became a chart-topping solo instrumentalist. His book, *Play In A Day*, inspired thousands to take up the instrument and was the starting point for performers like Paul McCartney, Phil Collins and Brian May.

Bert was a keen fan of the TV series *Kojak*, but rarely saw an

episode as it was always shown when he was working. One

Saturday evening he had a rare night off, and he settled down to watch the show. Five minutes before the pay-off his front doorbell rang, and he grudgingly answered it. It was a filthy night, rain streaming down, and the walk to his front door was up a long drive. There at the door were two blokes, water pouring off them and a smell of booze around them.

'You're Bert Weedon, aren't you?' said one.

'Yes,' said Bert, one eye still on *Kojak*.

'We've been having an argument down the pub,' said the other. 'Can you settle it for us?'

'I'll try,' said Bert.

'How old is Ivy Benson?'

Bert issued an expletive followed by an imperative and closed the door. When he got back to the telly the titles were rolling. 'What happened?' he asked. 'It's far too complicated to explain,' said Mrs Weedon.

'How old is Ivy Benson?' became a running gag among Bert's mates and was brought to a glorious conclusion on a Water Rats' Boat Trip. Bert was King Rat at the time and, surrounded by his subjects, was thoroughly enjoying his evening on the Thames. In the middle of the festivities a river police launch came alongside the floating boozer.

'Permission to come aboard?' was the request from the aqua rozzers. They boarded and an unhealthy silence greeted their arrival. 'We're looking for a Bert Weedon,' said the biggest and most unsmiling one.

'I am he,' said Bert, half-rising. The policeman slowly crossed to the Weedon table. 'Just one question, sir – how old *is* Ivy Benson?'

The river trip *and* the surprise interrogation had both been organised by Water Rat Peter Regan.

R.P. Weston and Bert Lee Two of music hall and variety's unsung heroes who were basically songwriters, with more than two thousand songs published, but, on top of this fantastic output, they wrote hundreds of sketches, 75 stage shows, dozens of pantomimes and 17 films. Beginning to write together just before the First World War, they kept going through to the 1930s and produced hit after hit, from the immortal 'Good-bye-ee' to 'What A Mouth'. They wrote material to order and their list of satisfied clients is an impressive one – Harry Champion, Billy Williams, Whit Cunliffe, George Lashwood, Ernest Shand, Clarice Mayne, Harry Fragson, Florrie

Forde, 'Wee' Georgie Wood, Violet Lorraine, Stanley Holloway, Billy Bennett, Randolph Sutton, Robb Wilton, Bobby Howes, Gracie Fields and the Crazy Gang.

I wrote a stage salute to them, called *Just A Verse and Chorus*. Billy Dainty played Bert Lee and I played R.P. (Bob) Weston. Billy showed everyone what a wonderful actor he was in this little show, and we were all set for a West End run when, sadly, he died – at a very early age. I miss him every day.

When I was researching the two lads' lives, Stanley Holloway was a terrific help. Stanley, even in his nineties, had instant recall and, as Bob and Bert were responsible for his big hits, 'With 'er Head Tucked Underneath Her Arm', 'My Word! You Do Look Queer' and 'Brahn Boots', he remembered them very well indeed. Amid all their other activities the partners were also constantly being called in to rewrite scenes for shows that weren't going too well. The business called them 'The Plumbers' because of their ability to patch up leaky productions, and this talent lead to them being employed to anglicise the American show, '*Hit The Deck*'. Stanley was in that show and remembered:

> By the late twenties Bob Weston's hearing had got very bad and, because he always carried a huge battery-operated hearing aid loaded with wires and earphones, I christened him 'Weston Electric'. In 1927 *Hit The Deck* opened in Glasgow and didn't go at all well. Today we'd call it 'a turkey'! The producer, oh dear, had organised a first-night supper party for the cast and writers. Bob, of course, sat next to Bert, with his hand behind his ear straining to hear what was being said. As we waited for the arrival of our governor the atmosphere was, to say the least, a trifle strained too. When the boss did arrive he was not a happy man. He launched straight into Bob and Bert. 'What about this lot tonight?' he roared. 'What have you done? I've given you two a wonderful cast, a marvellous orchestra, a fabulous theatre, beautiful dresses and scenery – *everything* that money can buy. And what have you given me? A flop! A failure! A total unmitigated theatrical disaster!'
>
> Bob leant across to Bert and asked in a loud voice, 'Did he like it?' After more work by the great team, everybody *did*.

Jimmy Wheeler Most of the stories about Jim, a variety hero and truly a legend, are unprintable, but I've managed to glean a few of the less salty ones.

Peter Elliott, the Executive Administrator of the Entertainment

Artistes Benevolent Fund, was a 'turn' himself for many years, notably as Dick Emery's straight man and as half of the double act, Edmundson and Elliott. Peter adored Jimmy, and can do at least an hour on the man. This one story just whets my appetite.

In 1967 Peter and his partner, Jimmy Edmundson, were working for the summer at the Opera House Jersey. Jimmy Wheeler was doing the season at the Watersplash nightspot. Two nights after the show opened came the very first occurrence of what was to become a nightly happening. At Peter's dressing-room door was Jimmy Wheeler with another bloke 'he'd found somewhere', three crates of light ale and two bottles of Scotch. The jolly quartet stayed, swapping stories and getting through the booze, till 4.30 in the morning. Eventually it was time to leave and Jimmy headed for his hired grey Jaguar. Peter tried to stop him.

'Not tonight Jim,' he said. 'You'll knock somebody down.'

'What time is it?' asked Jim.

'Four-thirty in the morning,' Peter advised.

'Listen,' said Jim, 'anyone who's out at half past four in the morning deserves to be knocked down,' and drove off at sixty miles an hour.

This classic tale is remembered by one of Jim's best friends, Frankie Vaughan. Jim introduced Frank, at the Kingston Empire, on his variety début and they remained great pals all Jim's life.

Frank was made King Rat of the GOWR in 1968. Jim, who was staying in Paris with his wife at his daughter and son-in-law's, rang Frank to tell him he would be at his installation as the Order's King. 'I'll fly over in the afternoon and be back with the family the same night.'

Jim duly arrived and, as always, the installation night was a good one. Every night for Jim was a good one! Eventually Jim, escorted by several of his brother Rats, was deposited at the airport. There was a delay on the Paris flight. Jim told his pals to go home – he would be all right.

He promptly fell asleep and was only woken by a fellow traveller nudging him and saying, 'Would you like to order dinner?'

'Dinner?' snorted Jim. 'They don't serve dinner on the Paris trip.'

'Paris!' said his neighbour. 'This plane's going to Karachi!'

How Jimmy Wheeler ever got on the flight to Karachi we'll never know. I don't think his missis ever forgave the Rats for that one.

Jim's comment to the manager of the Shepherd's Bush Empire on lack of business has become a much used cliché: 'I think it's the polo at Hurlingham that's affecting us.'

Albert Whelan This Australian music-hall entertainer, it is said, invented the signature tune. He would always enter for his act to 'The Jolly Brothers' waltz. As the orchestra played the tune he would whistle along while removing his hat, gloves and scarf. Sir Oswald Stoll booked him, but would give him only a short spot. Albert was upset and on his first night he walked on whistling as usual and, slower than ever before, removed his 'props'. By then he was half-away through his allotted time so he promptly, still whistling, put on his hat, gloves and scarf and exited.

June Whitfield She is a first lady of comedy, whom I have been lucky enough to work with for the past eight years not only on Radio Two's *The News Huddlines* but in panto as well. Indeed June became part of our *Huddlines* team through a panto. We were together in *Dick Whittington* at Richmond. June and I would share a drink after the show and one night she asked me what I was up to next. 'I'm doing another lot of *Huddlines*,' I said, 'but we're in trouble this time. We haven't got a girl for the show.'

Our ladies had included Janet Brown, Alison Steadman and Denise Coffey but they had all moved on to other things and now, after trying all sorts of others who weren't quite right, we had no one.

'We've tried every girl in radio,' I bleated.

'Well,' said June, 'I've done a bit of radio.'

A *bit* of radio, I thought – the lady who invented Eth Glum – a *bit* of radio! 'If you can do an impression of Margaret Thatcher,' I said, jokingly I assure you, 'I reckon you're in with a chance.'

The next afternoon the big fight scene in the panto was introduced by a fairy who sounded exactly like the Iron Lady herself. It got such a big laugh we kept it in the panto, and June has been with the radio show ever since.

For many years June and Terry Scott made up the popular TV team for *Terry and June*. At the same time she was featured in a long series of Birds Eye Frozen Food commercials. One evening she was going into the TV Centre to record an episode of the sitcom when she passed the queue for *Top Of The Pops*. She was spotted by a waiting teeny-bopper who screamed: 'Oh look! It's an advert.'

Bryn Williams Bryn is the doyen of toastmasters. Enough said. He always officiates at the Annual Water Rats Ball and here's his version of a very special night when Water Rat Danny Kaye attended.

It was quite a palaver getting a huge international star like Kaye to the Ball, and the agent who arranged it said in return for the 'favour' the Order must have one of his acts in the cabaret. This was agreed and the act duly appeared. They were a family flamenco team comprising a very ancient mother and father and their seven middle-aged and not terribly attractive offspring.

On the large raised stage they arranged themselves a semi-circle of chairs on which they sat when they were not actually dancing. At the end of each dance they all stood and took a bow. After the seventh, or it may have been the seventeenth, of those feet-clattering, hand-clapping, castanet-clicking marathons, which all sounded exactly the same, the mainly showbusiness audience started to get restless. Backstage we were sweating. We knew there were loads more dances to come. We *had* to get them off or face a riot.

It was our compère, a great little comic called Jimmy Jacobs, who saved the day. Gathering a posse of Rats around him, he said, 'Follow me. When they stand up to take their bow, we'll run on and pinch their chairs. They can't carry on then.'

We did as instructed, to the uproarious delight of the crowd and the unbelievable fury of the act. That night we learnt every swearword in the Spanish language. They threatened to go to the Embassy, sue us – the lot. We didn't care, we'd got 'em off.

Later on in the cabaret the audience became restless again but Jimmy stopped the noise and the show when he advised them, 'Shut up and listen, or I'll bring back the bleedin' Spaniards!'

Bryn has a story which has stayed with him for forty years concerning a very popular act in the cabarets of the 1950s and 60s. The act was the roller-skater Roy Dexter's, and it was called variously The Skating Dexters and The Skating Royals. Roy and his lady partner would perform on a specially prepared mat all sorts of fancy skating tricks.

Audience participation is always good in cabaret and Roy had a good gimmick. He would invite any of the punters: 'Go for a spin with Roy.' He would hold them from behind, lift them gently, give them a few revolutions and let them stagger back to their tables. The audience loved it. He would take on all comers, but one night at the Connaught Rooms he met his match.

The volunteer was a tiny little old lady. A sensational 'spin' looked in the offing and it certainly turned out that way. Neither Roy or Bryn knew that the volunteer had imbibed rather too unwisely. She was as light as a feather so Roy gave her the works. Faster and faster she spun, until her legs were horizontal. Spurred on by the shouts of the crowd he 'waved' her up and down. It was at this moment that her liquid intake became an out take!

Suddenly, there was the most almighty stampede of the people sitting at the tables nearest the floor to the back of the room. Pandemonium reigned. The poor lady was spraying everyone within quite a considerable range. There was total uproar and Roy, totally unaware of the waltzing water, was inspired by the roars of laughter to even greater efforts. Round and round and up and down she went. The floor was now drenched and the crowd were in hysterics.

Roy finally stopped to discover all the tables deserted and nearly the entire room crowded together, against the walls, crying with laughter. The little old lady star, unable to stand, crawled back to her table. She had no idea what had happened! As Bryn says, 'I don't think the Skating Dexters ever went so well.'

Wilson, Kepple and Betty They are remembered for their legendary sand-dancing speciality act, 'Cleopatra's Nightmare'. Wilson and Kepple, thin as pencils in their nightshirts and fezes and the beautiful Betty (the act had fourteen different ones over its many years) are still remembered with great affection by many variety lovers. Legend says that when they played that circus in the desert, Las Vegas, they took their own sand!

Arthur Worsley recalls being on a bill with them in Bristol. He often chatted to the two old lads in their dressing-room which, Arthur says, you could hardly move in. There were two huge

American wardrobe trunks, a full-size theatrical skip; suitcases, bags, and clothes – clean and dirty – everywhere.

One night he was in the room as they were getting ready to go on. Joe Kepple sat on a chair and removed his socks. He then produced a roll of white fivers, which he put inside a sock and then threw backwards over his shoulder.

'Why did you do that?' asked Arthur.

'Oh,' said Joe, 'in case of burglars. *I* don't know where the hell it is so what chance have they got!'

Robb Wilton The author of the famous catch-phrase, 'The Day War Broke Out', was a master of timing as his recordings still prove. He was a funny man off stage, too.

He once shared digs with Arthur Askey in the days when landladies would cover the walls of their halls with photographs of 'stars' who had stayed with them. As they arrived at their lodgings they saw in the middle of all the acts' photographs a large painting of the Last Supper.

'Ah,' said Robb, inspecting the picture, 'I see you've had Dr Crook and His Crackpots.'

'She slung us out there and then,' said Arthur.

Robb was sitting in a pub one evening and noticed, at the other end of the bar, a huddled figure quietly sobbing into his drink. Robb was a kind man and walked over to the bloke. 'Whatever's the matter?' he enquired.

'Oh,' said the man, 'it's being here by myself.'

'Well, I'm here now,' said Robb.

'I mean being by myself in life. I'm so lonely, so terribly lonely.'

'Oh buck up, old son,' said Robb. 'What'll you have to drink?'

'A large brandy,' replied the miserable figure.

'A large brandy?' said Robb. 'No wonder you're bloody lonely!'

In the last days of variety Robb had a visitor in his dressing-room at the provincial music hall he was working. The visitor looked around the cold uncarpeted cell, noted the missing pane in the window, the fly-spotted unshaded light bulb and the broken mirror. The variety game was obviously up.

'Oh Robb,' said his friend. 'You've got a few bob tucked away. Why do you carry on?'

Robb rubbed his hand over his chin in the familiar gesture,

looked around his palatial surroundings, and said, 'I think it's the glamour.'

The xylophonist Syd Wright was working a week at the Glasgow Empire with Issy Bonn and was told that two weeks earlier Robb had 'died the death' there. He had 'died' at every single performance of the entire week. As the next company took their band call on the following Monday morning, Robb suddenly appeared from the wings. He slowly walked down to the footlights, looked out at the empty auditorium, gave an enormous shudder and walked out of the theatre. He'd purposely stayed on for the weekend to do it.

One night, in the middle of his act, a storm began. There was first rain, then hailstones on the corrugated iron roof of the theatre, and then several huge claps of thunder. Robb battled on. Suddenly the sound of a brass band rehearsing next door filtered through to the auditorium. Robb paused, rubbed his hand around his face, and said, 'I think they're training me to be a police horse.'

Thanks to Bill Martin for this final example of Rob's unique thinking. One week's variety at the Finsbury Park Empire had three acts joint top of the bill: Robb, Jimmy Wheeler and the pianist, Charlie Kunz. After the first house on Monday night Jimmy and Robb repaired to the back bar in the theatre. A man approached Jimmy and said, 'I've just been in to see the show, Jimmy. You were so funny. I've been a fan of yours for ages. Will you have a drink?'

Jimmy, surprisingly, accepted. Robb sat at the table, completely ignored by the man who'd 'just been in to see the show'. He carried on lauding Jimmy Wheeler to the sky, and eventually turned to Robb. 'Were you in the show?' he asked.

Robb quietly replied, 'Yes I was.'

'Oh,' said Jimmy's fan, 'and what do you do?'

Said Robb, 'I'm Charlie Kunz's accompanist.'

Victoria Wood This girl changed the face of stand-up comedy in this country. She was the first really successful lady to do the job. Her original songs, thoughts and perceptive writing have all combined to make her, I think, a great of today. Victoria and her husband, the magician Geoffrey Durham, sent me this highlight of her early career.

I was booked to do a 'one woman' show at a small village

hall in the Pennines for £75. Geoff and I set off in our Mini, which had no suspension (I blame Geoff) and a radiator full of egg-white which some prat had told us would seal leaks. We arrived in the pouring rain to find the whole village deserted, like something out of *The Avengers*. There was just one poster that was so small it could only have been read by a moth, and the only person around was the woman who had been booked to do the interval teas and coffees: so convinced was she of my vast popularity she was well prepared for the rush, and had brought half a pint of milk from her own kitchen. We sold five seats. The show was cancelled and we drove home in the filthy rain. The windscreen wipers packed up and Geoff had to keep getting out to rub the windscreen with a potato (some prat had told us this would clear the glass). We ended up pushing the car through the streets of Morecambe at three o'clock in the filthy morning, snarling at each other. (What! and give up showbusiness?)

'Wee' Georgie Wood The diminutive music-hall star – whose solo acts and sketches, with Dolly Harmer as his mother, made him popular all over the world – was a highly intelligent, witty, articulate man who, all his life, courted men of letters, politicians and judges. His non-acceptance of his role as a midget led to a certain bitterness but I liked him and his sense of humour. His ability to namedrop was a byword and he once said to a friend of mine:

> In 1923 Woodrow Wilson gave me a photograph on which he'd written: 'You were the greatest ambassador Britain ever sent to the USA.' In 1929 George Bernard Shaw said: 'With another physique, you could have been a wonderful Macbeth, Lear, Othello or even Doolittle.' In 1932 Norman Birkett, QC, said about me: 'The Law has lost a great advocate to the music halls.' General Smuts, in 1937, said of me: 'This little man has been the greatest example of the sort of friendship that is needed between the Union and the UK I have ever known.' And in 1923, Fanny Brice said: 'You're a little shit!' Odd isn't it that all these marvellous people, and there were lots of others, could be 'taken in' by me.

Ted Ray, in an issue of *The Trap* (the occasional magazine of the Water Rats) reported a classic ad lib of George's at a Lodge meeting. One Rat stood up and made a complaint about another 189 who was from Liverpool. 'Look at him!' said the complainer. 'He's obviously going on to work somewhere but, I ask you, he's wearing black suede shoes with evening dress!'

'Sit down!' said George. 'In Liverpool that *is* evening dress!'

George was a Catholic convert and they of course never stop doing the 'hard sell' for Catholicism. George would preach its merits to anyone who'd listen and with even greater vehemence to those who wouldn't. He had an audience with the Pope and the story goes that while most people spend about a minute in His Holiness's company, George was with him for so long that the Cardinal who waited outside began to worry. He opened the door to the inner sanctum, just a crack, to hear the Pope say: 'But Mr Wood – I *am* a Catholic!'

Captain Joseph Woodward (and his Sealions)

In 1888 Joseph (not yet Captain) and his father were in America to suss out their chances in circus and stage entertainment. Joseph was convinced he could train and present an act with sealions, something never before achieved. He bought a sealion and found (like all the best animal trainers do) that with a combination of encouragement and bribery he could harness the animal's natural behaviour into an entertaining act. Over the next ten years he 'taught', with the help of a constant supply of herrings, his ever-expanding troupe to balance, juggle and even applaud themselves. He purloined the handle 'Captain' and his sealions became a top of the bill act.

This fascinating story was told to me by the comedian, now columnist, Freddie Sadler.

In 1916 German U-Boats were causing havoc and appalling casualties to Allied shipping. Captain Woodward learnt these facts while playing music halls in Chatham, Plymouth, Southampton and Portsmouth. He wrote to the Admiralty, offering to train his charges to detect submarines in motion below the water. He cited his success as pioneer in understanding what made sealions tick as proof that it could be done. Surprisingly, the Admiralty gave this Spike Milligan-type suggestion a cautious thumbs-up. Captain Woodward received the news while he was working the week at the Glasgow Empire, where the sealions were certainly going better than any English comic ever did.

He started his experiment in Glasgow Baths. His troupe – Queenie, Buller, Bluenose, Dorondo and Billaben – were joined by two chums from the local zoo and they did well. He began by placing appliances that made a buzzing sound similar to a submarine's engine under the water. These were baited with fish. Once the sealion touched an appliance the fish was released. Soon the troupe were finding the appliances like lightning.

The experiment was successfully transferred to a large lake in Alexandra Park, and the Captain was asked to show the navy bigwigs what he could do in Westminster Swimming Baths. The pool was stocked with trout and all sorts of sealion snacks, but the Captain's charges ignored the lot and instantly homed into the buzzing appliances. They did it again at the Bala Lake in Wales, so an area of the Solent was selected for the final trial. All shipping was excluded and British submarines were introduced into the area. The sealions, each attached to a brightly coloured buoy, scored ninety per cent direct hits.

This was it. Our fishy finders were let loose in an area where the U-Boats were known to be. Alas, a fatal flaw marred the one and only true 'Operation Sealion'. The troupe had been trained to find just one single sound. The area they were searching was full of naval vessels, merchant ships and even the occasional plane and so total confusion reigned with sealions locating every single sound they heard!

It wasn't a case of back to the drawing board, but back to the music hall boards where the good Captain and his, oh so nearly, war heroes continued to draw the crowds and react to the single sound they loved best of all – applause.

Arthur Worsley Retired now, he was, quite simply the very best ventriloquist I have ever seen. He was not only very funny but he had the very best technique of them all. The weird idea (shades of Michael Redgrave in *Dead Of Night*) of the dummy being in charge and doing all the talking never seemed creepy when Arthur did it and you really couldn't see *his* lips move. At technical run-throughs, band calls and especially during rehearsals, Arthur would allow his 'minder', Johnny Green, to let loose a stream of invective and rudery that would leave directors and floor managers white and shaking – 'God! is he actually going to say that?'

The classic story that every ventriloquist quotes actually happened to Arthur. It would have happened to him because no one else ever made their dummy live as he did. In the middle of a sound rehearsal for a radio show the producer gave the instruction: 'Not quite clear enough, Mr Worsley. Could you put the dummy closer to the microphone?'

Arthur was leaving the Palace Theatre, Blackpool, one night during a run of the Frankie Vaughan Show. Arthur thought he'd escaped the usual crowd of autograph hunters, when one of a pair of large ladies grabbed him shouting: 'Get his!'

'Who's he?' said the other.

'You know who he is,' shrieked her friend, 'the one with the effigy.'

One of Arthur's early comic heroes was the infamous Claude Lester, who once advertised in the trade paper *The Performer* thus:

> Claude Lester
> Last week Hippodrome, Manchester
> This week Empire, Glasgow
> I will give 10 per cent of my wages to anyone who can tell me where I am next week.

Harry Worth The lovable, bumbling, kind-hearted hero of *Here's Harry* and a string of television sitcoms is still remembered for the unique business with his reflection in a shop doorway that started his shows.

Harry was playing *Jack and The Beanstalk* in Birmingham with Cilla Black. Nightly Cilla would chop down the beanstalk and, standing over the fallen Giant, would enquire of the audience: 'What shall I do with him?'

'Kill him!' came the answer from a thousand charming children's throats.

One night, for no reason, she added, 'How shall I kill him?'

A solo Brummie voice advised, 'Sing to it!'

Harry told everybody that one, and so did Cilla.

Mark Wynter The former pop singer, who has matured to become one of our most sought after actor/singers, was working in a revue and, in the middle of a duet, his leading lady's top set came adrift and clattered into the footlights. Mark, in his own graceful way, retrieved them, (without gloves) and surreptitiously tried to return them to the owner. The lady refused but hastily whirled Mark upstage, squeezing his hand in hers. 'A case,' says Mark, 'of being bitten by the hand that led me!' Ouch!

One summer I did a season at the Winter Gardens, Margate with Mark.

(Before I continue, I must explain that my mother died during the war and my father, on his return from the army, married again. My brother was adopted by an aunt and I, to my great joy, was brought up by my gran. It was my gran who first took me to the Croydon Empire and so sent me off on the slippery showbiz slope. My father and I hadn't been in any sort of contact for many years.)

The finale of the first half of the show was an old time music hall scene which culminated with yours truly making a big entrance in drag and leading the company in a medley of Florrie Forde songs.

One night, as I prepared for this finale, Mark knocked on the dressing-room door and with a rather pathetic Eamonn Andrews impression announced, 'Here's someone you haven't seen for twenty years – your father!' He threw open the door and there was my father, whom I *hadn't* seen for twenty years.

I sat there in purple fishnet tights and basque, high heels, long red wig, Kathy Kirby lips and huge passe-partout eyelashes. I saw in the mirror my father stepping into the room. I paused as I screwed a diamanté earring on to my lobe.

'Hallo, Dad,' I said.

'Hallo, son,' said Dad.

GLOSSARY

ad lib: An unscripted remark. The life-blood of music hall, variety and especially pantomime.

band call: The first rehearsal with the orchestra. In variety days, on Monday mornings, whoever put their band books (the folders containing the music) next to the MD (musical director) the earliest would get to rehearse first.

billing: The position and size of a performer's name on the posters. Like who gets the number one dressing-room it could be, and still is, a real bone of contention. I have seen agents and promoters poring over a poster with a slide rule to prove that a certain name is the most prominent. Daft – but it gives them something to do.

bill matter: The phrase that would appear under an artiste's name. It was supposed to give the audience an idea of what he or she did. Some bill matter became as famous as the act it described: e.g. George Robey 'The Prime Minister of Mirth' Max Miller 'The Cheeky Chappie' Ted Ray 'Fiddling and fooling' Billy Bennett 'Almost a gentleman' Kardoma 'He fills the stage with flags' My favourite was The Three Aberdonians 'Too mean to tell you what they do!'

camp: Impossible to define exactly. Sometimes it refers to a homosexual – 'She's as camp as a row of purple bivouacs' – but I prefer it to mean something eccentric, out of the ordinary, different or bizarre.

civilian: Someone who is nothing to do with showbusiness. A customer or punter.

corpsing: Being unable to carry on with the act or play because you are laughing. See Chris Emmett.

dots/charts/parts: The, usually specially arranged, hand-written music used in an act. In the early days of the working men's clubs accompanists would often refuse to play from manuscript, dismissing it as 'London music'. One legendary club organist would only play from printed copies with 'a picture on the front'.

drag: A man dressed as a woman or, less usually, a woman dressed as a man. The term is nearly always applied to female impersonators *not* pantomime dames.

feed/straight man: The partner of a comedian whose function is to point up the comical qualities of his pal. It is a highly specialised art and, though it rarely happens, a good one is worth as much as, sometimes even more than, the whimsical part of the act.

flat: A piece of scenery usually placed at the side of the stage to stop the audience seeing backstage.

flies: The area above the stage where the painted cloths are kept before they're required to be seen. They are then 'flown' into view.

front cloth comic: A comedian who could appear onstage in the minimum of space, in front of a cloth as opposed to one who needed the whole stage to function. 'Can you open (start) and close (finish) in number ones?' was a constantly asked question in variety. It meant 'Can you do your act in front of the first row of curtains?'

gig: Originally a musician's term but now adopted by all sorts of performers. It simply means a job.

'low' comedy: Overdrawn, slapstick characterisations. Slapstick comedy – broad visual stuff – takes its name from the specially constructed stick which, when used to hit people with, makes a terrific crack but doesn't hurt. You still see it used in pantomime schoolroom scenes, but its origins go back to Ancient Greece.

orchestra pit: The place between the front of the stage and the front row of the audience where the musicians are situated. As it is mostly just their heads that are seen, the 'orchestra pit' is a place where white socks and Doc Martins are worn with evening dress and more crossword puzzles are completed than ever are on the 7.45 from Tunbridge Wells.

pratt fall: Falling on your backside without hurting yourself.

pro: Civilians still sometimes blanch when they hear someone referred to as a 'pro'. Folk memories of 'pro' – prostitute. It simply means a performer who gets paid for entertaining. Well, that's the bald description but actually a true 'pro' is a performer who is not only good at the job and knows the game inside out but is generous and helpful to his fellows and has a sense of humour too. It is the greatest compliment to be called 'a real pro'.

props: The portable bits and pieces essential to the act, hats, canes, juggling clubs or whatever.

tabs: Curtains

tag/pay-off: The last line of a joke or a sketch, and one always hopes it will be the line that gets the big laugh.

taking a call: Returning to the stage at the end of the act to receive your applause.

Index